# The
# Place-Names
# of
# South Ronaldsay
# and
# Burray

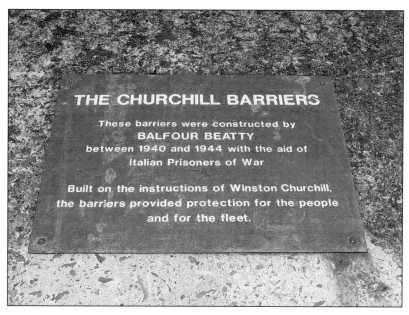

*The Road to the Isles*

# The
# Place-Names
## of
# South Ronaldsay
## and
# Burray

## Gregor Lamb

*Bellavista Publications*

ISBN 0 9550586 2 7


Copyright Gregor Lamb 2006


First published in 2006

Published by
Bellavista Publications, 3 Sabiston Crescent, Kirkwall, Orkney, KW15 1YT
Telephone 01856 878196

E-mail Address: bellavistabb@yahoo.co.uk


Printed by Cromwell Press Ltd., Aintree Avenue, White Horse Business Park, Trowbridge, Wiltshire, BA14 0XB

# *Contents*

# By the same author

*Come thee Wiz,* Kirkwall Press, 1978*

*Nivver Spaek,* Kirkwall Press, 1980*

*Orkney Surnames,* Paul Harris, 1981*

*Hid kam intae Words,* Byrgisey, 1986*

*Orkney Wordbook,* Byrgisey, 1988 (hardback)*

*Sky Over Scapa 1939-45,* Byrgisey, 1991*

*Aviation War Diary, Orkney, 1939-45,* Byrgisey, 1992*

*Naggles o Piapittem, the place-names of Sanday, Orkney,* Byrgisey, 1992*

*Testimony of the Orkneyingar, the place-names of Orkney,* Byrgisey, 1993*

*Orkney Wordbook,* Byrgisey, 1995 (paperback)*

*I mind hid aal fine,* Byrgisey, 1996 (editor)*

*Lamb's Tales,* Byrgisey, 1996

*The Orkney Dictionary,* Orkney Language and Culture Group, 1996 (with
     Margaret Flaws); 2nd Edition, 2001

*Langskaill,* Byrgisey, 1998

*Orkney Family Names,* Bellavista Publications, 2003

*Lamb's Tales—another wag,* The Orcadian (Kirkwall Press), 2004

*Orcadiana,* Bellavista Publications, 2004

*Whit Like the Day? understanding Orkney dialect,* Bellavista Publications,
     2005

*Carnival of the Animals,* a study of the role of animals, animal images and
     animal disguise in Northern Europe, Capall Bann, 2005

* out of print

# List of Illustrations

# Dedicated

to all those in
South Ronaldsay and Burray
who have helped
to make this
collection possible.

# Acknowledgements

A T A TIME when the population of Burray and South Ronaldsay is changing so rapidly it is more important than ever to record the place-names of these islands. Fortunately there are several native islanders left who have retained a great interest in the history of the islands and it is only with their generous help that this study of the place-names of South Ronaldsay and Burray has been made possible. For many years George Esson of St. Margaret's Hope has taken a keen interest not only in his native island but in the whole of Orkney as his huge collection of Orkney books testifies. When we met in 2003 I casually mentioned the fact that it was a great shame that no one had ever collected the place-names of South Ronaldsay and Burray, islands which had held a great fascination for me although I had had little contact with them. I had a collection of names from Ordnance Survey maps, details of which had been recorded in the 1870s, but I felt sure that there were many more to be found. After some weeks, George presented me with a long list of all the place-names of South Ronaldsay and Burray which he had painstakingly extracted from Census Records and along with this he included a list of the coastal place-names of Grimness which had been collated by Isa Ritchie of Limbo. Subsequently George's contacts drew further valuable contributions from Steven and Helen Manson, William Budge, Anita Montgomery, William Mowat, William Norquay, John Mackenzie and Karen Wood. In the final proof reading, William Budge's contribution in noting omissions and correcting several errors in the interpretation of coastal place-names has been invaluable. The role of South Ronaldsay and Burray in two World Wars is probably without parallel in Orkney and therefore it was also decided to include within the collection details of war-time defences. I am most grateful to George for allowing me to include from his research relevant valuable information otherwise not easily obtainable.

An article which I published in the newspaper *Orkney Today* on the subject of relatively modern South Ronaldsay place-names introduced me to Johnny Tomison of England, South Ronaldsay who had made his own collection of names with the help of others on the island who shared this interest. He would particularly like to thank James Ritchie, William

Dunnett, William Sinclair, Robert, Dora and Cyril Annal, Charles Nicholson, George Brown, Jimmy Sabiston, Peter Sabiston, John McIvor, Elma Rosie, Herbert and Ingrid Mackenzie and John Norquoy. Both George Esson and Johnny Tomison provided detailed maps of the place-names they had collected and I do not underestimate the amount of time which they have devoted to this project. I am extremely grateful to all these native islanders for the help that they have given me.

The location of many houses in Burray, in particular the new developments, presented some problems. Hazel Wylie, George Laird, my nephew Colin Sclater and daughter Debbie initially filled in many blanks and I should like to thank them very much for their help. Above all I should like to give special thanks to Irene Sutherland who must have spent many hours producing a large map of Burray, locating and listing precisely every house on the island. This valuable map and list will be deposited in the Orkney Archives for the use of other researchers interested in this island.

Ray Fereday, former history master at Kirkwall Grammar School, has provided a great incentive to the young of Orkney to encourage them to undertake local history projects. Erlend Wood's project on Berriedale Farm is one such success and I sincerely acknowledge the use of material drawn from Erlend's study.

In any project of this nature the Department of Archives in the Orkney Library is a primary source of information and the invariably quick response by library staff to puzzling queries is to be commended. Several photographs in this book have been drawn from their fascinating archive of film material.

Magnus Spence of Northfield Farm has made a dramatic contribution to the Burray skyline with the erection of a 44m. high wind turbine. He kindly loaned for our use a striking photograph of the structure by Rushbrook Designs Ltd. Magnus also helped to explain the interesting developments at his fish farm on Weddell Sound.

I should like to thank an old sporting adversary, John Findlay of Kirkwall, whose detailed knowledge of the island of Swona helped to solve many problems. Included in the book are several fine photographs which he has contributed. In the list of references at the back I have specifically included his superb video entitled *Swona—a memorial to a lost way of life*. It succeeds in brilliantly capturing the atmosphere of an island which has witnessed the passage—and indeed end—of so many vessels and which has itself become a kind of *Marie Celeste* of the Pentland Firth. This video cannot be recommended too highly.

Lastly, a special word of thanks to the publisher, Stewart Davidson, for his superbly professional approach. His eagle eye has spotted many errors. He has also toured the islands taking photographs for inclusion in the book, something far beyond his responsibility as a publisher. It has been a great pleasure to work with him.

# *Introduction*

THE interpretation of place-names is fraught with difficulties. The passage of years has corrupted many names to such a degree that their origins can only be guessed at and in a number of cases no guess can even be attempted. Even the interpretation of relatively modern names can be extremely difficult and many avenues have to be explored before a final suggestion is tentatively offered. As an example of the latter, let us consider the Burray place-name Cellardyke, first recorded in 1821 in the form 'Silver Dyke'. 'Dyke' is obviously Scots 'wall' and 'siller' is Scots for 'silver'. This raised the possibility that a wall here had been built by someone with the surname 'Silver' just as a wall in Sanday is called Galloway Dyke after the builder. Unfortunately the surname Silver has not been recorded in Burray, though, admittedly, there is a puzzling old place-name Silvars Quoy in South Ronaldsay. If we assume that the surname Silver does not explain the place-name, other possibilities had to be examined. The next consideration was that a wall had been built at enormous expense and had cost a lot of money but that was not convincing. When another place-name Sillerdyke appeared in a list of names from Windwick in South Ronaldsay a new search began to find out what these two places had in common. Crossing the beach at several points in Birsay are volcanic intrusions which are referred to locally as Iron Dykes. There are similar intrusions in Burray and South Ronaldsay; were they locally called 'Silver Dykes' in the belief that silver could be mined from them? When I came across an old silver mine in Montana, USA called Silver Dyke I realised the possibility that both these names had been brought back to the islands by Orkneymen who had gone to USA as prospectors, who had earned some money and who had named their house after the mine in which they had worked. The conclusion was that these house names fell into the same category as Klondyke and Balarat (sic) on the islands and the interpretation rested at that—until it was realised that the earliest recording of Silver Dyke in Burray is 1821 and silver mining did not begin in Montana until the 1860s! After these many deliberations it was discovered that there was also a house in Deerness called Cellardyke, which, in the 1841 Census took the form 'Silordyke'. It was clear that these three houses had something in common, but what was the common factor? For want of any better suggestion, it was finally concluded that all Silver Dyke place-names fall into the category of simple houses which were given fine names to enhance their status such as Goldhall in Flotta or Diamond Cottage in Stenness. It was subsequently discovered that this interpretation was also wrong! Stumbling by chance on work on some place-names in Fife, I learned that 'Silver Dyke' was a Scots nickname given to fishermen's houses when herring (the silver darlings), were split and laid on walls to dry. It was common to dry herring in those days rather than salt them because of the exorbitant cost of salt. The walls shone in bright sunlight giving the impression that they were rich veins of silver to be mined! In South Ronaldsay, one wonders what these houses were called on Sundays for on that day it was explicitly forbidden by the church to dry fish! 'Silver Dyke' was usually corrupted to 'Cellardyke' in its written form. It is significant that the three occurrences of this place-name in Orkney—in Burray, South Ronaldsay and Deerness, are all places associated with the herring industry when that industry was in its heyday in the 19th century. If we follow the movement of the herring shoals down the east coast of Scotland we come to the former herring fishing village of Cellardyke, now part of Anstruther in Fife.

There is no doubt that some of the place-names of Burray and South Ronaldsay are over one thousand years old. This cannot be proved; we can only assume this from the date of the settlements of the islands by the Norsemen. We note how they chose descriptive names from their own language to replace what we assume to be the Celtic place-names of the early settlers. They made a thorough job of the substitution in Burray and South Ronaldsay for there is not one definite, original Celtic place-name in evidence in the islands. With the coming of the Scots, a new language supplanted Norn, the native form of Old Norse, but, astonishingly, the bulk of the Old Norse place-names was retained. Why the Norse wiped out the language of the earlier settlers and the place-names and the Scots wiped out the language and left the place-names almost untouched, is impossible to explain. Fortunately for us we are left with a marvellous legacy of our history.

To study the old place-names of the islands it is the Old Norse language we have to be familiar with and the value of the ground-breaking work of Jakob Jakobsen in Shetland and Dr. Hugh Marwick in Orkney in interpreting the Old Norse place-names of the Northern Isles is sincerely acknowledged. Despite the close proximity of South Ronaldsay and Burray to the mainland of Scotland there is a striking absence of Gaelic place-names, a characteristic these islands share with the northern tip of Caithness itself. For the student of Orkney place-names, South Ronaldsay and Burray are ideal subjects of study since they may fairly be said to represent a microcosm of typical Orkney place-names both Norse and modern; indeed there are few place-names in these islands which do not have their counterpart elsewhere and every attempt has been made throughout the text to illustrate this.

*Look closely at the split herrings lying on the 'cellardyke'; also shown is a typical old gate, Old Norse 'grind', Scots 'slap'.*

# Section 1

# Around the Coasts

THE most common coastal place-name in Orkney is 'geo' or 'goe' from Old Norse *gjá* ravine. There are over one hundred and twenty such place-names in Burray and South Ronaldsay alone such as Fedi Geo, Ham Geo and Skipi Geo. Sometimes if the lower strata in the cliff face are softer than the upper strata the geo will become an elongated cave. At Shortie Geo in Barswick there is such a cave which may have been where Sveinn of Gairsay sought refuge when fleeing from the islands after the murder of his namesake Sveinn Breast Rope. Sometimes the roof of a cave collapses to form a so-called 'blow hole' through which spindrift is blown during times of storm. In Orkney, such features are called 'gloups' from Old Norse *gloppa*, a big hole. There is a fine gloup at Halcro Head which rivals the more famous gloup in Deerness but the fame of the latter rests perhaps on its accessibility. South Ronaldsay folk believe that their gloup is by far the more impressive! This gloup, which is unmarked on Ordnance Survey maps, is known locally as the 'Gloup o Root'. A smaller version of the gloup at Halcro Head can be found on Swona.

The coastal place-names Sinilie and Senoldies are also of great interest in that the first element contains a rare Norse word. Today the Norwegian verb *sine* is to 'dry up' applied to cows which stop lactating. In Shetland dialect the word *sinna* referred to a small kiln for drying corn. When corn was being dried, these kilns looked like very large smoking chimneys. The word *sinna* applied to a kiln must have been in use in Orkney too since in the names Sinilie and Senoldies the cliffs are compared with kilns since they 'smoke' during a storm just as the old grain drying kilns did. Blow holes on the Rousay coast called Sinyans o Cutclaws contain the same element. The element *sinna* also appears in Sinmire, a dried up marsh on the north side of the Ward Hill in South Ronaldsay. Near Redland in the parish of Firth there was a well by the name Sinniekelda, a dried up well. By a strange twist in the use of language, dried up pools came to be called 'kilns'! This explains why, when we go over the Redland Hill in Firth and down into Harray, we find dried up pools by the name 'Kilns o Rowamo'. 'Kil' was the common pronunciation of 'kiln' in Orkney dialect and Caddie's Kil (Sc. *caddie* a pet lamb) is a coastal depression in Grimness in South Ronaldsay and seems to have originally been a gloup which has partly collapsed in on itself in historical time. In Trae Geo on the north coast of Muckle Skerry on the Pentland Skerries the place-name 'The Kiln' is found. In a strong north easterly gale there is little doubt that this particular feature 'smokes' just as a grain drying kiln did! The place-name 'kiln' is also found on the north coasts of Birsay and Rousay at the Kilns o Skae and the Kilns o Brimnoven respectively, the latter name containing the Old Norse word *ofn*, literally 'oven' but used here in the sense of 'kiln' as in Norwegian *(tørk)ovn*.

The element 'lie' of Sinilie deserves a special mention. We shall refer to it presently with the meaning 'slope', from Old Norse *hlíð*. When used in coastal place-names it can carry the meaning 'cliff'. Bratlee Ber in Burray; a small precipice on the south-east coast, is one such instance. It has an exact equivalent in Brottalees in Unst in Shetland. The first element is Old Norse *brattr* steep. The 200 foot cliffs of Copinsay are known as Broad Lee where 'broad' is probably a corruption of *brattr*. These cliffs gave rise to the expression 'running the Lee', i.e. descending these cliffs on a rope to collect the eggs of seabirds.

The word 'taing', from Old Norse *tangi,* refers to a point of land as in Scarf Taing or Ossi Taing. One of the most common word for rock(s) in Old Norse is *berg.* Rocks lying off the coast have names derived from *berg* which take a variety of 'ber' and 'bar' forms as in Broti Ber, literally 'steep rock', on the Pentland Skerries or Angly Bar in Grimness. Ber Taing on Hunda is 'rock point'. A common word for a reef in the North Isles is 'ba/a'. It derives from the Old Norse word *boði* which really means a 'warner' (of hidden rocks). A good example comes from Baa Taing on Auskerry. We also have several examples in this area such as Wester Bows on Swona and Baaes, an underwater reef, south of Harrabrough Head in South Ronaldsay. On Blaeu's 1654 map and Mackenzie's 1750 map a rock, or possibly a sandbar, off the eastern entrance to Water Sound, between Burray and South Ronaldsay is marked Lippa. Here the 'pa' element is almost certainly a corruption of 'ba'. This reef has vanished, apparently carried away by a winter storm.

'Skerry' is the common name for a reef and in the case of the Pentland Skerries applies to a very large collection of reefs, the graveyard of many vessels. Skerries and taings are favourite places for cormorants to rest and

*Scarfs gather on Scartan Point.*

dry their wings hence the common Orkney place-name Scarf Skerry from Old Norse *skarfr* a cormorant. The gathering of cormorants at favoured points on the coast gives rise to two unusual place-names on Muckle Skerry. 'Tennis court', recorded by the Ordnance Survey in the 1870s, suggests a corruption of 'taing's court' from ON *tangi* a point of land where the 'court' of cormorants met! The place-name 'Parliament Square' on Scartan Point (Old Norse *skarfa-tangi* a peninsula favoured by cormorants) on that same island suggests another such meeting place!

Norse words for the sea breaking over reefs add colour to our coastal place-names. The second element of Skerloom, a coastal feature in Grimness, might suggest that this is a resting place for the red-throated diver. In Norse, this diver was called *lóm* and in Orkney dialect 'loom'. However the bird is called by this name because of the very striking call it has which was said to betoken rain. Its name means 'the sounder' from *hlamma* to sound. This also helps to explain the word Skerloom where it refers to the breaking of the surf there. Louther Skerry on the Pentland Skerries likewise derives its name from Old Norse *hljóðaðr* sounding. Loth in Sanday is derived in the same way. The Norse word *sund*, a stretch of water between two land masses, is related to English 'sound', to make a noise. Being an archipelago, Orkney has plenty of channels called 'Sound' derived from the Norse word *sund* and several of these are around Burray and South Ronaldsay such as Hunda Sound, Water Sound and Hoxa Sound,

*Hunda Sound showing the 'Reef', a natural shingle spit which was reinforced during World War II from the quarry on the island to make part of the Hunda Barrier, a second line of defence within Scapa Flow; left foreground Littlequoy; right The Ruff, a derelict croft.*

the latter being world famous as the principal entrance to Scapa Flow and heavily protected by boom defences during two world wars. The noise of the sea is also recorded in two other coastal place-names. The element 'root' in the Gloup o Root is derived from Old Norse *rjóta* to roar and it can be understood why, in his *Orkneys and Shetland* published in 1883, Tudor said of this gloup, 'even in the calmest weather the much resounding sea sends a deep boom through this tunnel'. Denni Geo which is referred to in the paragraph below has the alternative name Duni Geo. Old Norse *duna* is 'a thundering noise'.

There is plenty of seaweed around the Orkney shores so it is not surprising that the Norse word *þari* appears in place-names as in Tarri Clett or the Reefs o Turriegeo. Seaweed provided valuable nutrition for the land in olden days and Tarland in Grimness and Burwick records the old agricultural practice of spreading seaweed on the land to enrich it. 'Ware', the Scots word for seaweed, is found in Warebanks in Burray and reminds us of the old Orkney saying, 'The ware time is a sair time,' meaning that the spring time carting and spreading of seaweed on the land caused great physical pain. The amount of effort required in this operation is brought out by the entry in the diary of Patrick Fea in Sanday for 16th March, 1796; '. . . had 19 horses in the ware at Quoyness and one horse putting ware on Halksness'. Edible seaweed, *rhodymenia palmata,* is known in Orkney as 'dill', hence the name Dill Geo on Hoxa. When seaweed rots, as it frequently does when trapped above the high water mark or deep in geos, it gives off a most objectionable smell in the warm days of summer. Denni Geo in South Ronaldsay is derived from Old Norse *deyning* stink, and Fedi Geo to which we have already referred is from the verb *feygva* to decay.

One word for 'sand' in Old Norse is the similar word *sandr* hence the district name Sandwick. Yet another word for sand is *melr*. We find this word in the South Ronaldsay place-name Meall and in a corrupted form in Westermill, Burray. Meal was the old name of Newark in Sanday and Graemeshall in Holm. Shingle spits which are called *eyrr* in Norse usually take the form 'ayre' in Orkney place-names such as the Ayre o Cara and Liddel Ayre in South Ronaldsay. When a shingle spit joins one land mass to another the resulting form is an isthmus. A fine example of such a feature connects Hoxa to the rest of South Ronaldsay. The final 'a' of Hoxa is all that remains of what we know from records to have been an original *eið* or isthmus. The name Scapa in the parish of St. Ola presents a direct parallel; its original form, which we know from the *Orkneyinga Saga,* was *Skalpeið*.

*Vágr,* a bay, takes the form 'wall' as in Widewall. We find the same transformation in the place-name Kirkwall and in Walls on the island of

*A tranquil scene at The Hope.*

Hoy. *Vágr* is found too in a form nearer the original in *voe* as in Ronaldsvoe which is recorded in the *Orkneyinga Saga* as *Rögnvalds-vágr*. Names are in a constant process of change as is evidenced by 'Ronsa', the local pronunciation of Ronaldsvoe by older people today. Before long the name 'Ronsa' will vanish altogether. Old Norse *hóp, bay,* is preserved in the name St. Margaret's Hope and on the island of Hoy as Longhope. A small indentation in the south-west coast of Swona is known as The Haap which is also the old name of the Bay of Sandside in Graemsay. The Norse word *vík,* bay, assumes the form 'wick' in the islands and is much more common. In South Ronaldsay the 'w' of 'wick' is not sounded in the case of Barswick, Burwick and Windwick. Sandwick is an exception and is pronounced in the same way as the West Mainland parish of that name.

# Coastal Names as Evidence of Bygone Activities

N interesting feature of these coastal place-names to which we have referred above is that many of them give us a permanent record of human activities long since forgotten such as the trapping of wild salmon at Laxigar on Hunda. There is no one alive today who can recall, even through folk memory, the growing and preparation of flax which prospered in Orkney from the end of the 17th century into the 19th century but the place-names Lint Pows in Grimness and Hanni Pows in Wind Wick recall such an industry. A beautiful old ballad which must go back to the beginning of the 19th century at the latest, records the growing of flax near the Gloup o Root. It begins:

> On the rigs twa three
> 'Tween the gloup an the sea
> Lint grew there
> For ma mither and me.

A fine linen dress was made by the mother of a poor illegitimate girl from the flax which was grown there and the girl looked so beautiful in it

*Down the Windwick Road; nearest the camera Melhaven, Windwick and South Windwick; to the right Millhouse and in the distance Quoyorally.*

that she won over the heart of the local laird who married her and so raised the family from poverty!

The keeping of sheep, a universal activity in Orkney, was often associated with the coast since seaweed could be an important part of the animal's diet. It was also easy to pen animals at or near the shore such as at Soo Taing in Grimness (here 'soo' refers not to dialect 'soo', meaning 'sow' but to Old Norse *sauðr*, sheep) or Caddies' Kil, a depression on the coast in the same area to which we earlier made reference. On the coast too can be found a number of 'Croo/Crew' place-names which stems from the Old Norse word *kró*, a pen. As in Iceland, sheep were brought together annually at specific points for shearing and marking. These were known by the Old Norse name *rettr*. The Sand o Right is such a place.

In those days when salt was not freely available, salt pans provided a coarse salt for local use, especially for the preservation of food. Pickling Skerries is an extensive rock shelf on the west of Swona where fish would have been placed in barrels and 'pickled' with salt. Place-names throughout Orkney record the winning of salt such as Salt Pan on the coast of Orphir, Pan Hope in Flotta and Salt Ness in Shapinsay and Walls. South Ronaldsay had its own sea-salt extraction pond at Salt Geo, apparently another name

*Wreck of the Norwegian brigantine Adele on Kirk Taing, South Ronaldsay in January, 1902, the last sailing ship to be wrecked on the island; her cargo of pit props was washed into the Pool o Cletts.*

*Pit props from the wreck of the Adele; in the background right, the base of one of South Ronaldsay's windmills; on the left is Millhouse, an interesting, derelict 18$^{th}$ century two storey house with external stone staircase.*

for Ham Geo. There was never enough salt for local use however and much had to be obtained elsewhere. In the 1710 inventory of the 'Place' of Burray it is revealed that Sir Archibald Stewart obtained three tons of salt yearly from the Salt Pan in Flotta. Salt also came from much further afield. The sloop *Lady Charlotte* of Kirkwall with a cargo of salt came to grief on the coast of Grimness in 1794, one of many hundreds of vessels stranded on the coasts of South Ronaldsay and Burray. Throughout the text the reader will find many references to such strandings. Foreign sounding names such as Penang Geo, La Plata Hole and Marengo Road ensure that the sad fate of at least three of these vessels will not be forgotten.

Writing in his *History of the Orkney Islands* in 1805, George Barry, the Minister of Shapinsay, said of South Ronaldsay:

> *Even the bowels of the earth seem to contain treasures. In proof of this, it may be observed, that a promising vein of lead ore was long since discovered near Grimness Head on the north and another on the south-west, near Widewall; but owing to different causes they have not as yet been very advantageous.*

This was one of several attempts made four hundred years ago, to discover reserves of lead in Orkney. Other attempts were made in Deerness and Stromness. Coastal cliffs made the initial digging of the tunnel easier and today local South Ronaldsay people know well the old mine shaft in Grimness to the north of Manse Bay where, after apparently much endeavour, the operation was abandoned. Nothing is known of this activity in Widewall. It seems that, despite Barry's hope, the bowels of the earth have little to offer in South Ronaldsay!

The many fine buildings in South Ronaldsay and Burray demonstrate that the islanders are fortunate in having excellent building stone. In view of this fact, it is ironical that the stone for one of South Ronaldsay's finest buildings, Tomison's Academy, came from Orphir! It is often overlooked that, just as rock exposures on the coast made attempts at mining easy, it also made quarrying a fairly simple matter. The building stones for many houses were actually quarried from the shore. A well known Stenness lady, Maggie Paplay, built her own house in this way, the ruin of which may still be seen near the Brig o Waithe. A coastal place-name, Balaclava's Quarry, in South Ronaldsay records the fact that the house of Balaclava was also built from stones quarried on the beach. Some of the finer strata also provided sandstone roofing slates. 'Quarrel' is an old dialect word for 'quarry' and can be found in the coastal place-name Quarrel Geo. Here, in the 17$^{th}$ century, thin flagstones were quarried to roof St. Peter's Kirk. Hoxa Head and even Banks Head (formerly Liddell Head) also provided roofing slate for this church. In 1664 members of the Kirk Session were angry that some 1,200 slates, almost certainly from the latter quarry, had been lying at St. Mary's Kirk in South Parish for three years and no attempt had been made to repair the roof! In his book *The Church in Orkney*, John Smith says that the first Presbyterian ministers were compelled by the parishioners to preach in St. Mary's even though it was roofless! The fine building stone in the island quarries has been put to other uses too. From its quarries the island of Burray made a huge contribution to the construction of the Churchill Barriers. Elderly residents can well remember the ceaseless, dusty trundling of lorry loads of stone from Northfield, Links, Warebanks and Pole to form what is now the islands' lifeline.

With several fine harbours, immediate access to good fishing grounds in the east and the more sheltered waters of Scapa Flow to the west, it is not surprising that the inhabitants of Burray and South Ronaldsay have a long tradition of seafaring. In 1746 a house by the name Skebigo was recorded in Grimness. This house has vanished but we can guess that it lay near what today is called Skipi Geo from Old Norse *skipa-gjá,* a ravine into which a ship can be brought. There are several such ravine names in Orkney, the pure Old Norse name showing their long association with vessels. Lammer Geo in Hoxa has a similar association. It derives from Old Norse *hlað-*

*The motor mail-boat Hoxa Head pre 1906.*

*hamarr*, a flat rock where boats can load or unload. The coastal place-names Lober in Hoxa and Lobers in Grimness and Sandwick derive from *hlað-berg* which carries the same meaning. In dialect this word took the form 'loadberry/loadberrie'. In his *Kirkwall in the Orkneys*, Hossack records that, towards the end of the 18th century, the people of Kirkwall were furious when a local merchant, James Stewart, 'enclosed a Loadberrie (at Quanterness) at which, many of the inhabitants of Kirkwall, time out of mind, boated their peats.' Horse Geo in Burwick suggests that this geo was a suitable place to load and unload horses. In 1776 a large boat ferrying 37 horses across the Pentland Firth to Burwick and no doubt destined for this geo, capsized with the loss of the five crew, two women passengers and all the 37 horses it was carrying. Although today, only South Ronaldsay has a ferry connection, before the construction of the Churchill Barriers, ferries operated too from Westshore in Burray to Cara in South Ronaldsay and from Boats Geo in Burray to Holm. Here too tragedies were experienced. In 1775 the Burray ferry capsized east of Glims Holm with the loss of four lives.

   In the 1799 Statistical Account of South Ronaldsay and Burray, Rev. James Watson wrote, 'The passion of young men for a seafaring life nothing can exceed . . .'. We should not think however that, in the matter of seamanship, all that a Burray and South Ronaldsay man aspired to was being a ferryman or an inshore fisherman. Many risked their lives further afield, voluntarily joining the Navy, enlisting on larger fishing vessels going to Iceland or on merchant vessels. As early as 1568 we learn from Norwegian records that John Ronaldsa was the captain of a vessel which was trading at Ryfylke in Norway. No doubt he was one of many who continued trading there long after the islands were ceded to Scotland. In South Parish the field-name 'Jamie Green's' records the site of a vanished house. Jamie Green was captain of the *Dunbar,* a full rigged ship, which foundered at the entrance to Sydney Harbour on 20th August 1857 with the loss of 63 passengers and 59 crew. Many of the crew were Orcadians and from South Ronaldsay in particular. The sole surviving crew member was named Thomson and may have been from the island.

In the remarkably detailed Census of these islands made in 1821, there were 123 boats in St. Peter's Parish, 23 boats in St. Mary's and 5 boats on Swona. The large scale development of the herring industry in the 19th century, gave South Ronaldsay fishermen further impetus. In 1838, South Ronaldsay alone had 245 herring boats! This development also led to the growth of coastal villages in Burray and at Herston and St. Margaret's Hope in South Ronaldsay.

*The number thirteen apparently held no fears for these thirteen fishermen of Windwick who proudly show off a fine halibut.*

# Hills and Streams

**W**E move inland from the coast to find topographical names typical of the whole of Orkney such as Fea in Burray from old Norse *fjall* hill, and *varða* a beacon, a name we find in Ward Hill in the middle of South Ronaldsay, Warbister on Swona, Ward Point in Burray and The Wart, the hill to the west of St. Margaret's Hope. A *varða* was the equivalent of modern-day 'watch-tower'. There is a good example from the *Orkneyinga Saga* of watchmen on guard on a hill in South Ronaldsay. When Earl Harald the Young was granted the Earldom of Orkney by King Magnus of Norway, to assert his right, he first of all had to remove Earl Harald the Old. Accordingly he sent his brother-in-law Lifólf on a covert mission from Caithness to Orkney. This is what the *Orkneyinga Saga* says:

> *Lifólf landed east in Rognvaldsey and ascended a hill where*
> *he found three of Harald's watchmen. Two of them he killed*
> *and the other he took with him for information. Lifólf saw the*
> *Earl's fleet which consisted of many ships, most of them*
> *large. Then he went down from the hill to his boat. . . .*

He would have landed in Wind Wick and climbed the Ward Hill where he disturbed the watchmen. From that vantage point he would have had an uninterrupted view of Scapa Flow where the Earl's fleet lay at anchor. An interesting lookout point on The Mainland of Orkney was the farm now called Gaitnip in St. Ola. During Norse times it was called Geitaberg from the verb *geita* to keep watch. It has a perfect view of Scapa Flow too and we learn in the *Orkneyinga Saga* that it was here where Borgar, clearly on watch, saw Sveinn Asleifson's cargo boat leaving with the captured Earl Paul.

Beacon fires were lit on hilltops to warn of imminent dangers; to quote from the *Orkneyinga Saga* once more:

> *Earl Paul had beacons lit on Fair Isle and North Ronaldsay*
> *and on most of the other islands so that each could be seen*
> *from the other.*

A Norse term for such a fire was *bál*, a word also found in Scots in the form 'bale'. Ball Hill in South Ronaldsay would have been an old bonfire site. Muckle Billia Fiold in Harray, Bailie Hill in Firth and Yonbell in Birsay are other examples. It is not known whether these were the sites of beacon fires or ceremonial fires such as those traditionally held at mid-summer which in olden days was known as 'Johnsmas'. St. John's Geo in South Ronaldsay may relate to the old custom of lighting a Johnsmas Bonfire on the nearby headland.

There are a number of words for 'slope' in Old Norse. *Brekka* accounts for the place-name Breckin and shows the Norse definite article as a suffix. *Brekka* is often part of a compound name such as Windbreck in South Ronaldsay or Yeldabrek in Burray. We should be careful in interpreting the name 'breck' however since it can refer to the Scots use of the word 'breck' (which is from a different root) to mean 'rough heathland' as in Barebreck or Barebrecks. *Hlíð*, as we have seen, is another common word for a slope but it is very often impossible to distinguish between this word in place-names and Old Norse *hlið* meaning 'gate'. Note that the latter has no accent on the 'i' as in *grind-hlið,* a gate made from spars of wood which gave its name to Grindley in Burwick. There are only a few instances of Old Norse *bakki,* slope, in the island place-names possibly because most of them have been converted into English 'banks', a word of similar origin. We do find it however in Backaquoy and Geo Back. There is a fine example of another *bakki* place-name and that is Oback which we shall discuss presently.

Our Norse ancestors commonly used names of parts of the body such as head, skull, nose, ear, tongue, neck, chest, back and backside to describe physical features in the landscape. One commonly used word in Orkney was *ökkla*, ankle, used metaphorically of the spur of a hill. *Ökkla* appears in a variety of forms such as Ackla in Orphir, Aglath in Stenness, the Braes o Aglath on Hoy, the Braes o Aglath in Harray, Etyalith in Birsay and Aitkilith applied to the hill above Guithe in Dounby. The final 'th' of some of these place-names represents the Old Norse neuter definite article '*(i)t*' of *ökkla*, in which case the word would have taken the form *ökkla-t* meaning 'the spur'. This final 't' was normally pronounced 'th' in Orkney dialect. The letters 'k' and 't' were also sometimes interchanged in dialect as in Norse and so in South Ronaldsay we find the variant Atla/Attley. In the latter instance the designation 'upper' in front of Attley has introduced the form Upper Rattley, a name far removed from the original *ökkla*!

Norse names for the type of land surface have also survived in place-names. The word *grjót* was applied to stony surfaces and helps to explain the name Grutha. *Jörfi* described gravelly soil and takes the form Yarpha in Orkney place-names. The old house of Yarpha in Grimness has vanished but there are still Yarpha place-names in Deerness, Orphir, Harray and Sanday. The word *geldr* in Norse was used of an animal which was barren. In

Orkney place-names the word is applied metaphorically to barren soil hence the place-name Youlday in South Ronaldsay and Yeldabrek in Burray. The similar place-names Yuildadee and Yeldabreck (sic) are found in Sandwick (West Mainland) and Birsay respectively. The Norse word *skarpr* described a similar soil type and the word 'scarpy' applied to heathland is still known among the older generation. The name survives in Skerpie, Burray and was recorded in Poolsherp, the old name of Pole in Burray. Up until the 16th century there was an old farm by the name Quoysharps which is believed to have lain near Cara in South Ronaldsay.

The Norse had several words for moorland one of which was *mosi*. Normally the English 'moss' form is used as in Dale Moss, Northtown Moss and Blows Moss. The first element of the latter name is particularly interesting. It is a derivative of Old Norse *blása* to blow and suggests a wind-blown landscape similar to the heathland on which Macbeth encountered the witches, addressing them with the words 'why upon this blasted heath you stop our way?' The same Norse word is found in the farm name Blanster. Orcadians of old would have used a similar word *blen* to describe a mirror-like sea by saying 'Thir's no a blen on the sea the day,' meaning that it is completely unruffled by the wind. We find identical 'windy' elements in the Blomuir place-names of Flotta and Holm, the latter written in the form 'Blowmore' in an 18th century document! Another word for moorland in Norse was *mór*, a word which appears in the original form of Masseter which was Morsetter. Sometimes the 'r' of *mór* was lost in Norse and the same occurred in Orkney, hence the Mo or Moa place-names. When the definite article is appended as a suffix to this Norse form we usually find the name Moan or in the case of South Ronaldsay, Mon. Particularly wet land was referred to by the Norse as *dý* which literally meant a 'quaking bog'. Lurdy in Burray and Youlday, a vanished South Ronaldsay farm carry this Norse word, the former meaning 'clay bog', the latter 'barren bog'.

Flowing down from the island hillsides are streams which carry Norse names. The word *gil* which is applied to a stream flowing in a narrow bed is found in several place-names such as Gillietrang and Gilbroch in Burray as well as Crookagill in South Ronaldsay. The element *þröngr* in Gillietrang actually means 'narrow'. Crookagill indicates a settlement at a bend in a stream. The place-name Graemston Laik shows a rare use in Orkney of the Norse word *laekr* to describe a stream. Leoquoy in the Brough district was recorded as *Leika kwi* in a 14th century document written in Norse and may contain the same element. The common Norse word for stream is rendered simply by the one vowel *á*, the genitive and plural form of which is *ár*. In

Orkney place-names such words are usually represented merely as 'O' 'Woo' or 'Or'. Where a settlement has been established on a stream bank it is called Oback from Norse *ár-bakki*. There is an Oback in Widewall and the Oback Burn in Windwick derives its name from the old house of Oback, now a field-name to the north of Masseter. The reader should be aware that the streams which gave us many of these names have, with artificial drainage, long since disappeared.

Bridges were rare in Orkney in Norse speaking times but they did exist. On the main road near the Harray Post office is the Brig o Brenaniar. Brenaniar is *brygga-n ný(r)* the new bridge, which suggests that at least two were built in Norse times! Such bridges may not necessarily have taken the form we think of as a bridge today. They may have been merely a walkway paved with thick flagstones which were used to ford the stream when it was in spate. Orcadians still call the paved way around houses 'brigstones'. One of the names used for such stepping stones in former times was *hlað*. In Stronsay a stretch of shore which is apparently 'paved' is called Cubbie Roo's Lade, Cubbie Roo being a North Isles 'giant'. The name is the exact equivalent of the Giant's Causeway in Northern Ireland! The Olad place-names of Widewall and Sandwick in South Ronaldsay represent Old Norse *á-hlað*, stepping stones across a stream. A similar place-name describes a field through which a stream passes in the Netherbrough district of Harray. Significantly the nearby farm in Netherbrough is called Furso i.e. *fors-á*, stream waterfall or stream torrent. *Vaðill* was the Norse name for a ford which could be traversed by horses and it is tempting to suggest that the farm of Weddell in Burray takes its name from the fording by horses of that

*Weddell Sound now spanned by Churchill Barrier No. 3; in the background Churchill Barrier No. 2 and in the foreground Weddell Fish Farm, one of only three locations in Britain farming sea trout.*

stretch of water now spanned by No. 3 Churchill Barrier. The writer is assured by Burray seamen that this would have been impossible in Norse times even at low water unless in the meantime there had been some major geological change. It would seem that 'shallow water' an alternative meaning of *vaðill*, is most likely to apply here.

Neither Burray nor South Ronaldsay are served by powerful streams yet despite this, five corn mills driven by water existed at one time in South Ronaldsay, at Brough, Cara, Sandwick, Widewall and Windwick. There was

*Many Orkney meal mills have been converted to private dwellings; this is the former*
*Widewall Mill, now in private hands and known as Kirkhouse Mill.*

also one in Burray. To cover the cost of the erection and operation of the mill, tenants were discouraged from using their own hand operated quern stones to grind grain. In this way they became 'thirled' to the mill. So many took exception to this, believing the millers to be 'swicks' that they ignored the directive with the result that in the 17th century many landowners ordered querns to be smashed. Broken quern stones from that period may be found all over Orkney. At one time South Ronaldsay provided its own millstones too as the place-name Millstone Geo in Herston testifies. There were, in addition to corn mills, many threshing mills with their associated dams. Where these mills still exist, all are disused. To overcome the lack of powerful streams, enterprising South Ronaldsay men experimented with windmills. By 1795 there were two windmills in South Ronaldsay grinding bere but it was clear that local tradesmen could not design machines which would stand up to the frequent storm conditions often experienced in the grinding season. The remains of one of these mills may yet be seen on Kirkhouse Point near St. Peter's Kirk where plenty of power would have been available in a strong south-east wind! In the late 19th century, a modest windmill, a photograph of which exists, was built at Cleat but it seemingly suffered the same fate as the others. No trace of it now remains.

After these failures it seems that the power of the wind has finally been harnessed. A vision of the future may be seen in Burray where enterprising Orcadians have succeeded in constructing on Northfield Farm a 44m. high 850 kw. turbine capable of supplying 440 homes. Since South Ronaldsay and Burray currently have 488 occupied homes, a few more kilowatts would make the islands self-sufficient in energy provision! Unlike

*The only extant photograph of the windmill which existed at Cleat in South Ronaldsay; it drove a threshing mill and, with similar gearing, was clearly intended to replace a horse driven mill; on the left is Tom Budge and on the right a Mr. Miles.*

many parts of Orkney, South Ronaldsay and Burray were poorly endowed with peat and the sparse reserves which existed rapidly became exhausted. As far as we know, the power of the wind in Burray is everlasting.

*Wind Turbine, Burray, with Weddell Farm in the background.*

# Early Settlement

**I**N common with the whole of Orkney, there is evidence everywhere in the place-names of these islands of the hand of man fashioning the landscape and it is to this we turn now in a more specific way. If we think in terms of the pre-historic landscape, the farm name Stensigar (*steins-garðr*) in Sandwick in South Ronaldsay takes its name from the nearby standing stone. The farm of Stews presents a puzzling name until we realise that its name is derived from the nearby stumps (*stúfar*) of standing stones. Both these areas are without doubt ancient ritual sites. The old place-name Viga/Vigga which lay near Grindley in South Ronaldsay, suggests a derivative of Old Norse *vigja* to consecrate a piece of ground. There was another Vigga (now called Barnhouse) in Birsay and a similar place-name in Holm. There are Viggar place-name in Burness in Sanday and North Ronaldsay. Viggar in Sanday has 'kirk' places in the vicinity whereas Vigga in Holm is in the Paplay district of that parish.

Hoxa and Howatoft contain the Norse element *haugr*, a word related to English 'high' and describe mounds which are sometimes prehistoric burial sites, sometimes ancient house sites or the grass covered remains of Pictish brochs. In the case of Hoxa the large mound is indeed a Pictish broch. In the *Orkneyinga Saga* it is stated that Earl Thorfinn Skullsplitter was buried on Hoxa and Rev. George Low in his *Tour through the Islands of Orkney and Shetland* declared that there was a local tradition that a King of Norway had been buried here. Despite such assertions, no Earl's grave has been found. We should remember that several mounds in Orkney are said in folklore to be the burial place of Earls; in Papa Stronsay we even have the Earl's Knoll! Burray and South Ronaldsay, like most of the Orkney archipelago, is well supplied with brochs; in fact the name Burray means the 'island of brochs'. There were two brochs on this island, both situated by the sea.

The place-name element 'toft' as in Howatoft stems from Old Norse *topt*, an old house site. In disguise, Hottit has the same derivation. The location of these places suggests that they are very old. This is further suggested by the addition of Norse first names to some of these 'toft/taft' place-names such as Taftshurrie (Sigurd), Taftinga (Inga) and Ontoft, the latter meriting special consideration. It represents the site of a house at one time owned by Örn. The farms of Onziebust in Egilsay and Wyre contain the same personal name. The meaning of the <u>word</u> *örn* is 'eagle' and took the form *onyo* in the dialect of Orkney where it referred specifically to the white-tailed eagle which was extremely common in the islands at one time as the contents of the so-called Tomb of the Eagles in South Ronaldsay testifies! When these beautiful birds were not fishing they had favourite resting places, usually on elevations which still bear their name. Unya Tuack on Shapinsay and Erne Tuag, a hill in Stromness parish for example, mark such sites. South Ronaldsay had three such favourite resting places— Arneip near Burwick, Earny Coulags on Kirkie Hill and Ernes Tower in the Eastside. The names 'Tuack', 'Tuag' and 'Tower' are all forms of Old Norse *þúfa*, mound, 'Tuack' and 'Tuag' having the typical South Isles diminutive whereas 'Tower' is a corruption of the Norse plural form *þúfar*. The belief that these birds carried away not only lambs but also unattended babies meant, unfortunately, that they suffered the same fate as the wolf in Scotland.

In his *History of Orkney* Barry includes in the Appendix details of a number of 17th century Acts, one of which dramatically explains the disappearance of this eagle. Here is that Act paraphrased:

*Act 31, Kirkwall, 1626, Anent Slaying of the Earn*
*It is statute and ordained that whoever slays the earn or*
*eagle shall receive eightpence from every house in the parish*
*that has sheep and twenty shillings if a nest is destroyed.*

It is said locally that the last sea eagle to breed in South Ronaldsay nested on the cliffs at Mouster Head. Motivated no doubt by the reward, men from Stews descended the cliffs and 'blew the eggs' i.e., pierced the eggs and blew the contents. Presumably the blown eggs were used as proof to the local constables that the nest had been destroyed. At any rate the eagle never returned.

The Tomb of the Eagles at Isbister in the extreme south-east of South Ronaldsay is among the most impressive of the many ancient monuments in Orkney. It is an example of a stalled chambered tomb, i.e. a tomb in which the remains of humans—and in this case birds—have been placed in stalls similar to what can be seen in a cowshed. Interred here were the skeletons and skulls of more than three hundred people and the bones of eight white-tailed eagles and other birds. The significance of the entombment of these birds is not known. In a chambered tomb which lay close to the East Broch of Burray, the remains of seven dogs were found. These birds and animals may have been part of a funerary rite in which the

*Unlike many others who entered the Tomb of the Eagles five thousand years ago, this man has a return ticket!*

evil spirits in the deceased were transferred to the eagles and the dogs. Anthropologists have noted that in some cultures chickens were used for such purposes.

Scattered throughout the Orkney landscape are crescent shaped heaps of stones which invariably show signs of being subjected to intense heat. They are more than 2,500 years old and are referred to by archaeologists as 'burnt mounds'. Often in the vicinity of these mounds there is a well and sometimes too, a flag-lined pit. In Orkney alone there are some 230 of these, more than 30 of which are in South Ronaldsay and Burray but only those burnt mounds marked on the Ordnance Survey Map are included in the gazetteer. In Orkney the finest example of all is found at Liddel in South Ronaldsay. What is the origin of these burnt mounds? It is usually explained that the stones have been heated in a massive bonfire then dropped into the water-filled trough to raise the temperature to boiling point so that meat could be cooked for communal gatherings. Why such complex culinary arrangements were made when the meat could be much more succulently prepared over the fire itself is not explained! A simpler explanation is that they have been used for ritual purification ceremonies, almost a universal feature of belief systems. Despite their distinct composition, the Norse did not seem to have a particular generic name for burnt mounds; the Knowe o Brenda in Twatt in the West Mainland does however suggest *brendr-haugr*, literally 'burnt mound'.

# Chapels and Churches

RKNEY is liberally sprinkled with ancient chapel sites but it is doubtful if any area in Orkney can compete in this respect with South Ronaldsay and its satellite islands. Like most of the early immigrants to Orkney, the earliest missionaries would have passed through these islands from the nearby mainland of Scotland. Today the site of some of these chapels is uncertain, of some there is no trace, many are merely low mounds and others at best, low ruinous walls. The nearest part of South Ronaldsay to Caithness on mainland Scotland is the Pentland Skerries group with its chapel dedicated to St. Peter. If however we measure the distance from the island of Stroma (which is part of Caithness), the nearest part of South Ronaldsay is the island of Swona. Here we also have a chapel dedicated to St. Peter and perhaps an even more ancient foundation in the

*Twinly Kirk, Swona; nothing is known of this chapel on the southernmost tip of the island and which, from its position, might stake a claim to being the first Christian foundation in Orkney.*

south of that island with an unknown dedication and referred to locally as the Twinly Kirk. A case could be made for any one of these chapels to be the first chapel site, not only in South Ronaldsay, but in the whole of Orkney, but there are other very strong contenders for this status at Burwick in South Ronaldsay—St. Mary's and the nearby site of St. Colm's. St. Colm was a disciple of St. Ninian who is credited with bringing Christianity to the north of Scotland and it may be assumed that this is the site of the first chapel. On the other hand, for over five hundred years St. Mary's has been associated with the famous footprint stone which no doubt pre-dates Christianity. It was Pope Gregory I who urged Christians to incorporate pagan symbols wherever possible and to build at or near pagan sites, not so much in a spirit of tolerance, but rather to win over adherents more easily. The Stenness Kirk, built beside the Stones of Stenness, is another good example of the pagan in close association with the Christian.

St Mary's Kirk has an uncorroborated association with Earl Rognvald. Although it is stated in the *Orkneyinga Saga* that the body of the Earl was interred at St. Magnus Cathedral, the 17th century Danish scholar Thormodus Torfaeus claimed that when the Earl's body was brought from Thurso, it was interred initially at the 'Holy Virgin's Temple' (i.e. St.

*An old photograph of St. Peter's Kirk, Eastside, South Ronaldsay; this church has a centrally placed pulpit which is rare in Orkney.*

Mary's) before it found its final resting place. This is not altogether impossible. It can be imagined that much planning was required for the ceremonial burial of the Earl at the cathedral which he had founded and that the site of St. Mary's was a fitting place for the Earl's remains to be laid while preparations were underway.

In addition to the dedications already mentioned, a chapel to St. Peter was established in the Paplay district, two other chapels were dedicated to St. Colm and one each to St. Mary, St. Margaret, St. Andrew and St. Ninian. There was also a Chapel of the Holy Rood and a Lady Chapel. Despite its size, the island of Burray has the remains of only one chapel which is dedicated to St. Lawrence. Though there is no doubt that all the forementioned chapels are ancient foundations, St. Lawrence chapel is the only structure with a date. The year 1621 marks its building, or in this case most likely, its rebuilding.

As if South Ronaldsay and Burray did not have enough religious sites, the confusion which occurred in the Church of Scotland from the 18th century onwards resulted in even more church building! The problem arose from an insensitive government enactment of 1712 that ministers should be appointed to their charges in country districts by the laird and in towns by the magistrates. Not unnaturally the wrath of congregations and ministers throughout Scotland was raised. In 1740, many ministers with their congregations broke away to form the first of a series of Secession Churches and soon the effects of this schism was felt in Orkney. In 1745, the parishioners of Orphir were furious when they discovered that they had no say in the appointment of their minister. They rioted and locked the church door to prevent the ordination. The following year when the ordination was re-attempted, soldiers were brought from Caithness to forestall any trouble but despite this, another riot ensued and one woman was killed. It took many years before these changes impacted on South Ronaldsay but eventually, in 1827, a large Secession Church was built at Garth. In 1843, simmering discontent with the continued system of patronage led to the so-called Great Disruption when 40% of churches in Scotland broke away from the established church to form the Free Church of Scotland. Meanwhile all the Secession movements had united to form the United Presbyterian Church! In 1856 the relatively new Secession Church at Garth in South Ronaldsay was demolished and a new United Presbyterian Church was built at St. Margaret's Hope using the same stones! The new United Presbyterian Church which was built in Burray in the same year led the established Church of Scotland to do something about its own flock who had had little attention since their own St. Lawrence Kirk had been abandoned in the early 1800s. A new church and manse were accordingly built near the centre of Burray in 1874. In 1876 there were further developments in South Ronaldsay when the people of South Parish, who had aligned with the Free Church of Scotland, built a church and manse near Tomison's Academy. The union of the United Presbyterian Church with the Free Church of Scotland in 1900, led to the United Presbyterian Churches in Burray and St. Margaret's Hope and the Free Church in South Parish being renamed 'United Free Church'! Although patronage, which had caused the original split in the Church of Scotland was abolished in 1874, the different sects of the church which had gone their own diverse ways eventually saw sense and most came together once more as the Church of Scotland. As Stuart Picken, minister of South Ronaldsay and Burray, said in his *Soul of an Orkney Parish*, 'it left a heritage of bitterness and a legacy of numerous church buildings for which little justification can presently be found.' Today, with the exception of one church and one manse which serve the whole of South Ronaldsay and Burray, all other churches and manses are privately owned.

*A former Free Church of Scotland building built in 1873; in 1929 it was renamed St. Mary's (New) Church of Scotland; today it is in private ownership and is known as Eastward House.*

# Parishes and Districts

**A**LTHOUGH the boundaries of most of the Orkney parishes are clearly demarcated, in the case of the two parishes in South Ronaldsay, the boundary line is less clearly defined. There is a general agreement that it lies approximately on a line drawn from Mucklehouse in Sandwick to a point in the middle of Newark Bay. The eastern boundary would seem to be confirmed by the fact that in former times a ba' game was played on the sandy links near here on Christmas Day. The competing sides would have been drawn from St. Peter's Parish and from St. Mary's Parish respectively. A similar game was played between the parishes of Orphir and Stenness on the western boundary of these parishes near the Hall of Clestrain.

Throughout Orkney, we find frequent reference to smaller units than the parish. Many of these units hark back to a time when administrative divisions even older than the parishes existed. In the case of South Ronaldsay we have in North Parish for example Ronsa (the area to the west of St. Margaret's Hope), Grimness, Widewall, Herston and Sandwick. In South Parish the three most clearly defined districts today are Burwick, Barswick and Windwick. Although outside the scope of this study, an interesting observation can be made about some of these districts. Jo Ben, writing in the 16th century, noted that there was a general nickname for the inhabitants of every parish. Such parish nicknames are still known today. Although Sanday, Westray and Stronsay in the North Isles also had parishes, there are no separate nicknames for the inhabitants of the parishes in these islands; if they did exist they have been forgotten. Only island nicknames are known. In contrast, the inhabitants of the South Isles parishes had separate nicknames. On the island of Hoy, inhabitants of the parish of Hoy were called 'Hawks' whereas residents of Walls were called 'Lyres' (shearwaters). Burray folk were referred to as 'oily bogies', fish oil bags! A 'bogie' is a form of Scots 'bougie', the dried stomach of a sheep. South Ronaldsay is unique in that, though South Parish inhabitants had the nickname 'Teeacks' or lapwings, in the case of North Parish, nicknames were applied to the inhabitants of districts. These districts and nicknames were:

Grimness: 'Gruties', the 'oily' folk, a reference to the residue of fish after the oil has been pressed out.

Eastside: No old nickname exists for the folk of this locality but it is said that they call themselves 'Beauties' (to rhyme with, and in contrast to, their neighbours the 'Gruties'!)

The Hope: 'Scouties', apparently the bird, the scoutie-alan, dialect name of the Arctic skua; a similar nickname 'scootie' was used for the people of Kirkwall and referred to the bird, the starling; 'scoutie'/'scootie' means 'diarrhoeic', a characteristic of these birds.

Widewall: 'Witches', probably a reference to early witch trials though no witch trials related specifically to this district..

Herston: 'Hogs', yearling sheep; Shapinsay folk were also referred to as 'sheep', both carrying the meaning 'stupid'.

Sandwick: 'Birkies'; Scots 'birkie' is a 'smart youth' but in Orkney dialect the word carried the meaning 'dirty'; perhaps a variation of dialect 'barkèd', encrusted with filth.

As can be seen from the examples, some of these nicknames are uncomplimentary. The origin of such island, parish and district nicknames is uncertain. Many are truly ancient, being first recorded, as we have noted, in the 16th century. The inhabitants of many parishes and districts in Shetland also had objectionable names which would seem to point to a Norse connection but such nicknames are unknown in Norway. To compound the mystery, it has also been established that no such nicknames were ever used in the Western Isles which were under Norse domination for many centuries.

# Farm and House Names

**I**T was said in the introduction that South Ronaldsay represents a microcosm of Orkney place-names and this is particularly true of the farm names. There is a *bú* farm in Burray (The Bu) and several *bú* farms in South Ronaldsay but to judge by the early Rentals of the islands only the Burray *bú* seems to be an original Norse creation, the others being composites created from a number of farms. *Staðir* farms which are common on the Orkney Mainland such as Clouston and Tormiston are represented by Herston. There is a multiplicity of *kví* (quoy) names in South Ronaldsay as in Brandyquoy and Ossquoy. These referred normally to animal pens outside the tunship but some *kví* names in Orkney are applied to quite large districts such as Sutherquoy in Sandwick or Beaquoy, both in the West Mainland. It seems that, in Orkney at any rate, the word *kví* could be used for a much larger area. A good example of this comes from the island of Swona where the wall called the Quoy Dyke which cuts off the south-western tip of the island separated off a 'quoy', from the rest of the island. If we include the extensive foreshore, this 'quoy' covers an area of approximately 2 hectares which can scarcely be described as an 'animal pen'. Old Norse *saetr* has something in common with *kví* in that they were animal shelters too but seemingly only in seasonal use, something akin to the Gaelic *airigh*. Unlike 'quoy', it is never found applied to a large area. They are usually located on hills and former moorland. The word *saetr* is represented in South Ronaldsay by Blanster, Masseter and Quoyhorsetter. Blanster and Masseter both carry 'moorland' names.

Quoyhorsetter is of particular interest since it appeared in its original form as Quoyschorsetter. The middle element *schor* can be found in Nynorsk as *skur* and in Icelandic as *skjár*, both meaning 'hut'. In Nynorsk this word loses the final 'r' to take the additional form *skjaa*. The same development occurred in Orkney, the words *skyo*, *skeo*, *skio* and *skoo* describing a shelter, words used by a number of people even in the late 1980s when the writer was collecting Orkney dialect words. In the south-east of Swona this place-name is written in the odd form *Sk-yeows* on the Ordnance Survey map! Here such buildings were used for drying fish. Such forms account for the South Ronaldsay place-names Scews and Scows and with the Norse definite article as a suffix explains the farm name Schusan. In the West Mainland of Orkney there are Scuan place-names in Harray and Stenness and across the border in Orphir we find Scows. The farm of Skogar in Birsay which was compulsorily purchased to enable the construction of Twatt aerodrome in the 1940s contains the same element. Another Norse word for hut was *búð* which the reader will recognise as a word related to English 'booth.' With the definite article at the end it took the form *búð-in*. This word explains the South Ronaldsay place-name Quoyboon. Notice that the 'ð' consonant has disappeared. Normally this word appears in Orkney place-names as Bewan or Buan. The name of an old enclosure in Birsay was called by the related name Quoybune and its position today is marked by a significant adjacent standing stone known as the Stone o Quoybune. The Harray place-name Bu-house shows *búð* without the definite article. A rare Orkney place-name is Old Norse *sel*, a hut. Rossel Howe (*hross-sel haugr*) in Sandwick, West Mainland, marks the site of an old horse shelter near a mound. Vensilly in South Ronaldsay and Sellyland in Burray may mark the site of old huts but it is sometimes difficult to distinguish between *sel* meaning 'hut' and *selja* meaning 'willow'.

There are surprisingly only a few *bólstaðir* place-names in the whole of South Ronaldsay and Burray. The original meaning of *bólstaðir* is 'pens for animals' but since farm buildings became associated with these enclosures the word assumed the meaning 'farm'. In North Parish we find Wasbister, Midbister and Isbister which represent the 'west, 'mid' and 'east' farms respectively. There are several Isbister place-names in Orkney and the initial 'Is' is derived in a number of different ways. In the case of Isbister in South Parish the element 'Is' suggests its 'outermost' position from Old Norse *yztr-bólstaðir*. Warbister on Swona and Rigbister on Pentland Skerries, because of their position, could never have been farms. They would seem to carry the original meaning of 'pens for animals'. In the case of Rigbister, it is likely that sheep were transported there for summer grazing and simple shelters were constructed on the island for them. There is only one *bae* i.e. 'farm' place-name represented by Sebay but there is some doubt about whether it is an original place-name or transferred from a place of that name in St. Andrews since it does not appear in early records. The name Cleat (*klettr*) which is widespread in Orkney is found in South Ronaldsay and as the reader will note in the place-name entries, its use inland is interpreted as the location of a stone building, in some cases perhaps the cell of an anchorite. This Norse name is also found compounded in Linklater, a place-name found elsewhere in Orkney and which can take other forms such as Linklet, Howclet, Benzieclett and so on. The farm of Benzieclett lay in Sandwick in the West Mainland and was requisitioned during World War II to build Skeabrae aerodrome. The real meaning of Benzieclett is 'prayer house' from Old Norse *baena* to pray.

In the old system of landholding, each settlement had in close proximity to the dwelling a field which, unlike the rest of the land in the locality, was not shared by the neighbours. In Norse such a field was called a *tún-völlr* which is probably best translated as 'home field'. In Orkney this name became completely corrupted and in old deeds usually takes a variety of forms such as 'townmail', 'toomal' 'tumal' or 'tumol'. Farmers in the West Mainland of Orkney can still point to fields which they call the 'toomal'. This word rarely appears in place-names with the important exception of Longtownmail in St. Andrews. In a list of Burray farms drawn up in 1750 after the death of Sir James Stewart of Burray no less than seven Tumol place-names were recorded. All these names have vanished. In Fea's Rental of 1750 there was a Tumol o St. Columbus (St. Colm's) in Grimness. There is only one Tumal field-name in South Ronaldsay today near the farm of East Masseter. Two farms still retain the word *völlr*, meaning simply 'field'. Farewell (*faer-völlr*, sheep field) matches the farm of Faravel in Birsay. Broll, the earliest recording of which was Burrowell, would originally have been *borgar-völlr* the field (by the) enclosure; sadly the name of this old farm has been changed. The word 'acre' in English relates to a field of a particular size. It is an ancient Indo-European word which is found in Latin in the form *ager* and even in Sanskrit as *ajra* and means merely 'field'. In the *Orkneyinga Saga* it said of Sveinn that after his plundering trips in the Hebrides and Ireland he returned just after mid-summer (to Gairsay) when his *akrar* had been cut. In Norse *akrar* or *ekrur* meant 'cornfields'. Today the South Ronaldsay district name Aikers tells us that it was good farming land in Norse times. We also learn that Thord had a fine arable field at *Þordar-ekr*, (now Thurrigar) and there was good land too at *Gossakir* (now Gossigar) owned by Gási.

South Ronaldsay, in common with a number of Orkney parishes, has a farm by the name Flaws and similarly named fields. Flaws place-names in Orkney have presented a problem to those researching place-names but there is no doubt in the writer's mind that it was originally an area with poor shallow soil which was stripped in an extravagant process to make a kind of compost to enrich the better fields. Thin turves from shallow soils were also used for thatching roofs. This process in Orkney was called 'poning' and is related to Norwegian dialect *panna*, a roof tile. The Old Norse word *flag* was an area stripped of turf. With the neuter definite article as a suffix it took the form *flag-it*. Flecketsquoy (now Doverhouse) in the Northside of Birsay contains this element. Its old name was Flagith. In the parish of Harray the place-name Flaws o Yeldavil is interesting since Yeldavil, means 'barren field' and the 'Flaws' would have been an ideal place to cut thin turf.

Today the Orkney landscape is criss-crossed by countless roads and paths. In the olden days there must have been many more paths but a striking feature of Orkney place-names is the almost total absence of words for road or path. In Harray and Birsay we find instances of the word *leið* which takes the form Lyde. In one or two places such as Sanday and Tankerness the word Messigate includes the word *gata*, a path, in these instances a pass to 'Mass' i.e. to the church. Neither of these words is found in Burray or South Ronaldsay but an interesting 18th century place-name Trofer in Burray merits interest. It compares with Troffers in Evie, a word applied to paths there. It is probably a corrupt form of Old Norse *traðir*, literally 'trodden' places and is used here in the Icelandic sense of 'lane'. A very common word for a path in South Ronaldsay is *clivvy*. It refers specifically to a path which follows a cleft in the rock face. The word is derived from Old Norse *klufðr* a cleft, and is used generically in South Ronaldsay to describe such a path today. These paths were used regularly to get access to fishing rocks or to gather what local folk called 'beach', i.e. gravel, more generally referred to in Orkney dialect as 'chingly stones'.

It is not only in terms of Norse place-names that South Ronaldsay and Burray mirror the whole of Orkney. These islands also contain some fascinating more modern place-names and by that is meant place-names which have been born, and in many cases have died, within the last two to three hundred years. These include many transferred place-names such as Canada, New Zealand, California, Klondyke, Balarat (sic), Sedan, Kronstadt and Havanah (sic). The house known as Little Stews, now used as an agricultural building, was jocularly referred to as Crowsnest at the beginning of the 19th century. It was later renamed Egypt which gave locals the opportunity to rename the small stream which passed it 'The Nile'! All these names reflect the wanderlust of Orcadians as seafarers or as returned emigrants.

These islands also share with the rest of Orkney fanciful names given for a variety of reasons. By the end of the 17th century a new fashion arose throughout Britain in which owners chose house names which were thought to add some dignity to their dwelling. This development took root in Orkney too. South Ronaldsay did not escape the rash of Mount Pleasant place-names which began to litter the English speaking world or the popular Scots names Mounthoolie and others such as Blinkbonny and Blinkglee.

Many such names included the word 'bank' as in Daisybank, Merrybank, Bonnybank and because of the popularity of the flower, the rose, the common name Rosebank. There are at least six Rosebank house names in Orkney. In South Ronaldsay we also find Rose Lea and Rose Cottage, the latter being one of the most popular house names in Britain!

Other house names were clearly not given by the occupier but sneeringly perhaps applied by neighbours. Names which fall into this category are Crowsnest to which we have referred above, Cauldhame, Windywalls (another 'cold home'!), Ploverbrake and Tebrake (teeick = lapwing). 'Brake' here refers to poor, heather covered land, very poor as in the case of Barebrecks. The name Whistlebere (now 'Whistlebrae' in Paplay) was used by the Scots to describe similar land, the element 'whistle' here referring to exposure to the wind! The old house of Cathole in Burray recorded in 1821 must have been a poor dwelling indeed. Today it would be called a 'dog hole'. Perhaps one of the most objectionable names applied to a house was Dog Tuag, a name also found in Westray as Dog Too and in Burray and Shapinsay in the form Dog Toos. It probably referred to a house made entirely of turf since a number of such houses still existed in the 19th century. A 'dog tuag' was a tuft of grass against which a dog would urinate! A more acceptable name for such a turf house was

*This humble dwelling which has vanished was known only by the name Maggie Broon's, from the name of the occupant who poses for her photograph; notice the benlins which held down the heather thatch, the small window behind the boorwid tree and the bourtisement which not only sheltered the door but, in this case, also apparently held up the wall!*

'Griceback', meaning 'pig's back', a reference to the shape of the house. It is the exact equivalent of English 'hog's back', often applied to rounded hills. There were at one time four such 'houses' in South Ronaldsay. We can read a description of such a house in Stronsay in Daniel Gorrie's *Summers and Winters in the Orkneys* relating to a period at the end of the 19th century:

> *The walls (of Effie Spence's house) are composed mainly of turf with a few layers of slabs beneath; the roof is turf; the small chimney top is wisped with rotten straw ropes; there is no window in the walls and a solitary nobbed pane of green glass is the only bull's eye of the dismal abode.*

The name Limbo in South Ronaldsay fits into a pattern of similar house names found throughout Orkney such as Hell and Purgatory. They often referred to land that was initially difficult to work. A dramatic example of such is the aptly named field called Murder which lies to the west of Quoyorally! Sometimes such names referred to the dwelling house itself or the occupants! An instance of this is the house of Hell which stood in Albert Street in Kirkwall near the site of the present day Woolworths. Next to it was Mounthoolie which presumably represented heaven! We find a similar juxtaposition of Heaven and Hell in Shapinsay, nicknames given to the houses of Veantroe and Comelybank respectively; apparently prayer meetings were a feature of the former and blazing rows of the latter!

We cannot leave reference to house nicknames without a passing mention of Heathercowspunk in Burray! A 'heather cow(e) spunk' is a spark flying from a piece of burning heather bush! It must have been applied initially as a nickname to a former inhabitant who described such a spark when it flew from the open fire, the name subsequently being applied to the house! She must have been a poor soul indeed, burning the heather covered 'fails' which had been 'flayed' from the peat bank before the peat was cut, rather than the peat itself.

# *Personal Names*

HERE sometimes is a very close relationship between the names of places and the people who lived there. We have already noted how some of the old 'toft' place-names carry first names. South Ronaldsay and Burray place-names have preserved the first names of many long-gone inhabitants, names which are no longer in use. Men by the name *Brandr* lived at Brandyquoy and at Brance, *Bersi* at Quoybirse and Bersiedale, *Gási* at Gossigar, *Örn* in Ontoft, *Hramn* in Ramsquoy, *Hámundr* in Hamisquoy, *Hrókr* in Rockerskaill and *Sigurðr* in Taftshurrie. Those Orkney farms which had the Old Norse element *staðir* in them appear to have been particularly significant for four reasons: 1. two of them, *Skeggbjarnarstaðir* (regrettably vanished) in Deerness and *Jadvarrarstaðir* (now Gaitnip) in St. Ola are recorded in the *Orkneyinga Saga*. 2. the latter farm was in the possession of a daughter of Earl Erlend. 3. all of them have a personal name element in them. 4. many of them became district names. The sole example we draw from South Ronaldsay is Herston, the first

*An old photograph of St. Margaret's Hope taken from the Ontoft Road leading to Ronsa.*

recording of which in 1492 is Harthstath. Here *Harðar*, clearly an important Norseman, must have farmed. Like all the other *staðir* farm names in Orkney, it too became a district name. Perhaps one of his contemporaries was *Rögnvaldr* who owned a great swathe of land to the west of St. Margaret's Hope. He must have been a mighty man indeed for he gave his name not only to Ronsvoe but to the whole island of South Ronaldsay. There is no mention of him in the *Orkneyinga Saga* which demonstrates that this name pre-dates the 11th century.

Women's names are not commonly found in Orkney placenames. *Jadvarrarstaðir* above is one such example from the *Orkneyinga Saga*. One of the earliest recorded examples of a place-name carrying a woman's name exists in a document written in Norn in 1329 and which will be referred to in more detail presently.

> j Stufum xx skillinga kaup oc i Kuikobba .xx. skillinga kaup. Jtem j Klaete tolf mærkr jtem sex peninga land i þordar ekru firir aeina mork oc xx. Jtem .iij. peninga land j Borgh firir .ix. mærkr jtem j Leika kwi vj marka kaup oc j Lið xx skillinga kaup jtem a Haughs æiði x skillinga kaup jtem Petlandz skær vttan bus firir xx mærkr.

*An excerpt from the document written in Kirkwall in 1329 in which, for the first time, certain South Ronaldsay place-names are mentioned. These are underlined. The original is held in the Danish National Archives.*

It refers to Kuikobba in South Ronaldsay which suggests an enclosure belonging to *Jakoba*. With regard to similar place-names, we can be reasonably sure that Oss(a)quoy was the home of *Ásleif*, a female name which persisted right up until the 19th century in the form Ossilla or more commonly Osla. Ossilla Sclater was born in Burwick in 1658. One of the few Norse names to have survived right through the centuries is Inga and is found in old South Ronaldsay place-names such as Taftinga and Inyequoy the latter appearing later in the form Quoyinga and Quoyenas. In the parish of Firth the remains of the broch known as Ingashowe would have stood at one time on the land of a lady by the name Inga. Later personal names in South Ronaldsay include 'Cathy' in Cathysquoy and 'Eden', the latter from the Old English name *Eadu* and recorded in the place-name Quoyeden. This rare girl's first name was used by the Leith family in South Ronaldsay in the mid 16th century and the place-name Quoyeden is likely to be as old as that if not older. Actually the name was first recorded in Orkney in 1460 and has something of an aristocratic ring about it since, in that year, Edane Paplay exchanged her lands in Paplay in Holm for Sebay in Tankerness, the property of Earl William. Another rare name for a girl was Geiles or Gilius, a form of Giles. Geiles Flaws married Donald McBeth in St. Peter's Kirk in 1660. This first name is fossilised in Gylliosquoy an old name of the farm of Schusan.

No less than twenty five of the farm names/districts in turn provided surnames seven of which still exist. These are Banks, Berston, Windwick, Flaws, Halcro, Leith and Linklater. Banks, Berston, Flaws and Linklater also originated elsewhere in Orkney but Windwick, Halcro and Leith are unique to South Ronaldsay. There is some doubt about whether the farm of Meall in South Ronaldsay or Westermill (earlier Westermail) in Burray gave birth to the surname Meil. John Maile lived in Burray in 1658 but that name could have originated from Meall in Holm, the old name of Graemeshall. We should remember that the island name Burray also provided a surname. It is now extinct but it existed for a good number of years in the North Isles. William Burray was one of a number of distinguished men who sat on a court at the farm of Sebay in Tankerness in 1552 and in that same district is the old farm name Quoyburray. The surname Ronaldsay is recorded only once. We have already made mention of John Ronaldsa who was the captain of a vessel at Ryfylke in Norway in 1568. He appears to be the same man who was witness to the sale of a house in Kirkwall in 1573.

# Norsemen and Scots

THE close proximity of South Ronaldsay and Burray to the Scottish mainland gave it not only a strategic significance but also, positioned as they were on a trade route and with some excellent soils, made them a desirable place for important families to take up residence. We have already noted that Earl Thorfinn Skullsplitter was said to be buried in Hoxa. There is no proof of this but it raises the interesting possibility that he lived there just as his namesake, Earl Thorfinn Sigurdarson, lived in Birsay and was buried there. There is definite proof of Viking presence, if not settlement, in Burray. On the 22nd April 1889 George Petrie of Little Wart was cutting peat near the Green Sleigh, a small stream above Ourequoy in Burray when he came across a wooden bowl buried in the moss containing tarnished pieces of metal and coins. It was later established that he had stumbled upon a Viking hoard which included silver torcs, armlets and 10th and early 11th century Anglo-Saxon coinage, the latter helping to pinpoint the burial to the earlier part of the 11th century. Surely only a resident Viking pirate would have concealed treasure here, the use of a domestic bowl suggesting further proof. There is certainly evidence of such activity elsewhere on the islands.

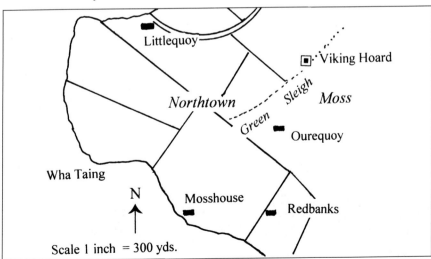

*The location of the Viking Hoard*

According to the *Orkneyinga Saga* three men lived on Swona; they were Grim, a poor farmer and his two sons Asbjorn and Margad. One might read too much into the word 'poor' applied to these early Swona residents. The 'poor' merited little attention in the sagas. The word used to describe the father and his sons in the *Orkneyinga Saga* is *fé-lítill* which is ambiguous. It can mean that Grim was poor in the sense of having no money but it could merely mean that he had no sheep. I strongly suspect the latter. These men, like all Swona men would have been skilled navigators and probably made a living from rich pickings in the Pentland Firth. One can imagine them challenging the masters of smaller vessels with the threat, 'Allow us to pilot you through at a price or if you don't we'll have your cargo.' This assumption about their means of livelihood is borne out by the fact that all three were powerful and influential men. They were all very much in the mould of their close friend, Sveinn of Gairsay, and like him, pirates, since the island was well placed to intercept traffic going through the Pentland Firth. It says elsewhere in the saga that Sveinn gave Grim a gold ring for taking him from Swona to Scapa which was surely, in the context of the time, one of the most expensive ferry crossings ever! The giving of a gold ring—even though it was probably looted—was a mark of great personal affection. Sveinn used Margad as an intermediary between himsel and Earl Erlend and when Sveinn fled to the court of King David of

*A sight familiar to Grim, Asbjorn and Margad—the east side of Swona with its 40 m. high cliffs and with coastal features named The Bishop and Slates of the Altar.*

Scotland he took Margad with him, on the way plundering the monastery on the Isle of May! They were given a warm welcome by King David who might have been expected to become very angry when he learned of this typical Viking raid on his subjects but the value placed on the Orkneymen by the king is demonstrated by the fact that he made reparations to the monks for their losses! No tears need be shed for these 'poor' early inhabitants of Swona!

After the *Orkneyinga Saga*, there follows a long lacuna in historical information about the islands until the 14th century when the earliest historical records of South Ronaldsay are found. They were written in Kirkwall in 1329 in the Norn language and dealt with a land transaction in which Katerina, Countess of Orkney and Caithness and widow of Earl Magnus V, bought from Herra Erling Vidkunnsson, the King of Norway's Steward, land in Stews, Aikers, Cletts, Gossigar and Thurrigar in addition to the Pentland Skerries. It is not known whether the Countess lived in South Ronaldsay at any time, but the transaction definitely shows aristocratic influence, if not residence.

Many Scots settled in Orkney even when it was part of Scandinavia but when it was transferred to the Scottish Crown, they came in increasing numbers. Since the principal ferry route from the Scottish mainland to Orkney was from Caithness to South Ronaldsay and Burray it is not surprising that the first recording of many Scottish surnames are in these islands. These surnames about which we have definite information include Bain, Budge, Cromarty, Croy, Currie, Donaldson, Doull, Esson, Gutcher, Laird, Leslie, Lyall, MacKay, MacLeod, Mair, Rorie, Rosie and Scott. Several of these, such as Budge, Cromarty, Currie, Doull, Gutcher and Rosie are still seen as typical South Ronaldsay names. The Cromartys take their name from that part of the Highlands normally linked with Ross County. They arrived in South Ronaldsay soon after it became Scottish and are said to be either Douglases or Urquharts who sought refuge here. They were among Orkney's first asylum seekers and whatever their background, they soon made a huge impact on South Ronaldsay. We have little knowledge of the many Jacobites who took refuge in Orkney after the failure of their rebellion but an interesting story is told of the Allans who lived on Swona for almost two centuries. It is said locally that the original settler was Allan Stewart who, to avoid the terrible persecution of the Jacobites after the defeat at Culloden, assumed a new identity in the form of Stewart Allan. As interesting as this local tale is, we should point out however that there were already Allans in Burwick in the middle of the 17th century.

# *Fine Dwellings*

**B**RANCHES of important Orkney families, usually associated with residence elsewhere, settled here too such as the Fletts, the Irelands, the Heddles, the Richans and as, Storer Clouston argues, the Cloustons, whom he maintained, adopted the territorial surname Cara. Does it surprise us then that, outside Kirkwall, no part of Orkney could rival these islands for fine dwellings. By far the most significant was the mansion house or 'Place' in Burray, the 18th century home of Sir James Stewart

*An old photograph of The Bu in Burray.*

which, according to an Inventory of 1710, contained much oak furniture, silverware and many items made of silk. Sir James supported Bonnie Prince Charlie in the 1745 rebellion and paid dearly for it, dying in prison in London. A few remains of this Palace may yet be seen in its successor, the

Bu of Burray. The Caras lived in the Great House of Cara, a two storey mansion house which, with its adjacent St. Colm's Chapel, served the whole of Grimness. It could boast having one of the five water mills in South Ronaldsay and the very important ferry rights. Later, when this estate was divided into two, half through marriage became the estate of Brecks, home of Sir James Sinclair, who led to victory the soldiers of so many important Orkney families in the encounter with the Earl of Caithness and his forces at the Battle of Summerdale in Stenness in 1529. Cara later became associated particularly with the Cromarty family.

Another fine building, apparently occupied by the Sinclairs, was a mansion house, perhaps even a 'castle' said to have lain in what is now the farm yard of Mucklehouse in Sandwick; nearby lay the Holyrood Chapel. The building was occupied by a Lady Wemyss who, supposedly, had a French maid. If this seems the stuff of fairy tales it should be remembered that, in the middle of the 16th century when Marie de Guise was Regent of Scotland, much French influence was felt throughout the kingdom, Monsieur Bonot being appointed Governor of Orkney! There is no trace of Lady Wemyss Castle today but the name seems to have been transferred to the remains of a broch known as Weems Castle nearby.

(Old) Grutha in Grimness was occupied by the Fletts and was a very important, large house in its day. It was sufficiently important to merit the attention of the Royal Commission on Ancient Monuments in the 1930s who estimated that the extant structure then dated from the 17th century.

Further south, in the east of the island, little remains of a residence which was sufficiently imposing to gave its name to a whole bay and the stream which flows into it. The mansion house was known as 'New wark' or Newark, where 'wark' (Old English *weorc*) had the meaning 'imposing building'. It was built, probably in the 16th century, apparently by an important merchant family, the Pitcairns, who had interests in Kirkwall and in Shetland. In the middle of the 17th century it was occupied (though not owned) by Matthew Mowbray, a wealthy man and Chamberlain of Orkney, who is buried in St. Peter's Kirkyard. The history of this house is

*The arms of Matthew Mowbray, a wealthy Kirkwall merchant and property owner, who settled at Newark in South Ronaldsay and was buried in St Peter's Kirkyard. He died in the 1640s.*

remarkably similar to the history of the mansion house of Newark in Deerness and its associated chapel built by Earl Patrick Stewart towards the end of the 16th century and which gave its name to Newark Bay there. In the 17th century the Deerness Newark was occupied by Lord Lindores, a relative of the Earl. Just as there is little trace of the South Ronaldsay Newark today, little trace of the Deerness mansion or chapel was found by the Royal Commission on Ancient Monuments when they surveyed the area in the 1930s.

Of all South Ronaldsay families, there is little doubt that the Halcros stood head and shoulders above all others. They wielded great power as landowners all over Orkney and Shetland and produced a series of distinguished church men. Their domicile was that part of South Ronaldsay known at one time as 'Holland alias Halcro'. In 1627, Hugh Halcro owned all the lands belonging to these chapels—St. Colm's in Burwick, St. Colm's in Hoxa, St. Ninian's at Stews, St. Peter's Chapel on the Pentland Skerries, the kirk lands at Stensigar as well as of course the lands attached to his own Chapel of Our Lady at Halcro. With such wealth and influence one can imagine that his fine 17th century mansion house known as the Hall of Holland was a very fine building indeed. In the vestry of St. Mary's Kirk can be seen one of the oldest Orkney tombstones which records the death of Sir Hugh Halcro (great-grandfather of the former) in 1554.

*The initials H H clearly identify this as the Arms of Sir Hugh Halcro, rector of South Ronaldsay, who died in 1554; his tombstone is in St. Mary's Kirk.*

The Graemes of Graemeshall in Holm married into the Halcros and also built nearby a fine mansion house. In Craven's *Church Life in South Ronaldsay and Burray in the 17th Century* we read, '18th July, 1690, George Graeme of Gramstoun (sic), husband to the Lady Halcro, depairted this lyfe'. At the beginning of the 20th century the ruins of this house could still be seen.

# *Schools*

HERE is a surprising number of references to schools in this study of the place-names of South Ronaldsay and Burray and education in these two islands is worth a special mention since, outside Kirkwall, they were in the forefront of educational provision in Orkney. As early as 1658 a school was established in South Ronaldsay with Donald Clerk as schoolmaster. It apparently catered for all the pupils on the island. In 1659 Archibald Stewart built a school in Burray where education was provided free of charge and every child was compelled to attend. Such a thing was unknown until the passing of the 1872 Education Act! A school specifically serving South Parish was built in the Windwick district of South Ronaldsay in 1663 and two years later North Parish was catered for by the establishment of what appears to have been a new school in St. Margaret's Hope with Walter Kynnaird as master. By 1683 a private school was also operating in South Ronaldsay. All early parish schools were intended to be supported by those who owned property and since many heritors defaulted in payments, these schools continually suffered from lack of funds. An organisation known as S.S.P.C.K. (Scottish Society for the Propagation of Christian Knowledge) often came to the rescue. Such a school was established in South Ronaldsay in the early part of the 18th century but was closed in 1732 when it was realised by the society that providing a charity school was a disincentive for the heritors to pay up and it appears that South Ronaldsay was without any school for a long period until 1790 when the S.S.P.C.K. once again felt compelled to re-open a school. Although in the 17th century the heritors of South Ronaldsay and Burray were among the first to provide education for their children, by 1810, through persistent default in payment, it was the only area in Orkney without parish schools! When James Stewart, a Kirkwall merchant, left almost £1,000 in a legacy for the poor of Kirkwall to be educated, it gave two other Orcadians, Magnus Twatt of Orphir and William Tomison of South Ronaldsay, both employees of Hudson's Bay Company, an opportunity to provide education for the children of their parishes. Magnus left a portion of an annuity to be used by the people of Orphir to build a school which opened its doors in 1804 and which is today a substantial private house known as the Old Schoolhouse. William Tomison joined Hudson's Bay Company as a mere labourer in 1760 and rose to become Governor of North West Territories. In this endeavour he accumulated a large fortune to become one of Orkney's richest men ever. In 1793 he had already begun to pay £20 yearly towards the salary of a schoolmaster, ten years before an Act of Parliament made such a salary payment compulsory. On his retirement in 1812 he went further by building near his house, a school which eventually came to be known as South Parish School. When he died in 1829, half of his personal estate which in total at that time was valued at £12,000 was left to provide an even better school to be maintained in perpetuity from his legacy.

It was apparently Tomison's private initiative which spurred the heritors of South Ronaldsay and Burray to meet in that same year with a view to providing a parish school which would serve both islands. The site of the old house of Brandyquoy in South Ronaldsay was chosen and the building was designed in such a way that the schoolmaster lived on the same premises. The school offered eight subjects which included French, Latin, Greek and Navigation and parents were expected to make a contribution to the education of their children. The first schoolmaster was James Forbes who, during the summer months, laboured at his duties from 9 o'clock in the morning until 5 o'clock in the afternoon with a break of only an hour. In the winter, because of poor light, the school opened at 10 o'clock and closed at 3 o'clock. James must have been grateful for his five

*Tomison's Academy today.*

weeks' holiday which began only when harvest was ready, this arrangement ensuring that the more able bodied children could help on the farms. It was in this school where the celebrated doggerel poet William McGonagall received some of his education when this Irish family stayed briefly in South Ronaldsay in the 1840s. Since poetry was not on the curriculum of the school, Forbes cannot be held responsible for McGonagall's effusions! The school came to be known as Forbes' School and subsequently became a dwelling house when the new parish school was built in St. Margaret's Hope. Today, Forbes' School is known as the Old Schoolhouse. The building of Forbes' School delayed until 1851 the implementation of Tomison's bequest. Tomison's Academy, as it came to be known, was eventually built in 1851 and remained in use until the 1960s. Today, sadly, it remains empty but the original school, which came to be the School House, is occupied as a private dwelling.

When the Second Statistical Account of Orkney was published in 1841, the local minister, Reverend Gerrard, was able to declare that there were ten schools in operation on the island. A house in St. Margaret's Hope known as Cullocks, which has now vanished, became a school as did South Liddell and West Flaws, the latter also referred to as Miller's School. With the passing of the 1872 Education Act, government schools providing free and compulsory education were established in the islands. Generous provision was made here with new schools being built in St. Margaret's Hope and in the districts of Herston, Widewall and Grimness in South Ronaldsay. New schools were also built in Burray and on the island of Swona. Today, when from a passing ferry we look at the forlorn island of Swona, it is difficult to believe that in 1878 the new school opened here with 14 pupils on the register and continued to provide education for the island children for half a century.

# Summary

I n July 2006 when the manuscript was finally revised, there were 488 occupied houses in South Ronaldsay and Burray. In addition to these, 21 houses were seasonally occupied as holiday homes and 42 houses were empty, the great majority of which face an uncertain future. 32 properties are derelict and are likely to follow the 365 which have already vanished. Perhaps the fate of many more would have been sealed today but for the advent of immigrants from mainland Britain who have chosen to live here and who have, in many cases, restored houses unpretentiously in a manner which is in keeping with old building traditions. Local people lament the rapid change which has taken place in their community in the last fifty years but change has been a facet of life in these islands for more than two hundred years. When a Census was made of South Ronaldsay and Burray in 1821, the population was 2231. At that time there were 29 people living on Swona and 8 on the Pentland

*With the rapid development of Burray today few would recognise this picture of the east end of Burray village taken from the pier.*

*St. Margaret's Hope; 1974.*

Skerries. Today, only 1211 people live on South Ronaldsay and Burray; Swona and the Pentland Skerries are uninhabited. This population loss has to be seen in context however—similar losses have occurred elsewhere in the islands. Post-war, South Ronaldsay and Burray have emphatically benefited from their strategic position in two World Wars, guarding as they do the eastern and southern approaches to Scapa Flow. This is clearly shown by population statistics. No one laments the construction of the Churchill Barriers which, technically, has incorporated the islands into The Mainland and which, subject to the weather, allow free passage of vehicles. Without such a transport link the population would no doubt be much lower. Contrast population trends in Shapinsay, a mere Cubbie Roo stone throw from Kirkwall, with Burray and South Ronaldsay which, at their nearest point, lie nine miles away. Shapinsay has lost 28% of its post-war population compared with 13% for Burray and South Ronaldsay combined. This latter statistic conceals the fact that the post-war population of Burray itself has increased by 36%, a figure matched by few Scottish islands and clearly demonstrates that it has become an increasingly popular island in which to live. The construction of the Churchill Barriers has also enabled foot passenger and car ferries to revive the original short sea crossing route to ship passengers, goods and vehicles to South Ronaldsay and from there to all parts of The Mainland and no one can deny that South Ronaldsay has further benefited from this development. Should a Pentland Tunnel be built, the effect on these islands cannot be imagined!

A disturbing tendency in South Ronaldsay and Burray, a tendency which is echoed throughout Orkney, is the substitution of new names for houses and farms, names which go back more than a thousand years. This is particularly true of Norse names which take on another meaning if seen as English names. Such substitution is not new. Old Norse *melr*, sand, a fine sounding name for a farm in the original language, took the form Meall in Orkney which was deemed unsuitable when seen as an English name. Meall in Holm became Graemeshall and Meall in Deerness, Newark. These names were changed more than three hundred years ago. Examples of modern substitutions are found in the text. It does seem strange that preservation orders can be made on houses which in some cases are barely three hundred years old and at the same time little regard is paid to keeping alive names which are equally part of our heritage and in some instances, more than a thousand years old. Perhaps steps could be taken at county level to preserve what is left. Meanwhile it is to be hoped that this book will help to increase understanding of the significance of the great pool of old names which the people of Burray and South Ronaldsay are fortunate enough to have inherited in the hope that no more will disappear.

# Section 2

# Gazetteer of The Place-names of South Ronaldsay and Burray

*Many entries are extracted from Ordnance Survey Maps, 1882 edition, and relate to a period in the 1870s. House names with Census dates and some earlier dates were kindly supplied by George Esson, Linburn, St. Margaret's Hope in August 2003. The spelling of many Orkney place-names presents a difficulty. This is particularly true of the spelling of house names where occupiers prefer one form to another. The chosen form in this book does not represent the correct form but, in many cases, only one of many spelt forms. All foreign words and dialect words are in italics as are all cross-referenced place-names. Orkney has been the graveyard of many vessels and the opportunity has been taken to list details of many shipwrecks on and around the coastline of South Ronaldsay and Burray though this list is by no means definitive. The names of vessels are also italicised. All place-names in Burray, Swona and the Pentland Skerries are clearly identified. Where there is no island reference, the reader should assume that the entry refers to South Ronaldsay.*

*Where possible, all place-names have been given a Grid Reference number followed by a Map Page Number in Roman numerals. No houses in St. Margaret's Hope Village or in Burray Village have been given a Grid Reference; the reader is directed to the appropriate map page only.*

*Abbreviations:*

| | |
|---|---|
| ON | Old Norse |
| Nor. | Norwegian |
| Far. | Faroese |
| Eng. | English |
| Sc. | Scots |
| Ork. dial. | Orkney dialect |
| Sh. dial. | Shetland dialect |

**Aftonlea** St. Margaret's Hope; occupied; fanciful name; Map Page IV.

**Aikers** Eastside, 1492, 1500, 1545, 1564, 1595, 1653, 1665, 1750; occupied; also district name; ON *akrar,* plural of *akr,* fields in which corn is grown; the form Aikers shows an English plural; there is also an Aikers place-name in St. Andrews and a farm by the name Aikers existed in Orphir up until the 17th century; the South Ronaldsay Aikers is one of a number of Orkney place-names which provided a surname; Andrew Aikers lived in Aikers in 1665; 454907; Map Page VIII.

**Air** 1. Swona 1821, 1841; derelict; referred to later as one of four *Northouse* place-names on the island; there are many similar place-names in Orkney but they are usually spelt 'Ayre'; ON *eyrr* a sand or shingle spit; 392851; Map Page XII.

**Air** 2. Hoxa, 1750, 1821; the same house as *Barns of Ayre.*

**Air** 3. Grimness, 1821; see *Ayre o Cara.*

**Aird House** now *Cobbler's Cottage*; St. Margaret's Hope; occupied; Map Page IV.

**Aird Lea** St. Margaret's Hope; occupied; name derived from surname of a previous owner; Map Page IV.

**Aldene** St. Margaret's Hope; occupied; fanciful name; Map Page IV.

**Alla/Oula** 1736; see *Oula.*

**Aladale** Burray village; occupied; Map Page VI.

**Alladale** St. Margaret's Hope; holiday home; Map Page IV.

**Allibelly Geo** ON *ali-dýr* cattle; in Shetland the word *ali* was used on its own applied to domestic animals; ON *boeli* enclosure; *gjá* ravine; presumably at one time an animal pen existed near this inlet or, more likely, the geo was used as a temporary pen; for 'alli' element compare Ellibister in Rendall, formerly Alibuster; for 'belly', compare *Coos Belly, Staneisbul* and *Instabely*; 430853; Map Page X.

**Alma** Grimness 1891; also known as the *Heights of Alma*; called after the battle fought in the Crimean War in 1854 near the River Alma and fifteen miles from Sebastopol; in the very first 'Orcadian' newspaper published in November 1854, a reference is made to 'the battle on the heights of Alma'; it is remarkable that this name is still known in South Ronaldsay; Alma was also called *Issy Gutcher's*; the name is now changed to *West Cara*; there is an Alma Cottage in Sanday; 474929; Map Page VI.

**Alskahem** Burray; occupied; 472966; Map Page II.

**Altar (The)** coastal feature, the name suggested by the shape of the rock; the Altars of Linay is a coastal place-name in North Ronaldsay; 415904; Map Page IX.

**Anchorage** St. Margaret's Hope; now a public house serving meals; also known as *Galley Inn* fanciful name; there are several Anchorage place-names in Orkney; Map Page IV.

**Ancroft** Herston; occupied; 418920; Map Page V.

**Angle Cottage** St. Margaret's Hope; occupied; standing at an angle to the road; compare the house nicknamed Skaoowaoo in Sandwick, West Mainland, a house which also stands at an angle to the road; (Ork. dial *skaoowaoo*, not aligned); 444934; Map Page IV.

**Angly Bar** 1. coastal feature, Grimness; ON *berg* rock; the first element is probably Eng. 'angling'; all around the Orkney coastline certain rocks were favoured spots for using a rod, particulary to catch 'kuithes', i.e. one year old coalfish; 470859; Map Page XIII.

**Angly Bar** 2. coastal feature; Windwick; 469860; Map Page XIII.

**Ankersted** Burray village; occupied; Map Page VI.

**Annag's** named after Annag (i.e. Annie) Walls; the surname Wallis/Walls has existed in South Ronaldsay since the 17th century; 463893; Map Page XI.

**Annster** the house of *Biggings* in Eastside has been divided into two, half of which is now known by this name.

**Ardage** Burray; empty; fanciful name; 477959; Map Page VI.

**Ardconnel** St. Margaret's Hope; occupied; Map Page IV.

**Ardmohr** Burray; occupied; 475958; Map Page VI.

**Ardnacamus** Grimness; occupied; 484938; Map Page VII.

**Arneip** 1500; an early alternative name for the farm of *Burwick*; ON *örn* sea eagle; sea eagles were very common in Orkney at one time; compare *Earny Coulags*; ON *gnípa* cliff, as in Noup Head, Westray.

**Arp** Burray; derelict; there is also a house by this name in Flotta; a difficult name to interpret; it does not appear in old records which suggests that it is no older than the 19th century; almost certainly the nickname of a former inhabitant; from Sc. *erp, orp, wurp, yarp,* to grumble; 465955; Map Page VI.

**Ashby** Grimness; occupied; a transferred name from one of a number of Ashby place-names in England; 470947; Map Page VI.

**Ashley Cottage** Burray village; occupied; Map Page VI.

**Atla** Widewall 1595; 'besouth' the burn in Widewall, the burn presumably being the *Oback Burn*; Marwick thought the name had vanished but see *Upper Attley/Rattley*; this place-name appears in different forms in Orkney, e.g. Akla in Orphir, Ackalay in Westray, Etyalith in Birsay and Aglath in Stenness; ON *ökkla*, ankle, used metaphorically of the spur of a hill.

**Ayre** field name, *Roeberry Farm*; named from the nearby shingle spit; the house nearby is called *Barns of Ayre* today but was known as *Air* in 1821; 429937; Map Page V.

**Ayre o Banks** see *Ayre* above; 425914; Map Page V.

**Ayre o Burwick**; coastal feature, also known as *Burwick's Ayre* also known as *The Strone*; see *Ayre o Cara* below and *Burwick* for derivation; 438842; Map Page X.

**Ayre o Cara** 1. Grimness; a physical feature; ON *eyrr* sand or shingle spit; compare the Ayre Road in Kirkwall which follows the line of the old gravel spit blocking off the Peedie Sea from Kirkwall Bay; see *Cara*, Grimness; 1. a brigantine from Fort William with a cargo of coal was wrecked near here in 1732. 2. vessel *Margaret* (other details unknown) was wrecked here in 1837; 478949; Map Page VI.

**Ayre o Cara** 2. Grimness; a house; occupied; named after the above feature; in 1821 this house was known as *Air*; 477949; Map Page VI.

**Ayre o Westermill** Burray; see *Ayre* above; the 'mill' element is a corruption of ON *melr* sand; 475954; Map Page VI.

**Ayres/Ayresdale** Northfield, Burray, the site of *West Broch*; the 'dale' element is Sc. *dale*, piece of land, hence 'piece of land belonging to *Ayre (o Cara)*'; see *Dale*; 483988; Map Page III.

**Baaes** an underwater reef, an extension of *Barni Taing*; ON *boði* reef with English plural; compare *Wester Bows* and *Lippa*; 422901; Map Page IX.

**Backaquoy** vanished; because of its position, unlikely to have been a farm but merely an enclosure; ON *bakki* slope; *kví* enclosure; 434846; Map Page X.

**Back Big Hoose** field name, *Roeberry Farm*; 429932; Map Page V.

**Back Geo (The)** Swona; probably the geo behind *Geo Longo* relative to the *North Houses*; ON *gjá* ravine; 392854; Map Page XII.

**Back Hole o Garsnya Geo** Swona; see *Garsnya Geo*; 393847; Map Page XII.

**Back Road** St. Margaret's Hope; Map Page IV.

**Back Slates** the flat area to the back of the *Slates o Hest/Hess*; 465878; Map Page XIII.

**Bagall Toustie's** see *Barns of Ayre*.

**Bakehouse (The)** Burray village; occupied; Map Page VI.

**Balaclava** Grimness 1871; some remains may yet be seen; after the battle of that name fought at Balaclava in 1854 during the Crimean War; compare *Alma*, *Inkerman* and *Sebastopol*; there are also Balaclava place-names in Flotta, Shapinsay and Westray; see below; 480925; Map Page VI.

**Balaclava's Quarry** many houses near the shore were built using stones quarried from the shore if the strata were suitable; stones used in the building of *Balaclava* were quarried from the foreshore here; see *Balaclava* above; 482926; Map Page VI.

**Balarat** (sic) Widewall 1881; vanished; after Ballarat near Melbourne, Australia where large gold reserves were discovered in 1851; the house was probably built and named by a returned prospector; there is also a Ballarat in Harray; compare *Klondyke*.

**Ball Hill** ON *bál*, Sc. *bale* beacon fire; which suggests that this hill played the same function as the *Ward Hill* of South Ronaldsay in times past; compare the hills Muckle Billia Fiold in Harray, Bailie Hill in Firth and Yonbell in Birsay, the latter suggesting the site of the Johnsmas Bonfire; 424901; Map Page IX.

**Ballgreen** Burwick 1750, 1821, 1841; occupied; built on or near a 'green' or field set aside for playing the old style game of football; compare *Gammon(s) Park*; 454845; Map Page XIII.

**Banavie** St. Margaret's Hope; occupied; a transferred name from Banavie, near Fort William; Map Page IV.

**Bankburn** St. Margaret's Hope, 1861; derelict; see *Oback* for the ON form of such a place-name; 450928; Map Page IV.

**Bankburn House** occupied; 449928; Map Page IV.

**Bankhouse** St. Margaret's Hope; occupied; Map Page IV.

*Bank of Scotland, St. Margaret's Hope; in the 1970s?*

**Bank (The)** occupied; originally established in St. Margaret's Hope as a branch of the Union Bank of Scotland on 10th December 1866 with manager W. T. Norquay; post-war it operated as a branch of the Bank of Scotland; it closed some years ago and is now a private house; Map Page IV.

**Banks** 1. Burray; occupied; 464955; Map Page VI.

**Banks** 2. Herston, 1821; occupied; English form of ON *bakki* slope; 422914; Map Page V.

**Banks** 3. Liddel; there are at least nine Banks place-names in Orkney; the Orkney surname 'Banks' originated in South Ronaldsay in addition to other places in Orkney but which Banks in South Ronaldsay is responsible for the surname is not known; William Banks lived in Eastside in 1695 so it is possible that the surname derived from this particular Banks; see *Banks* above for derivation; 459834; Map Page XII.

**Banks Geo** ON *gjá* ravine; see *Banks* above for derivation; 458833; Map Page XII.

**Banks Head** formerly *Liddel Head*; thin flag-stones used to be quarried here for roofing; see *Banks* above for derivation; 460832; Map Page XII.

**Bankslea** St. Margaret's Hope; occupied; Map Page IV.

**Barebreck(s)** Widewall; now known as *Breck (The)*; occupied; 1821; Eng. *bare*, Ork. dial. *breck(s)*, originally poor quality (usually heather covered) land; see *Heather Brakes*; 426905; Map Page IX.

**Barebrecks** Grimness 1821, 1851; some remains may yet be seen; there is a Barebrecks in Orphir and formerly a Barebrecks, now known as Hillcrest, existed in Stromness Parish; see above for derivation; 485938; Map Page VII.

**Bardeflaws** field-name; ON *barð* edge of a hill (compare *Barth Head*); for explanation of 'flaws' element see *Flaws*; 484852; Map Page XIII.

**Barkville** Quindry/Ronsa district; 1891; vanished; from Barkville, Vancouver Island, British Columbia, Canada; probably named by a returning emigrant; compare *Canada*.

**Barnhouse 1.** Burray; occupied; 470959; Map Page VI.

**Barnhouse 2.** occupied; 455938; Map Page IV.

**Barni Taing** first element suggests ON personal name *Bjarni*; coastal features were sometimes named after an individual whose boat had foundered there but another possibility is that it is derived from ON *björn*, bear, since animal names were frequently used for coastal features; compare *Honey Geo*; 422902; Map Page IX.

**Barns of Ayre** Hoxa, holiday home; known as *Air* in 1821; called after the nearby 'ayre' from ON *eyrr* a sand or shingle spit; in the past this house has been known as *Bagall Toustie's*, named presumably after a previous occupant; 429938; Map Page V.

**Barron** vanished; a farm recorded in the *Aikers* district in the 17ᵗʰ century; probably lying towards *Vensilly Hill* hence Eng. 'barren'; compare Barrenha in North Ronaldsay.

**Barswick/Barthwick/Barwick** South Parish, 1492, 1584, 1627, 1821; occupied; Barswick is one of two Orkney farms from which knights have chosen their title (the other is Kirkness in Sandwick, West Mainland); John Arnot was a wealthy Scotsman who, after the execution of Earl Patrick of Orkney, laid claim to the extensive estates of the Earl to whom he had loaned a great deal of money; these estates included the lands of *Barswick*; when John Arnot was knighted by King James VI in 1604, he chose the title 'Arnot of Barswick'; why he chose to act as a banker to the Earl of Orkney and chose this title in preference to any other, points to a family connection with Orkney and specifically with South Ronaldsay since the Arnots were well established in Widewall in the 16ᵗʰ century though by the beginning of the 19ᵗʰ century, the name had died out; for origin of 'bar' element of *Barswick* see *Barth*; ON *vík* bay; 435857; Map Page X.

**Barswick Bay** this bay is referred to twice in the *Orkneyinga Saga*: 1. 'Earl Erlend and his men lay on board their ships in Barswick'. 2. 'When Sveinn of Gairsay was on the run, his vessel put into Barswick and stayed in a certain cave. Sometimes Sveinn took his meals at a house during the day but slept during the night down by his boat'; 433865; Map Page X.

**Barswick Haven** an alternative name for the above; onshore here is the location of a small, now ruinous, building where *Swona* residents attending church in South Ronaldsay changed from their sea clothes into their church clothes; Swona people were buried in *St. Mary's Kirkyard*.

**Bar Taing** Hunda, Burray; see *Bor Taing*.

**Barth** 1750; vanished; ON *barð* edge of a hill; the southern point of the isle of Bressay in Shetland is called The Bard.

**Barth Head**; the sailing vessel *Europe* was wrecked here in 1806 and the trawler *James Evans* of Granton sank off this headland in 1934; see *Barth* above; 426855; Map Page X.

74 *The Place-Names of South Ronaldsay and Burray*

**Barth Skerry** see *Barth* above; ON *sker* reef; 425856; Page X.

**Barthwick** see *Barswick.*

**Barwick** see *Barswick.*

**Batavia** Widewall 1871; vanished; probably named by a sea-faring man; dates from around 1800 when Holland was renamed *Batavia* by Napoleon.

**Bathing Rock** see *Crinilag.*

**Bayview** 1. Herston; occupied; there are several Bayview place-names in Orkney, all in commanding positions; 422918; Map Page V.

**Bayview** 2. St. Margaret's Hope; occupied; Map Page IV.

**Bayview** 3. Sandwick; 431893; Map Page IX.

**Bayview** 4. Burray; empty; 471955; Map Page VI.

**Bayview Cottage** St. Margaret's Hope, occupied; Map Page IV.

**Beach o Skolimar** Swona; see *Sgoilamar/Skolimar.*

**Beachview** Burray village; occupied; Map PageVI.

**Bed Green** field-name, *Cletts*; origin uncertain; 458908; Map Page XI.

**Beechwood Cottage** Burray; 472964; Map Page II.

**Bell Dag** a fishing rock, Windwick; ON *böllr*, a ball shaped rock; the same usage is found in Shetland; the second element is difficult to interpret, perhaps ON *dagr* day, i.e. this rock was used as a so-called day mark in relation to one particular farm; when the sun was above this rock, it was a certain time of day; in the old days every farm in Iceland had such 'day marks'; 459868; Map Page XIII.

**Bellevue Hotel** St. Margaret's Hope; common, fanciful name; 443937; Map Page IV.

**Bellevue House** St. Margaret's Hope; occupied; Map Page IV.

**Bendigo** Grimness; derelict; post-war dwelling base on an ex-army hut; there is a Bendigo in St. Ola, a transferred name from Bendigo in Australia; 479947; Map Page VI.

**Bent Geo** Burray; 'bent' refers to 'bent grass' on the nearby sandy links rather than to the shape of the geo; ON *gjá* ravine; 488978; Map Page III.

**Berriedale** Grimness; occupied; ON *berr* open, bare; 'dale' can be interpreted in a number of ways; here it is probably Sc. *dale*, piece of land; there are Berriedale place-names in Hoy and Westray; this is one of the most interesting South Ronaldsay farms; in Mackenzie's map of Orkney drawn up in 1750, a large square appears in the north of South Ronaldsay to the east of St. Margaret's Hope; it was the *Park of Cara*, a 410 acre enclosed piece of grazing land owned by Sir James Stewart of Burray; in the 1860s this was rented from the Earl of Zetland by William Cromarty, merchant in St. Margaret's Hope, land was reclaimed and a steading and mill dam built; by 1868 a farm of 450 acres had been established with modern farm buildings and incorporating *Little Berriedale, Berriedale Common* and *Quoys*; a searchlight, one of at least twenty on the island was positioned above Berriedale Farm during World War II; see also *Park o Cara*; 463939; Map Page VI

**Berriedale Cottage** 1. occupied; see above; 464936; Map Page VI.

**Berriedale Cottage** 2. occupied; see above; 462942; Map Page VI.

**Berriedale Cottage** 3. occupied; see above; 462942; Map Page VI.

**Berryhill** Burray; 462959; Map Page VI.

**Bersiedale** a croft; the original name of *Ladypark*; ON personal name *Bersi*; Sc. *dale* a piece of land.

**Bersiedale Burn** a small stream near *Ladypark*; 456879; Map Page XIII.

**Berston** Paplay 1677, 1821; occupied; there are Berston place-names in Westray and St. Ola; like *Burrowston* in South Ronaldsay, Berston seems a variation of the name Burroughstone in Shapinsay where it applies to a *borg* (a walled enclosure in this case) along with a *tún* (enclosure); the Orkney surname 'Berston' originated here; John Berstane (sic) lived in St. Margaret's Hope in 1695; 472921; Map Page VI.

**Betty Omand's** field name, *Kirkhouse*; named after the occupant of a house here which was already ruinous in 1877 when this area was surveyed; Betty Omand, aged 14, was a servant at Newbigging in Widewall in 1821; it is quite remarkable that this field has retained her name over such a long period; the only Omand family in South Ronaldsay in the 1820s lived at *Oback* in Widewall; 436920; Map Page IV.

**Betty's City** a lane in St. Margaret's Hope linking the *Back Road* to *Cromarty Square*; named after Betty Banks who lived nearby; according to the 1891 Census returns, she lived in *Burnside 1* and was described as a laundress; Map Page IV.

**Big Field** 439846; Map Page X.

**Big Hill** field name, *Roeberry Farm*; it borders *Hoxa Hill*; 433934; Map Page IV.

**Big Howe** an elevation of uncertain origin in a field; nearby lay *Little Howe*; ON *haugr* mound; 431908; Map Page VIII.

**Biggings** 1. Eastside; occupied; now a shared occupancy, half of which is known as *Annster*; Sc. *biggings*, buildings; this farm name is found in several Orkney parishes; 456910; Map Page XI.

**Biggings** 2. 449845; Map Page XIII.

**Biggy** 1821; vanished; lay near Banks/Windbrake in South Parish; origin uncertain.

**Big Ore** coastal stretch seemingly named after *Bigore Head* below; 469892; Map Page XI.

**Bigore Head** a prominent headland; ON *eyar* islands; see *Ours o Stews*; and *Little Ore*; 469892; Map Page XI.

**Bill's Toonlands** these fields were originally in the possession of a Bill Sinclair; the name *toonlands* probably means 'arable land'; in the old system of land holding the *tún* field or *toomal* as it was usually called was an arable field close to the farm and not shared by others in the tunship; compare *Sandy's Toonlands*; 463897; Map Page XI.

**Bill Rosie's** field name; the first Rosie family was recorded in *Masseter* in South Ronaldsay in 1601; 453845; Map Page XIII.

**Binniewindows/Bennywindows** occupied; first element seems a diminutive of Sc. *bune* above, paralleling West Mainland *appie* for 'upper' in place-names; Binniewindows lies on the slope above *Shorewindows*; the 'windows' element = 'wind house', i.e. a house in an exposed situation; the name has now been changed to *Garth Farm*; 457935; Map Page IV.

**Birbinks** Swona; coastal feature; ON *berg* rock; Sc. *bink* bench; in this case refers to flagstones; the old Orkney house often had in the end room a flagstone bench on which rested a wooden water tub called the *sae* (ON *sár*); the bench was called the *sae-bink*; 393847; Map Page XII.

**Bishop (The)** Swona; coastal feature; nearby are the *Slates o the Altar*; 392843; Map Page XII.

**Black Babby** Burray; a volcanic dyke exposed on the shore here; origin of 'babby' unknown; 482954; Map Page VI.

**Black Geo** 1. ON *gjá* ravine; see *Shortie Geo* for a name comparison; 458878; Map Page XIII.

**Black Geo** 2. see above; 472848; Map Page XIII.

**Black Rock** Burray 489976; Map Page III.

**Black Smiddy** St. Margaret's Hope; vanished; a blacksmith's shop which lay at the junction above the village; it ceased operating before the war; the house *Fairhaven* is built on the site; 449933; Map Page IV.

**Blanster/Blosetter/Blanksetter** St. Margaret's Hope 1492, 1501, 1595, 1644, 1668, 1841, 1861; forms of the first element suggest that it is related to 'blos' in *Blos Moss*; compare ON *blásin* stripped bare of turf and Shet. dial. *blan* wind; ON *saetr* seasonally used hut; see *Blos Moss*; much of what was Blanster Farm is now owned by the Golf Club and a new nine hole course with a club house has recently been opened; the old dwelling house which became a bothy is derelict but it could be restored; 448929; Map Page IV.

*An old photograph of Blanster House in St. Margaret's Hope.*

**Blanster House** St. Margaret's Hope; occupied; in 1868 it was described by Gorrie in his *Summers and Winters in the Orkneys* as a 'villa of superior class'; see above; Map Page IV.

**Bleet** field-name; *East Masseter*; ON *bleyta* mud; the old field-name Bletyadith near Dunsyre in Harray carries the same element; 449865; Map Page X.

**Blellain** Eastside 1881; vanished; origin unknown.

**Blinkbonnie** Eastside 1841; vanished; fanciful name; there are Blinkbonny (sic) place-names in Burray, St. Ola, Westray and Stronsay.

**Blinkbonny** 1. Herston; occupied; fanciful name; 417917; Map Page V.

**Blinkbonny** 2. Burray; 1821; holiday home; see above; 464957; Map Page VI.

**Blinkglee** Eastside 1871; vanished; fanciful name.

**Blitchen Slates** ON *bleyta* mud, *tjörn* pool (compare *Bleet* above and Blotchnia Fiold, the highest hill in Rousay); ON *slettr* 'smooth', of stones, etc; 459869; Map Page XIII.

*The hulk of the blockship Reginald, a 930 ton Irish steamer, at Churchill Barrier No. 3.*

**Blockships** 1. (*Churchill Barrier No. 2*); of the ten blockships sunk in *Skerry Sound*, only the following vessels are visible at low water: 1. The 2641 ton British vessel *Elton*. 2. The 2338 ton British vessel *Lycia*; 482999; Map Page II.

**Blockships** 2. (*Churchill Barrier No. 3*); of the five blockships sunk in *Weddell Sound*, only the remains of the Irish steamer *Reginald* may still be seen; some of the others appear at low water; 474985; Map II.

**Blockships** 3. (*Churchill Barrier No. 4*) of the nine blockships sunk in *Water Sound*, only two are now visible: 1. The 1780 ton Canadian vessel *Collingdoc*. 2. The 2733 ton British vessel *Clio* (visible only at low water); 478953; Map Page VI.

**Block Works** Burray; it was here where blocks were made for *Churchill Barrier No 4*; the detonator shed is still extant; 482955; Map Page VI.

**Bloomfield** Burray; occupied; fanciful name; the origin of this house is very interesting since it was built by public subscription for a widow and her children after her husband was drowned crossing *Water Sound*; there was a long tradition in Orkney of communities rallying round to help those who had suffered misfortune; see *Skae* for an illustration of this; 466963; Map Page II.

**Blos/Blows Moss** a derivative of ON *blása* to blow (compare Shakespeare's 'blasted heath'); there is a hill ridge known as Blossan in Rousay and a house named Blow(e)s in Deerness; a gravestone in Deerness churchyard records that an 'Aim died at Blowes'!; see *Blanster* above; ON *mosi* moorland; 452859; Map Page XIII.

**Blow Geo/Bloie Geo** see *Blos Moss*; Eng. 'blow'; ON *gjá* ravine; 404925; Map Page V.

**Blue Geo** Swona; there are also Blue Geos in Rousay and Sanday; probably ON *blár* black; 390839; Map Page XII.

**Bonnybanks** Quindry/Ronsa/Hoxa district 1861; vanished; fanciful name.

**Boat Dock (The)** 418934; Map Page V.

**Boat Dock** Burray; before the opening of the Churchill Barriers, the ferry to Holm left from this point; 484988; Map Page III.

**Boats Geo** Burray; compare *Skipi Geo*; somewhere near here the *Laurel* of Kirkwall with general cargo was wrecked in 1857; 486988; Map Page III.

**Boatyard** Burray; locally known as Duncan's Boatyard, now regrettably unused; 472955; Map Page VI.

**Bobby's** field name, *Roeberry Farm*; 430935; Map Page IV.

**Bonnington** St. Margaret's Hope; occupied; Map Page IV.

**Boony Geo** Swona; suggests dialect *bungy* a word recorded only in North Ronaldsay and applied to a seal; it is related to Norwegian dialect *bunka* a fat woman; 385841; Map Page XII.

**Bor Taing** Hunda; also marked *Bar Taing* on current O.S. Map; ON *bára*, wave but used in Orkney in the sense 'tidal race' as in the Bore o Papay; 430966; Map Page I.

**Bothy Geo** Burray, probably a fisherman's hut was located here; compare Boothie Geo on Flotta; ON *búð* hut; *gjá* ravine; 488981; Map Page III.

**Bothy (The)** St. Margaret's Hope; soon to be converted into a dwelling house; Map Page IV.

**Bow** 1. as marked on O.S. map; see *Bu (The) o Linkletter* above.

**Bow** 2. Hoxa; see *Bu (The) o Hoxa*.

**Bow of Linklater** see *Bu (The) o Linkletter.*

**Bowling Green** St. Margaret's Hope; Map Page IV.

**Bowman's House** vanished; a house on the land of *Cools* set aside for the use of a 'bowman', a Scots word for 'cattleman' but it was used generally for 'farm servant'; 444895; Map Page VIII.

**Brae** see *Brain.*

**Braebreck** 1821; Grimness; vanished.

**Braeface** 469916; Map Page XI.

**Brae Garth** Burray; occupied; 478957; Map Page VI.

**Braehead** 1. Burray; 467960; Map Page II.

**Braehead** 2. 1821, 1861; occupied; Sc. *brae* hillside, therefore 'hill top'; there are Braehead place-names in Holm and Westray; 443938; Map Page IV.

**Braehead** 3. Eastside; vanished; only *Nether Braehead* remains; see above for derivation; 456907; Map Page VIII.

**Braeland** Eastside (formerly *Borrowland, Brunaland* and *Brualand*) 1492, 1500, 1821; 1841; occupied; ON *borg* (with the sense 'walled enclosure') ON *land* land; 463893; Map Page XI.

**Braemore** Garth, St. Margaret's Hope; occupied; an introduced name; 455928; Map Page IV.

**Braeside** Ontoft Road, St. Margaret's Hope; 444936; Map Page IV.

**Brain/Brayne/Brae** Paplay; 1750, 1821, 1841; a difficult name to interpret; perhaps ON *breið-eng* broad meadow; now renamed *Orkadee*; 469920; Map Page VI.

**Brance** 1821; Grimness; occupied; see *Yorbrandis*; 485939; Map Page VII.

**Brandyquoy** 1. St. Margaret's Hope; occupied; the original Brandiquoy lay further south; see below; 458932; Map Page VI.

**Brandyquoy/Brandiquoy** 2. 1861; also known as the *Old Schoolhouse* or *Forbes' School*; the teacher's accommodation and the school occupied the same building; it was here where the famed Scottish poet William McGonagall received some of his education from the teacher, James Forbes; ON personal name *Brandr*, ON *kví* enclosure; there was also at one time a small croft in Kirkwall known as Brandiquoy; 457928; Map Page VI.

**Bratlee Ber** Burray; a precipice on the south-east coast; ON *brattr* steep, ON *hlíð* slope, but also used in Orkney in the sense 'cliff' as in the Lee o Copinsay, a south-east facing cliff over 200 feet high; 'Bretally' is an old house name in Knarston, Dounby but in that case it would have referred to a slope!; ON *berg* rock; 501962; Map Page III.

**Breaheas** Ronsvoe and St. Margaret's Hope, 1695; vanished; origin unknown.

**Breck** 1. Widewall 1821; occupied; formerly *Barebreck*, now known locally as *The Breck*; ON *brekka* slope; 426905; Map Page IX.

**Breck** 2. see *Suthergill*.

**Breck** 3. Burray; see *Breckhouse/Breck*.

**Breck (The)** 1. field name; 463915; Map Page XI.

**Breck (The)** 2. see *Breck 1*.

**Breckholm** Burray; vanished; 478963; Map Page II.

**Breckhouse/Breck** Burray; occupied; 469964; Map Page II.

**Breck House** Burray; 479963; Map Page II.

**Breckin(s)/Brechins** occupied; ON *brekka-n* the slope; there are several Breckan (sic) place-names in Orkney; 475945; Map Page VI.

**Brecks** Grimness 1584, 1821; 1861; derelict; Clouston states that, at one time, Grimness consisted of one estate which was subdivided into *Brecks* and *Cara*; Brecks was the home of Sir James Sinclair who, in 1529, led his army against the Earl of Caithness' forces at the Battle of Summerdale in Stenness and defeated them; there are Brecks place-names in Shapinsay and Deerness; such a name can be quite old e.g. in the *Orkneyinga Saga* it is said that *Rikarðr bjó* *a Brekkum i Strjónsey*, i.e. Richard lived at Brecks in Stronsay; ON *brekkur* slopes, with English plural; 479933; Map Page VI.

**Brekka** Cleat Road; occupied; 462845; Map Page XIII.

**Brenches** Swona; coastal feature; ON *bringa*, chest, used in place-names to apply to a grassy slope or slopes; compare Brinkies Brae in Stromness; Jakobsen recorded a similar place-name 'de Brongis' in Sandwick, Shetland; the place-name Brancherhouse in Birsay shows the Old Norse plural *bringur*; see also below; 380838; Map Page XII.

**Brenches (The)** Swona; compare the above; 392843; Map Page XII.

**Briarlea** Burray village; empty; there are several Briarlea place-names in Orkney; Map Page VI.

**Brick** Grimness 1750; vanished; Sc. *brik* ground broken up for cultivation.

**Broad Ebb/Broddebb** there is also a Broad Ebb in Eday; Sc. *ebb* foreshore; 493924; Map Page VII.

**Broadebb o the Cause (The)** Swona; compare the above; see *Cause;* 391853; Map Page XII.

**Broch** 1. Hunda, Burray; no longer visible; believed to have been sited at *Cairn Head (The)*; ON *borg* fortification; 435962; Map Page I.

**Broch** 2. the feature from which the farm of *Brough* got its name; 443833; Map Page X.

**Broch o Ontoft** Hoxa; no longer visible; ON *borg* fortification; see *Ontoft*; 442936; Map Page IV.

**Broll** Windwick (earlier *Burrowell, Burwell, Burwall*) 1492, 1500, 1595, 1750, 1821, 1841; occupied; the Orkney surname 'Burwall' originated here; Magnus Burwall lived in South Ronaldsay in 1601 but the name is no longer recorded; ON *borg* walled enclosure; *völlr* field; 452875; Map Page XIII.

**Brook (The)** 1. ON *brúk* rotten piles of seaweed on the beach; 458868; Map Page XIII.

**Brook (The)** 2. Swona; see above for explanation; 389849; Map Page XII.

**Broti Ber** coastal feature, *Pentland Skerries*; ON *brattr* steep; *berg* rock; 465785; Map Page XIV.

**Brough** 1. 1329, 1492, 1500, 1595, 1821, 1841; occupied; ON *borg* fortification; there are no definite remains of such a structure here today; a searchlight, one of at least twenty on the island was positioned here during World War II; 443834; Map Page X.

**Brough** 2. see *Broch o Ontoft*.

**Brough (The)** 1. ON *borg* fortification; 459873; Map Page XIII.

**Brough (The)** 2. Muckle Skerry, Pentland Skerries; some indeterminate structure was recorded here; 468785; Map Page XIV.

**Brough Geo** 1. Burray; 482988; Map Page II.

**Brough Geo** 2. Muckle Skerry, Pentland Skerries; named from a nearby indeterminate structure; 466785; Map Page XIV.

**Brough Ness** near *Brough 1* above; ON *nes* headland; a visual signal station overlooking the Pentland Firth was built here by the Admiralty during World War I; later it was the site of the Coastguard Station; 445834; Map Page X.

**Bruce's Barn** there were a number of Bruce families in South Ronaldsay in the 17th century but the name is no longer recorded there; the substance of a local tale is that Robert the Bruce sought refuge on this island and was responsible for the introduction of the name—it is even claimed that it was in this barn that he saw the spider and a further claim that the Halcros led a small contingent of Orkneymen to assist Bruce at the Battle of Bannockburn; see *Newark* for another interesting reference to the Bruces; 458849; Map Page X.

**Bruntbigging** Burray 1750; vanished, but see below; Sc. *brunt*, burnt, an obvious reference to a house or farm fire.

**Bruntland** Burray; may be the same as above; see also *Burntland*; 466958; Map Page VI.

**Bu (The)** Burray; 1492, 1500, 1821; occupied; one of the three original divisions of Burray; the other divisions were *Northtown* and *Southtown*; *The Bu* was the residence of the Stewarts of Burray and the site of a magnificently furnished 17th century mansion house, an inventory of which still exists; there are several *The Bu* place-names in Orkney; Scots scribes often wrote these place-names in the form *Bull* in the mistaken belief that that was the correct spelling and it is for this reason that *The Bu* often wrongly appears in the form *The Bu'* ( i.e. with an apostrophe); ON *bú* estate; 485971; Map Page III.

**Bu (The) o Hoxa** occupied; ON *bú* estate; 406933; Map Page V.

**Bu (The) o Linkletter** occupied; 1821; also written *Bow of Linklater*; ON *bú* estate; 451871; Map Page XIII.

**Bu Sand** Burray; the name applied to the sandy beach which faces the *Bu of Burray* and from which fine building sand is extracted; 487970; Map Page III.

**Bu (The)** Sandwick, 1821; vanished.

**Burma Road** St. Margaret's Hope; during air raids on Scapa Flow, ammunition was transported through St. Margaret's Hope via the Back Road to the batteries at Hoxa and Herston, sometimes in total darkness and it was feared that if the village were bombed, the Back Road would become impassable therefore in the early years of the war a military road was built to by-pass St. Margaret's Hope; it ran from the *Quindry* road, past *Farewell*, around the *Oyce o Quindry* to *Kirkhouse* in Widewall; by the time the road was nearing completion, the air-raids had stopped, thanks to the success of the so-called 'Scapa Barrage' when artillery units in Scapa Flow put up a curtain of gun-fire to thwart enemy aircraft; the road was named after the road which links Burma with China and which was of great strategic importance during World War II; there is also a Burma Road in Sanday; Map Page IV.

**Burn** 1. Liddel; occupied; Sc. *burn* stream; 455837; Map Page XII.

**Burn** 2. Grimness; holiday home; Sc. *burn* stream; 473932; Map Page VI.

**Burn** 3. Ronsvoe; vanished.

**Burnbank** Burray; see *Braegarth*.

**Burn Field** borders the *Newark Burn*; 463897; XI.

**Burn House** St. Margaret's Hope; also known as *House of Burn*.

**Burnlea** 1. St. Margaret's Hope; occupied; Map Page IV.

**Burnlea** 2. Eastside; occupied; 460893; Map Page XI.

**Burnmouth** vanished but the location is known; there is also a Burnmouth in Hoy; 467833; Map Page XII.

**Burn o Liddel** see *Liddel*; 456835; Map Page XII.

**Burn o Stane** see *Stane*; 455870; Map Page XIII.

**Burn o Stews** see *Stews*; 468893; Map Page XI.

**Burn o Sutherland** Burray; 478948; Map Page VI.

**Burnside** 1. empty; 453845; Map Page XIII.

**Burnside** 2. St. Margaret's Hope; the name given to a group of houses in the 1891 Census; an open stream, from which these houses took their names, formerly ran through *Cromarty Square*; one of these houses, *Burn House* above is now *Westlea*; Map Page IV.

**Burntland** Burray, 1821; occupied; see *Bruntland*; 467960; Map Page VI.

**Burnt Mound** 1. a burnt mound is a crescent shaped heap of stones which have been subjected to intense heat and are believed to have been used to heat water in a nearby pit for ritual purposes; there is frequently a well in the vicinity; in Orkney alone there are some 230 of these which are more than 2,500 years old, more than 30 of them in South Ronaldsay and Burray; only those marked on the Ordnance Survey Map are listed here; despite their distinct composition the Norse did not seem to have a particular generic name for them; the Knowe o Brenda in Twatt in the West Mainland does however suggest *brendr-haugr*, literally 'burnt mound'; 432906; Map Page VIII.

**Burnt Mound** 2. 420907; Map Page V.

**Burnt Mound** 3. 433861; Map Page X.

**Burnt Mound** 4. Liddel; a particularly fine example of a burnt mound with adjacent well and pit; 465840; Map Page XIII.

**Burnt Mound** 5. 435883; Map Page VIII.

**Burra View** Grimness; occupied; 472948; Map Page VI.

**Burray** 1375; administratively the island has always been attached to *South Ronaldsay*; it became physically attached to its southern neighbour with the construction of the *Churchill Barriers*; William Burray, presumably from Burray, was one of a number of distinguished men who sat on a court at the farm of Sebay in Tankerness in 1552; this surname is perpetuated in the place-name Quoyburray in Tankerness; ON *borgar* fortifications (referring to *East Broch* and *West Broch*); ON *ey* island.

**Burray Haas** coastal feature in east of Burray; ON *háls*, neck with an extended meaning 'ridge' presumably referring to the neck of an animal; there is an old dwelling in Birsay called The Hass which has a similar derivation; 493987; Map Page III.

**Burray Ness** ON *nes* headland; the Norwegian brigantine *Frithjof* of Tonsberg under ballast was wrecked here in 1876; because of its strategic position, a coastal battery was established here in World War I; see also *Wife's Geo*; 507965; Map Page III.

**Burray Pier** 473954; Map Page VI.

**Burray School** 474959; Map Page VI.

**Burray Village** developed as a result of the 19th century fishing industry; it is now a popular place to live and has expanded greatly recently; 473956; Map Page VI.

**Burri Geo** ON *berg* rock (Ork. dial. *berry*) rock; *gjá* ravine; 458873; Map Page XIII.

**Burrowston** Brough; (written as *Berston* in 1653); 1821, 1841; holiday home; there is a Burroughstone place-name in Shapinsay and the form 'Broughston' in Sanday and Westray are similar forms; Burghstonhill in St. Ola is another instance of this name; in most cases, the 'burrow/burgh' forms can be interpreted as ON *borg*, fort, i.e. 'broch' but this word was also applied in as general way to enigmatic stone structures; see also *Berston*; 449844; Map Page X.

**Bur Wick** traditionally the mail route to Huna in Caithness was from this bay; the *Three Friends* of Montrose with a cargo of wood was wrecked here in 1800; ON *borg* fortification, *vík*, bay; 440840; Map Page X.

**Burwick** 1. 1492, 1500, 1595, 1841; empty; earlier alternative name was *Arneip*; the Orkney surname 'Burwick' originated here; Andrew Burwick lived in South Ronaldsay in 1643 but this surname is no longer recorded; a searchlight, one of at least twenty on the island was positioned here during World War II; see above for derivation; 436839; Map Page X.

**Burwick** 2. a district name applied to the hinterland of *Burwick* above; 440843; Map Page X.

**Burwick Pier** seasonal terminal for the foot passenger ferry from John o Groats, Caithness; 438839; Map Page X.

**Burwick Loch** see *Burwick* above; see also *Loch Sheen* for reference to what was perhaps an older name; 441844; Map Page X.

**Burwick Post Office** located at the house of *Quoys 3.*; 452849: Map Page XIII.

**Bus Taing** Sc. *buss* seaweed, especially eel grass, growing on rocks and exposed at low tide; compare the area around the Brig o Waithe in Stenness called 'The Bush'; ON *tangi* point; 486945; Map Page VII.

**Button** 1. Grimness 1746; vanished; there is a Button place-name in Stenness and a Button in Holm near Netherbutton; ON *botn* bottom; as in English, used in the sense 'end' e.g. of a field, valley etc.

**Button** 2. Hoxa 1736, 1851; vanished; see above.

**Byers** St. Margaret's Hope 1851; vanished; most likely Sc. *byres*, cowsheds; there is no record of the family name Byers in South Ronaldsay although it is recorded elsewhere in Orkney where, in some cases, it became corrupted to 'Byas'.

**Cabin** Burray village; occupied; Map Page VI.

**Cableton** see *Cavelton*.

**Caddies' Kil** coastal feature; Sc. *kil* a kiln for drying grain, used metaphorically when applied to a blow-hole in a cliff top which 'smokes' during a storm; compare *Sinilie*; in this case it probably refers to a former blow-hole, partially collapsed in on itself, where *caddies* were penned; Sc. *caddie* a pet lamb; 491925; Map Page VII.

**Café** St. Margaret's Hope; vanished; originally a Church of Scotland canteen during World War II; in the 1960s it served meals and high teas and was a popular resort for people from all over Orkney; the house *Seaview* is now built on the site; Map Page IV.

**Cairn** 1. Burray; 453967; Map Page I.

**Cairn** 2. *Kirkie Hill*; 438902; Map Page VIII.

**Cairn** 3. 434897; Map Page VIII.

**Cairn** 5. 429892; Map Page IX.

**Cairn** 6. 441872; Map Page VIII.

**Cairn** 7. 465889; Map Page XI.

**Cairn Head (The)** Hunda, Burray; site of a former broch; 435962; Map Page I.

**Cairn Hill** Sc. *cairn* a low, man-made tower; 434853; Map Page X.

**Cairn Point** see *Cairn Head (The)*.

**Cairns** 445829; Map Page X.

**Cairns o the Bu/Cairns o Flaws** there is confusion in archaeological reports about the location and nature of these cairns..

**Cakie** coastal feature; seems to relate to some 'twisted' feature here; ON *keikja* to bend; 418904; Map Page IX.

**Calder's Point** relates to the surname 'Calder'; there were Calders in *Quoys* St. Margaret's Hope in 1821; 430942; Map Page IV.

**California** 1. Hillside; occupied; if this is a genuinely old name it may relate to the time of the Californian gold rush in 1849; compare *Klondyke* and *Balarat* (sic) and houses below; 432928; Map Page IV.

**California** 2. field-name; compare above; 455862; Map Page XIII.

**Callos** 1736; vanished; origin and location unknown.

**Calves' Park** field name, *Kirkhouse*; all larger farms set aside a small field near the farm buildings for young calves; 436914; Map Page IV.

**Camberbosk** coastal feature; ON *kambr* ridge; 'bosk' is a variant of Shetland 'bost/bust', a corruption of ON *bust,* literally 'bristle' but used metaphorically of the roof ridge of a house; in Shetland (and apparently Orkney) the metaphor was extended and applied to a steep rock face; compare Sinnabust in Sandwick, Shetland; see also *Kamberbosk*; 434843; Map Page X.

**Campick** coastal feature; ON *kambr* ridge, Ork. dial. diminutive 'ick'; 488934; Map Page VII.

**Camp Site** (disused); see Hoxa Battery under *Hoxa Sound*; 405929; Map Page V.

**Canada** Widewall 1881; vanished; such house names were usually introduced by emigrants who returned to Orkney and who built modest houses with their savings, compare *New Zealand*; there is a Canada place-name in Birsay.

**Cantack** Swona; coastal feature; Nor. *kant* projecting part; with local diminutive 'ack'. compare Cantick Head in South Walls; 390480; Map Page XII.

**Canton** Grimness 1851; vanished; from *Canton*, China; introduced perhaps by a sea-faring man; 481945; Map Page VI.

**Cara** 1. Grimness, 1514, 1563 and 1595, 1821; occupied; also known as the *Hall of Cara* and in the 18th century inventory of the estate of Sir James Stewart of Burray, the *Great House of Cara*; the Orkney surname 'Cara' originated here; Magnus Cara lived in South Ronaldsay in 1514; it was later long associated with the Cromarty family; Marwick believed that this farm which apparently lay close to *Garay* in Grimness is in fact the same place since the present farm of *Gairy* in Sandwick, South Ronaldsay was also called *Cara* in 1595; the name derives from ON *garðr*, an enclosed piece of land; see also *Garay*; see also *Brecks* for a related reference; 477946; Map Page VI.

**Cara** 2. Sandwick, South Ronaldsay; see *Gairy*.

**Cara Battery** because of the strategic position of *Cara*, 199 Coast Battery, R.A. (Royal Artillery) was established here to prevent intrusion into Scapa Flow; a 12 pounder quick-firing gun was positioned in this locality in March 1940 followed by another in March 1941; by November 1943, Churchill Barrier No. 4 had appeared above water and since no further attacks by U Boats were possible, Cara Battery was abandoned; 480947; Map Page VI.

**Cara Ferry** Grimness 1851; this was the main ferry between South Ronaldsay and Burray, it was used by the post and anyone making the journey north or south before the introduction of steamships and piers; Cara Ferry was one of three ferries on the route from The Mainland of Orkney to the Scottish mainland, i.e. Holm to Burray, Burray to *Cara* and *Burwick* to Huna in Caithness; *see Glims Holm;* 471948; Map Page VI.

**Cara Flats** occupied; these were formerly part of the old herring fishing station; 477949; Map Page VI.

**Cara View** Hoxa; occupied; 417937; Map Page V.

**Caraville** Grimness; originally a hut on *Cara Battery*; now a dwelling house; many Orkney houses which were built post-war had an ex-military hut as the basis; before Caraville became a dwelling house it was used by the young people of Grimness as a club hut for a number of years; 479947; Map Page VI.

**Carawell** St. Margaret's Hope; occupied; Map Page IV.

**Carlan Geo** Swona; Sc. *carline* witch, in Orkney place-names refers to a troll-woman; spirits were believed to inhabit such wild places; ON *gjá* ravine; there are *Carlin (sic) Geos* in Stronsay and on the Muckle Green Holm, Eday; see also *Gariel Hole*; 393848; Map Page XII.

**Car Park** 1. *Glims Holm*; 473987; Map Page II.

**Car Park** 2. Burray; 481955; Map Page VI.

**Car Park** 3. *Burwick*; 437840; Map Page X.

**Car Park** 4. *Windwick*; 456871; Map Page XIII.

**Castle** 1. Burray; house; vanished.

**Castle** 2. Grimness; occupied; an old house modernised; named from *Castle (The)* below; 472943; Map Page VI.

**Castle Dam** this dam was filled in in the 1980s; 473943; Map Page VI.

**Castle Field** a field near *Castle (The)* below; 470941; Map Page VI.

**Castle Park** adjacent to *Castle o Burwick*; 436843; Map Page X.

**Castle (The)** Grimness; an ancient building locally known as 'The Castle' stood here; it was built in the 17th century by Sir James Stewart of *The Bu* in Burray for his illegitimate daughter who married into the Caras of Cara; it apparently reached only the first storey; a searchlight, one of at least twenty on the island was positioned here during World War II; 472943; Map Page VI.

**Castle Geo** see *Castle* above; ON *gjá* ravine; 434842; Map PageX.

**Castle o Burwick** applied to a long peninsula parallel to the shore with traces of an ancient stone structure; ON *kastali* fortification; see *Burwick*; 434843; Map Page X.

**Castle Skerry** near the *Castle o Burwick*; 434842; Map Page X.

**Castle Taing** Sandwick; ON *tangi* point of land; see *Weems Castle*; 433888; Map Page VIII.

**Castleview** Herston Village; occupied; it faces *Roeberry Castle* in Hoxa across the water; Map Page IV.

**Castni Geo** origin uncertain; 457833; Map Page XII.

**Cathole** Burray, 1821; vanished; it lay near *Tofts*; probably a pejorative name for a poor dwelling; compare Eng. use of 'dog hole'.

**Cathysquoy/Cattysquoy** Widewall 1821; vanished; personal name Cathy (compare *Quoyeden*); ON *kví* enclosure.

**Cauldale** Quindry, Ronsa and Hoxa district, 1871; vanished; pejorative name, Sc. *cauld*, cold; Sc. *dale* a piece of land; there is a Caldale (sic) in St. Ola; 469919; Map Page XI.

**Cauldhame** Paplay 1821, 1841; occupied; pejorative name; Sc. *cauld*, cold, *hame*, home; there are Cauldhame place-names in Stromness Parish, Birsay and Eday; 469920; Map Page VI.

**Cause** see *Coss*.

**Cavelton/Cableton** Eastside, 1750, 1821, 1841; vanished; a very interesting name; its fundamental Norse meaning from the word *kefli* is 'a round piece of wood' such as a stick or a log hence it could mean 'an enclosure of sticks or logs', however the Scots word *cavel* which is from the same root referred particularly to a stick used in casting lots and, by extension of meaning, to a piece of property, the ownership of which was determined by casting lots; the latter is probably the correct interpretation.

**Cavern** vanished, but there is some doubt about whether this house actually existed; 470855; Map Page XIII.

**Cellardyke** 1. Burray, 1821; occupied; originally *Silver Dyke*; there was also a *Siller Dyke/Cellardyke* in *Windwick* and a Cellardyke in Deerness; 'Silver Dyke' was a nickname given to fishermen's houses when herrings were split and laid on walls to dry, the reflecting sunlight giving the impression that the wall was made of silver; in its written form 'Silver Dyke' sometimes appeared as 'Cellardyke'; a small village and former fishing harbour in Fife is called by that name; see the Introduction for a more detailed discussion of this place-name; 472961; Map Page II.

**Cellardyke** 2. South Parish; see *Sillerdyke*.

**Central Garage** Burray; formerly a Church of Scotland, built in 1874; 473966; Map Page II.

**Chair (The)** a pronounced rock on the coast; nearby lies *The Table*; compare *Grey Chair*; 412928; Map Page V.

**Chambered Cairn** 1. Burray; vanished; it stood 90m. west of *East Broch*.

**Chambered Cairn** 2. *Hoxa Hill*; 433936; Map Page IV.

**Chambered Cairn** 3. 430892; Map Page IX.

**Chambered Cairn** 4. (remains of); 464888; Map Page XI.

**Chambered Cairn** 5. see *Tomb of the Eagles*.

**Chambered Cairn** 6. (remains of) Swona; 385837; Map Page XII.

**Chapel Brae** relates to *Our Lady's Chapel* Halcro; 462855; Map Page XIII.

**Chapel Cottage** Burray; occupied; 478966; Map Page II.

**Chapel Geo** the ruins of *St. Colm's Chapel* are nearby; see the Introduction; 488934; Map Page VII.

**Chapel Hall** Burray; a former Baptist chapel now used as a store; 478966; Map Page II.

**Chapel Point** the ruins of *St. Colm's Chapel* are nearby; 488934; Map Page VII.

**Church** 1. Burray; Church of Scotland (also known as the *Mission Station*) with its adjoining manse was built in 1874; now a garage; 473964; Map Page II.

**Church** 2. Burray village; formerly United Free Church; after the union of the United Free Church and the Church of Scotland in 1930, this became the principal place of worship on the island; initially known as *South Church* it was subsequently renamed *St. Lawrence's* after the original *St. Lawrence* foundation in the east of the island; this church is no longer in use; Burray churchgoers now attend *St. Margaret's Church* in *The Hope*; 471956; Map Page VI.

**Church** 3. St. Margaret's Hope; formerly *United Free Church*; now *St. Margaret's Church*; see *United Free Church* for an explanation of this; 449934; Map Page IV.

**Church** 4. formerly Free Church of Scotland, built in 1873 with its associated manse; after 1900 it was renamed *South United Free Church* and, in 1929, *St. Mary's (New) Church of Scotland*; now a private house; see *Eastward House*; 442856; Map Page VIII.

**Church Hall** 1. formerly used by St. Peter's and St. Margaret's congregations; it is now a holiday home; 462923; Map Page VI.

**Church Hall** 2. St. Margaret's Hope; the hall attached to *St. Margaret's Church*; 449934; Map Page IV.

**Churchill Barrier No. 2** links Lamb Holm and *Glims Holm*; 481998; Map Page II.

**Churchill Barrier No. 3** links *Glims Holm* and *Burray*; 474985; Map Page II.

**Churchill Barrier No. 4** links *Burray* and *South Ronaldsay*; 478953; Map Page VI.

**Church Road** St. Margaret's Hope; Map Page IV.

**Clairlea** 1. St. Margaret's Hope; occupied; fanciful name; Map Page IV.

**Clairlea** 2. Burray; empty; 459968; Map Page II.

**Clava Clivvy** coastal feature; *clivvy* is derived from ON *kluför* cleft and in South Ronaldsay is a generic name for a path in such a cleft, especially on a cliff face and was used especially for collecting what is called 'beach' in the dialect of South Ronaldsay i.e. gravel; there are no less than seven named coastal clivvies in South Ronaldsay and probably as many more without a name, some of which are listed below; *clava* is probably a mere duplicated form; several such duplicated forms are found in Orkney place-names e.g. Meery Mawry, formerly a marshy area in Marwick, Birsay; another interpretation is that Clava is from the related ON word *kleif*, a rocky ascent; there is a place-name Clavie in Northmavine in Shetland which is interpreted in this way; Clova was an old farm which lay near Cannigill in St. Ola; like Cannigill, it must have lain near the edge of the Scapa cliffs; 468895; Map Page XI.

**Clay Banks** Quindry Ronsa and Hoxa district 1861, 1871, 1881; vanished.

**Claybraes** occupied; Sc. *braes* slopes; 456928; Map Page IV.

**Cleat** 1. Thurrigar, 1329 (when it was referred to as *i Klaete* in a Norse document), 1492, 1500, 1595, 1653, 1821; a district; ON *klettr* rock (plural *klettar*); when used inland this word carries the same meaning as Gaelic *cleit*, a stone house, in this case perhaps a vanished chapel; compare ON *steinn* rock which also carried the meaning 'cell'; some of these cells developed into chapels as in the case of the Chapel o Cleat in Sanday; there are several similarly named place-names in Orkney; see *Linklater*; see the reference below to other houses which bear this name; 457846; Map Page XIII.

**Cleat** 2. there are 8 houses named 'Cleat' along the road to *Isbister*; these were at one time individual crofts, the property of the Earl of Zetland who owned much of the land in the South Parish; numbers used to distinguish these cottages are: No. 1. occupied; 455845; No. 2. holiday home; 455845; No. 3. occupied; 457845; No. 4. occupied; 458845; No. 5. occupied; 459845; No. 6. holiday home; 462845; No. 7. holiday home; 461845; No. 8. empty; 460848; Map Page XIII.

**Clecksquoy** Eastside 1861; vanished; perhaps a form of 'Clerksquoy' as in Quoyclerks in Orphir; Eng. 'clerk'; ON *kví* enclosure.

**Clefters/Cliftors** Herston, 1736, 1746, 1750; vanished; Orkney dial. 'glifter', variant of ON *gljúfr* gully; compare Glifters o Pegal on Hoy.

**Clett (The)** 1. ON *klettr*, rock; 460872; Map Page XIII.

**Clett (The)** 2. see above; 428863; Map Page X.

**Clett (The)** 3. see above; 468889; Map Page XI.

**Clett o Crura** coastal feature; ON *klettr* rock; *krókar* plural of ON *krókr* corner or nook but which in an Orkney setting probably carries the Faroese meaning 'shelter'; see *Crook*; 463874; Map Page XIII.

**Clettack Skerry** one of the *Pentland Skerries*; ON *klettr* rock with dialect diminutive; 485775; Map Page XIV.

**Cletts** Eastside 1821, 1841; occupied; Eng. plural of ON *klettrar*, stone houses in this case, perhaps anchorite cells; see *Cleat* above and *Linklater*; 461911; Map Page XI.

**Cletts Geo** Swona; see *The Clett* for derivation; the steamer *Croma* of Newcastle with general cargo was wrecked here in 1899; see *Inverbiggings*; 388838; Map Page XII.

**Clickhimin** Sandwick 1881; occupied; fanciful name popularised by Sir Walter Scott referring usually to an old ale-house; the name literally means, 'click him in', where Sc. *cleik*, means 'hook' and probably referred in the first instance to touts 'hooking' men inside; this house name, like many others in Orkney, must have been applied to the house by local people rather than adopted by the occupier; there is a Clickimin (sic) in Sanday and there was formerly a Clickimin in the Ireland district of Stenness; in Kirkwall there used to be a Clickhimin near the pier-head, an appropriate place; compare *Dunkirk*; 437885; Map Page VIII.

**Clivvy 1** 476920; see *Clava Clivvy*; Map Page XI.

**Clivvy 2** 475919; Map Page XI.

**Clivvy 3** 475918; Map Page XI.

**Cloddyhall** 1. Sandwick; 1821, 1861; soon to be occupied; now *Cloudyhall/ Claudie Hall*; dial. *clod* a lump of peat, in this instance probably a reference to the fact that the original house was built of turf; Eng. 'hall' when attached in such circumstances in Orkney place-names always referred to a simple dwelling; see *Dog Tuag*; 435896; Map Page VIII.

**Cloddyhall** 2. Burray, 1821; see above for derivation; now *Klondyke*.

**Cloventots** coastal feature; ON *klofinn* cleft; ON *tota* a protuberance, with Eng. plural; 410914; Map Page V.

**Clot** 1821; Grimness; vanished; name probably has the same origin as *Cloddyhall*.

**Cloudyhall** see *Cloddyhall* above.

**Cloudie** Grimness 1851; a ruin; origin uncertain; perhaps a clipped form of another *Cloddyhall*; 488937; Map Page VII.

**Clousack** Grimness, 1821; vanished; origin unknown.

**Club Hut** Widewall, vanished; when bicycles were the normal form of transport this ex-army hut was, for many years after the war, used for weddings and recreational activites such as dancing and whist drives since it was conveniently placed for both South Parish and North Parish.

**Clump o the Ness (The)** Swona; coastal feature; at first sight the word seems to be English but the word 'clump' is also found in Shetland place-names to refer to a crag and elsewhere in Orkney e.g. Clump o Backber, Eday and The Clumps in Westray; Norw. *klump* apparently used locally in the sense 'rock'; 390852; Map Page XII.

**Coal Store** Herston; supplied the *Pentland Skerries Lighthouse*; 422917; Map Page V.

**Coastguard Lookout Station** now disused; 445829; Map Page X.

**Cobbler's Cottage** see *Aird House*.

**Coburg Roads** Burray; a deep water anchorage off Hunda; the name clearly applies to a vessel which lay here for some time and appears to date back to the 19th century; 451972; Map Page I.

**Coel Na Mara** 1. Burray; occupied; modern Gaelic name; 482970; Map Page II.

**Coel na Mara** 2. St. Margaret's Hope; occupied; Map Page IV.

**Collie** Widewall 1881; vanished but location is known; originally part of *Kirkhouse* of Widewall; two fields on *Kirkhouse* are known as *Upper and Lower Collie* but there is no trace of the original dwelling; said to derive from 'Collie' the surname of an Aberdeenshire family who settled here; (N.B. in the 19th century there was an influx to Orkney of Aberdeenshire farmers who settled on poor land believing that they could succeed where Orcadians had failed; most settlements were abandoned; 446924; Map Page IV.

**Common o Cara** marked on provisional edition of earliest O.S. map; an error for *Common/ty o Berriedale*.

**Common o Kirk** a house, now vanished, built on common land on *Ward Hill*; the 'kirk' referred to is probably *St. Ninian's Chapel* which lay to the north-east; 457884; Map Page XI.

**Commons of Quindrie** occupied; see *Quindrie*; 435924; Map Page IV.

**Commonty o Lally** 1881; the house on the commonty has vanished; Sc. *commonty*, common land; 453905; Map Page VIII.

**Common/ty o Berriedale** the house on the commonty has vanished; see *Commonty o Aikers* above and *Berriedale*; Sc. *commonty*, common land; 461931; Map Page VI.

**Commonty o Herston** 1821; centred on 415916; Map Page V.

**Commonty o Lady** 1891; the house on the commonty has vanished; see *Lally*; *Lady* refers to the *Chapel o Lady*, Halcro; Sc. *commonty*, common land; 475923; Map Page VI.

**Commonty o Lally** see *Commonty o Aikers* above; 476923; Map Page VI.

**Coo Hole** coastal feature; dialect 'coo' cow; the significance of the name is not known; 435839; Map Page X.

**Cools Burn** see *Coulls* below; 450894; Map Page VIII.

**Coo's Belly** coastal feature; refers specifically to a hollow in the cliffs; the name may be transferred from a former nearby enclosure; Sc. *coo* cow; ON *boeli* enclosure; compare *Allibelly Geo*; 445945; Map Page IV.

**Corbie's Nest** Hoxa; pejorative name; Sc. *corbie*, crow or raven; nearby lay *Crowsnest* (Hoxa); 436943; Map Page IV.

**Corn Cappags** depression in cliff line north of *Ossi Taing*; ON *kýrnar* cows; 'cuppags' is ON *koppr* hollow with dialect diminutive; the whole name suggests depressions in the cliff edge where cows sheltered in a south-east wind (a cliff edge is the most sheltered spot when a strong wind is blowing onshore); 462868; Map Page XIII.

**Corn Mill** 1. Burray; 473967; Map Page II.

**Corn Mill** 2. Widewall; 434914; Map Page IV.

**Corn Mill** 3. Cara; 467947; Map Page VI.

**Coss/Cause** Swona; ON *kös* heap; compare *The Keys*; 392855; Map Page XII.

**Cot/Cothouse/Cotthouse** now known as *Cottage*; St. Margaret's Hope 1851, 1871; 455933; Map Page VI.

**Cot of Ronaldsvoe** St. Margaret's Hope; see *Police Station*; Map Page IV.

**Cott** Burray; 1750; vanished.

**Cottage** see *Cot/Cothouse/Cotthouse* above.

**Cottage (The)** Burray; empty; (the most common British house name!); 466961; Map Page II.

**Coulls/Cools/Coulis** 1589, 1750, 1821; Sandwick; occupied; ON *kular*, hillocks, in this instance, with Eng. plural; compare *Earny Coulags*; the Orkney surname 'Cowlis' originated here; John Cowlis lived in South Ronaldsay in 1545; see also *Bowman's House*; 442893; Map Page VIII.

**Couparsquoy** 1736; vanished but the dwelling is believed to have lain near *Quoyboon*; there were several Coupar families recorded in South Ronaldsay in the 17th century; Elizabeth Cooper (sic) lived in *Whities* in Herston in 1821; ON *kví* enclosure; 442883; Map Page VIII.

**Coupar's** field name on *Roeberry Farm*; named presumably from the occupant of a vanished house; compare *Couparsquoy* above; 426933; Map Page V.

**Cove** South Parish 1871; vanished; Eng. 'cove', bay.

**Craa Stone** see *Croo Stone*.

**Craw's Nest** see *Crowsnest*.

**Craa Stone Geo** see *Croo Stone Geo*.

**Crabbi Geo** unlikely to be Eng. 'crab'; see *Tumol o Crapygoe* for possible explanation; 433887; Map Page VIII.

**Craft Centre** 1. Burray; 448964; Map Page I.

**Craft Centre** 2. St. Margaret's Hope; see *Loft Gallery*; Map Page IV.

**Craft Centre** 3. Hoxa; the *Tapestry Gallery*; established for a number of years, a local artist, Leila Thomson, produces here high quality hand-woven tapestries; 413937; Map Page V.

**Crafts** field-name; Sc. *craft* croft; compare 'The Crafty', a small field in Kirkwall where the Lammas Market was at one time held and later, the Phoenix Cinema was built; 463894; Map Page XI.

**Craigflower Cott** Herston; occupied; fanciful name; 422917; Map Page V.

**Crawstaing** Quindry, Ronsa, St. Margaret's Hope 1861; vanished; ON *kró* enclosure; ON *tangi*, point of land; compare *Croo Taing* and *Toung*.

**Creara Head** see *Clett o Crura* for derivation; 431850; Map Page X.

**Creel (The)** coastal feature which forms a sharp rocky point; the name suggests that lobster creels were at one time laid here; 434834; Map Page X.

**Creel Restaurant** St. Margaret's Hope; Map Page IV.

**Creet (The)** underwater reef in the middle of *Savi Geo*; a difficult name to explain since there is no Norse form of this word; similar place-names exist in Shetland which Jakobsen explained as having their origin in a number of Celtic words such as *cruaidh* a hard (rocky place); 420904; Map Page IX.

**Crew o the Slade (The)** Swona; ON *kró* enclosure; ON *slettr*, flat and smooth of stone etc; 386842; Map Page XII.

**Crews (The)** Swona; old enclosures; see above; 392853; Map Page XII.

**Crews o the Quoy Dyke** Swona; see above for interpretation; see also *Quoy Dyke*; 385839; Map Page XII.

**Crinilag** a difficult name to interpret; possibly ON *kró-in á laegð* the enclosure in the hollow; the place-names Cruan in Firth and Lagy in Evie include both these elements; 462868; Map Page XIII.

**Croft** vanished but the location is known; compare *Crafts* above; 441871; Map Page VIII.

**Cromarty Hall** St. Margaret's Hope; built in 1878; it acts as an entertainment centre for the island; named after the Cromarty family who were first recorded in South Ronaldsay in 1479; early in World War II this hall served as a mortuary but later reverted to its normal use for dances and films provided by the armed services who also ran a mobile service around the different camps on the island; the hall has recently been refurbished and extended; Map Page IV.

**Cromarty Square** St. Margaret's Hope; named after the community hall above; Map Page IV.

**Cronstadt** 1. Grimness 1861; some remains may yet be seen, from Cronstadt/Kronstadt in Russia, the commercial seaport of St. Petersburg before the 1880s; a name introduced probably by a sea-faring man; compare *Canton*; see also below; 479929; Map Page VI.

**Cronstad** (sic) 2. field name on *Roeberry Farm*, presumably originally a house name; it is extraordinary to have two Cronstad(t) place-names in South Ronaldsay; no explanation can be offered for this; 429928; Map Page IV.

**Crook** 1. Eastside 1841; occupied; Faroese *krok* shelter; there are Crook place-names in Rendall and Marwick and a Crookhutcheon existed in Stenness; 461913; Map Page XI.

**Crook** 2. Burwick; 1821; occupied; see above for derivation; 435853; Map Page X.

**Crookagill** Hoxa 1821; vanished; ON *krókr* a bend in this instance; ON *gil* stream running in a narrow channel.

**Croo/Craa Stone/Stane** 489941; Map Page VII.

**Croo Stone Geo** a ravine near the above feature; 490941; Map Page VII.

**Croo Taing** ON *kró*, small pen; *tangi* point, i.e. an enclosure on a point of land usually to pen sheep; compare *Soo Taing*; a searchlight, one of at least twenty on the island was positioned here during World War II; 415945; Map Page V.

**Crow Gersty** field-name; ON *kró*, small pen; *garð-staðr* turf wall; 441859; Map Page X.

**Crowtaing/Crootaing** Hoxa 1841; occupied; house named after *Croo Taing* above; there are Crow Taing place-names in Holm and Sanday; 417943; Map Page V.

**Crows** compare Croos in Sanday; see *Cruive*.

**Crow's Nest** Burray; coastal feature; 491983; Map Page III.

**Crowsnest** 1. Hoxa; occupied; pejorative name; nearby lay *Corbie's Nest*; there is a Crowsnest in Hoy and a Crownest in Flotta; 436943; Map Page IV.

**Crowsnest** 2. Eastside 1841, 1861; now *Little Stews*; see above for explanation of the name.

**Cruive** also spelt *Crows*; coastal feature; related to Sh. dial. *krobb*, a small enclosure; the form *Crows* represents Ork. dial. *kreus*, small enclosures; 484927; Map Page VII.

**Crura** see Clett o Crura; 462874; Map Page XIII.

**Crura Head** 462874; Map Page XIII.

**Crura Skerry** 462874; Map Page XIII.

**Cullocks/Coulloch** St. Margaret's Hope 1736, 1851; only low walls remain; the house name derives from the family name McCulloch; there were McCullochs in *Claybrae(s)* in 1821; the 'Mac/Mc' prefix of Highland names were sometimes omitted in place-names; compare *Kenzie's Field* in this respect; this small house was once a school; 444939; Map Page IV.

**Cumla Geo** ON *kuml* a (burial) mound which must relate to some vanished feature; (compare Cumlaquoy, Marwick, Birsay); ON *gjá* ravine; 458832; Map Page XII.

**Cumminsquoy** 1736; vanished; from the surname 'Cumming'; there were Cummings in *Taftnickie*, Widewall in 1821; ON *kví* enclosure.

**Cursey** Grimness 1695; vanished; location and derivation unknown.

**Daisybank** Burray; occupied; fanciful name; 463954; Map Page VI.

**Daisy Villa** St. Margaret's Hope; occupied; fanciful name; the Doctor's Surgery is now established here; Map Page IV.

**Dale** Widewall; 1736, 1821; empty; in Orkney place-names 'dale' has a number of meanings; here it most likely derives from Sc. *dale* a piece of land; there are at least seven other Dale place-names in Orkney; compare *Deall*; 432904; Map Page IX.

**Dale Moss/Moss o Dale** Widewall; see *Dale* above; ON *mosi* moor; 435906; Map Page VIII.

**Dam** 1. Widewall; also known as *Damside/Damseye*; derelict; 451913; Map Page IV.

**Dam** 2. Grimness, 1821; vanished.

**Dam** 3. Sandwick, 1750, 1821; vanished.

**Dam** 4. field name, *Kirkhouse*; it lies beside the old mill dam on the *Oback Burn*; 436913; Map Page IV.

**Dam o Collie** see *Collie*; 449915; Map Page VIII.

**Dam o Gutter** 1821; vanished.

**Dam o Hoxa** referred to as *Hoxa Bay* on the 1862 map of Roeberry Estate; formerly there were very many 'dam' place-names in South Ronaldsay, all normally taking their name from dams, most associated with threshing mills; this particular dam has no association with a water mill but refers, oddly enough, to the small bay <u>outside</u> the stretch of water dammed by a shingle spit; the name must have applied originally to the dam itself which, significantly, has no name today! see *Hoxa*; 428940; Map Page IV.

**Dams Ber** ON *berg* rock; origin of 'dams' in this case uncertain; 403927; Map Page V.

**Damseye** Widewall, 1901; see *Dam 1*.

**Damside** see *Dam 1* above.

**Danska Kirk/Danskirk** see *St. Margaret's Chapel*.

**Deadman's Hillock** this mound, now vanished, lay to the north of *Our Lady's Chapel*; the name suggests the discovery at one time of a cist burial.

**Deadwater Hole** 463875; Map Page XIII.

**Deall** 1736; vanished; see *Dale*.

**Denni Geo** an alternative name for *Duni Geo*; ON *deyning* stink, referring to rotting seaweed; compare Denwick in Deerness; ON *gjá* ravine; 470842; Map Page XIII.

**Dermont** St. Margaret's Hope; fanciful name; occupied; Map Page IV.

**Dettinton/Duttentown** 1750, 1821; near Holland; now merely a farm building on *Newbigging 2*; apparently from the Cheshire surname 'Dutton' though it does not appear in any South Ronaldsay records; 455850; Map Page XIII.

**Devil's Causeway** flat rocks, Grimness; where an extent of rocks assumes an unusual form (in this case a wide road) the construction is usually attributed to some supernatural agency; compare Giant's Causeway in Northern Ireland and Cubbie Roo's Lade in Stronsay; 492924; Map Page VII.

**Dill Geo** Ork.dial. *dill*, Eng. 'dulse', edible red seaweed, *rhodymenia palmata*; see *Dulse Skerry*; ON *gjá* ravine; 403928; Map Page V.

**Dinki Bows** a vanished house; origin of the name is unknown; this house was also known as *Wooldrage's* from the name of a previous occupier; the Wooldrages were slaters by trade in 17th century South Ronaldsay; 417937; Map Page V.

**Dog's Geo** Muckle Skerry, Pentland Skerries; there is a Dog Geo in Shapinsay; in Norse the use of animal names for coastal features was extremely common; both seem a direct translation of ON *hunda-gjá*; there is a Hunda Geo on the Birsay coast; 465785; Map Page XIV.

**Dog Tuag** Eastside 1861; vanished; ON *púfa* mound, plus dialect diminutive 'ock'; a pejorative name for a house; it means, 'tuft of grass where a dog would urinate' and probably related to a house made completely of turf; there was a house by the name Dog Tua in Shapinsay; both Sanday and Westray have Dogtoo place-names.

**Dogtoos** Burray, 1821; vanished; see *Dog Tuag* above for derivation.

**Dooacks Loch** see *Duacks Loch.*

**Doo Geo** Sc. *doo* pigeon; ON *gjá* ravine; 414931; Map Page V.

**Doos' Cave** Sc. *doo* pigeon; 489925; Map Page VII.

**Dornes** vanished; a farm in the Aikers district in 17th century South Ronaldsay; origin uncertain.

**Double Taing** ON *tangi* point; 417904; Map Page IX.

**Douglas Clog** Swona; coastal feature; Douglas families existed in South Ronaldsay in the 17th century; 'clog' seems akin to the Orkney 'Cloke' farm names which in turn are related to Norse *klakkr* type names meaning 'lump' or 'protuberance'; significantly this point marks the western extremity of a boundary of a wall which crossed the island in a south-easterly direction passing over the summit of *Keefa Hill*; 386846; Map Page XII.

**Duacks Loch** origin uncertain; 442866; Map Page X.

**Duck Caves** 470839; Map Page XII.

**Dulse Skerry** Burray; Eng. 'dulse', edible seaweed; see *Dill Geo*; 479988; Map Page II.

**Dunbreck** St. Margaret's Hope 1851; see *Dunsbreck.*

**Duncan's Boatyard** Burray village; this long established boatyard is now closed; Map Page VI.

*Duncan's Boatyard, Burray today.*

**Duncan's Cairn** Grimness; family name 'Duncan'; see below; 1861.

**Duncansquoy** Widewall, 1871; vanished but position is known; family name 'Duncan'; this family name has existed in South Ronaldsay for over 500 years; Christian Duncan lived in *Aikers* in 1601; ON *kví* enclosure; 425906; Map Page IX.

**Dundas Moor** South Parish 1841; vanished; from the family name 'Dundas'; see below.

**Dundas House** Burwick; 1821, 1841; occupied; former home of William Tomison who rose to become Governor of North West Territories, Canada and part of whose large estate was used to found *Tomison's Academy*; William Tomison was 80 years old at the time of the 1821 Census when he was living in this house; he was interred in the garden here; why the family name 'Dundas' was used for this house is uncertain; at first sight it would appear to derive from Sir Lawrence Dundas who purchased the Earldom of Orkney and Lordship of Zetland in 1766 and whose grandson, Lawrence, became Earl of Zetland in 1838; the family name 'Dundas' has however existed in Orkney since 1504, possibly in Holm, certainly in Evie and South Ronaldsay where the first recording is apparently in Cleat in 1666; in 1821 there was a Dundas family in Ossquoy; the early Dundas families seemed to have been important people, judging by the offices they held; 'Dundas' is also found in the abbreviated form Dass in the 1821 Census when there were Dass families in St. Margaret's Hope and Grimness; 444855; Map Page X.

**Duni Geo** an alternative name for *Denni Geo*; ON *duna* a thundering noise, describing the roar of the sea here; ON *gjá* ravine; 470842; Map Page XIII.

**Dunkirk** St. Margaret's Hope 1821; vanished; the only inn recorded in the 1821 Census and operated by a Cromarty family; in the Statistical Account of 1799, Rev. James Watson noted that there were four inns; in South Ronaldsay at the time of the Statistical Account of 1842, by which time the herring industry was established, Rev. John Gerard commented that there were sixteen inns and he was of the opinion that seven would have been sufficient; with regard to the name 'Dunkirk', it is said locally that it relates to the nearby site of *St. Margaret's Chapel,* and was originally 'Danska Kirk'(see *St. Margaret's Chapel* for a further reference to *Danska Kirk*), however it should be noted that there was at one time a cluster of small thatched roof houses named 'Dunkirk' on the seafront in Kirkwall, on the east side of the present St. Catherine's Place; Hossack was of the opinion that it was named after *Dunkirk,* the ship of Patrick, Earl of Orkney; a more likely explanation of this place-name is that, being right on the sea front, it was, like its South Ronaldsay counterpart, an inn; in English a 'Dunkirk' was a French privateer and the name was used by extension to apply to anything which relieved one of one's money, hence a likely nickname for an inn frequented by sailors where they could be 'robbed', just as they could be on the high seas; compare *Clickhimin*; 445935; Map Page IV.

**Dunromin** Burray; occupied; formerly *Tammie Norie's Cottage*; 467968; Map Page II.

**Dunrowan** Burray; 475959; Map Page VI.

**Dunsbreck** origin uncertain; vanished though location is known; 443943; Map Page IV.

**Duttentown** see *Dettinton*.

**Dyke End** 1. Grimness; occupied; 'wall end'; such places are usually found at the shore where a tunship wall reaches the sea, the tunship being an ancient administrative area enclosed by a turf wall; the *Orkney Seal Rescue Centre* is based here; there are at least five other Dyke-end place-names in Orkney; see *Gasender* for the Old Norse form; 475922; Map Page VI.

**Dyke End** 2. Swona; Sc. *dyke* wall; there is no evidence of any wall here today; this place-name represents the 'end of a wall', one of two which apparently divided the island into three; 385845; Map Page XII.

**Dykend** Burray, 1821; occupied; see above; 465954; Map Page VI.

**Eager (The)** see *Euger*.

**Earny Coulags** in Low's *A Tour through Orkney and Shetland*, he mentions hillocks by such a name just north of Sandwick, South Ronaldsay, perhaps on *Kirkie Hill*; ON *örn*, eagle, ON *kúla*, lump, plus dialect diminutive; compare *Ernes Tower* and *Coulis*.

**East Ayre** Hunda, Burray; see *Ayre* for derivation; 447973; Map Page I.

**East Broch** Burray; now a distinctive mound, excavations revealed that the walls were up to fifteen feet thick; one of two brochs which gave the island its name; both this broch and *West Broch* must have been quite distinctive in Norse times; 490988; Map Page III.

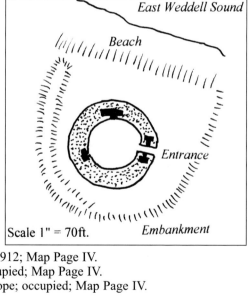

*Plan of the East Broch of Burray, with walls 15 feet thick and a central courtyard almost 40 feet in diameter. One of two brochs which gave Burray its name.*

**Eastdam** Widewall; occupied; 447912; Map Page IV.

**Eastend** St. Margaret's Hope; occupied; Map Page IV.

**East End House** St. Margaret's Hope; occupied; Map Page IV.

**Easter Biggings** see *Biggings*.

**Easterdale** 1750, 1821; Hoxa; vanished; see *Dale* for explanation of 'dale' element.

**Easter Deal** Grimness 1746; vanished; see *Dale* for derivation of name.

**Easter House** Sandwick 1861; vanished.

**Easter Holland**; occupied; see *Holland*; 461850; Map Page XIII.

**East Masseter** Windwick; occupied; see *Masseter*; 448866; Map Page X.

**Eastside** name given to the hinterland of *Newark Bay*; Map Page XI.

**Eastside Links** flat, sandy stretch inland from *Newark Bay*; a ba' game was formerly played on these links on Christmas Day; the competing sides would have been drawn from St. Peter's Parish and from St. Mary's Parish respectively since the boundary of these two parishes passes through these links; a similar game was played between the parishes of Orphir and Stenness on the western boundary of these parishes near the Hall of Clestrain; see *Gammons Park* and *Ball Green* for similar references; Sc. *links* sandy ground near the sea shore; 462900; Map Page XI.

**East Lynn** Burray; 462962; Map II.

**East Swartaquoy** see *Swartaquoy*; 433943; Map Page IV.

**Eastlynn** Burray; see *Overfaulds*.

**East Shaird** Sandwick; vanished though location is known; see *West Shaird*; 444903; Map Page VIII.

**Eastward House** South Parish; occupied; a former church; see *Church 4*.

**East Windi/Wini Skerry** see also *West Windi Skerry*; 387836; Map Page XII.

**Eastview** 1. St. Margaret's Hope, occupied; Map Page IV.

**East View** 2. Burray; occupied; 469966; Map Page II.

**Ebback** Sc. *ebb* foreshore; ON *bakki* bank; 460872; Map Page XIII.

**Echna Loch** Burray; seems originally to have been 'Etna Loch'; ON *jötunn* giant,

*Looking across Echna Loch, Burray. Foreground: Loch House/Lower Loch House;*
*Centre: Rufford, Beechwood Cottage, Upper Loch House;*
*Background: Cellardyke, Remuera, Slap, Howe.*

a reference to an association with some forgotten spirit; 'Eti Goni' was a
Shetland goblin; compare Yetna Steen, a standing stone in Rousay; 474967;
Map Page II.

**Echnaloch Bay** see *Echna Loch* above; 470975; Map Page II.

**Echna View** Burray; occupied; earlier known as *Peterhead*; 474966; Map Page VI.

**Egypt** a small stream running past this house was jocularly referred to as *The Nile*;
see details under *Little Stews*, the alternative name; 462892; Map Page XI.

**Eloner** St. Margaret's Hope; occupied; fanciful name; Map Page IV.

**Ellan Don** Eastside; occupied; 457913; Map Page XI.

**Enclosure** an old semi-circular piece of enclosed land on the coast near *Mayfield*;
432942; Map Page IV.

**England/Ingland** Eastside; 1677, 1821, 1841; occupied; one of a number of
Orkney place-names which provided a surname; Agnes England lived in South
Ronaldsay in 1613; her father was Rorie Ingland; later generations adopted their
father's patronymic 'Rorieson' as a surname which later became established as
the South Ronaldsay surname 'Rorie'; ON *eng* meadow, ON *land*, land; there is
also an England place-name in Iceland; 468919; Map Page XI.

**Enkeldorn** Eastside; occupied; the name suggests that it is transferred from
Enkeldorn, the former name of Chivu in Zimbabwe; 463926; Map Page VI.

**Ennisby** St. Margaret's Hope; occupied; built in the 1930s; Map Page IV.

**Erlend Terrace** St. Margaret's Hope; one of a number of housing developments in
St. Margaret's Hope which have been given the names of the Norse Earls of
Orkney; there are six houses in this development; 1. occupied; 2. occupied; 3.
occupied; 4. occupied; 5. occupied; 6. occupied; Map Page IV.

**Ernes Tower** Eastside 1861; vanished; this house must have taken its name from a
nearby knoll; ON *arnar* 'of the sea eagles' with English plural; 'tower' is a
corruption of ON *púfar* mounds; see *Earny Coulags*.

**Euger/Eager (The)** coastal feature; ON *eggyar* edges in the sense of 'banks';
compare Eggins, a beach feature in Yell in Shetland; 412917; Map Page V.

**Eversley** St. Margaret's Hope; occupied; Map Page IV.

**Eye (The)** coastal feature; 454832; Map Page XII.

**Failte** Burray village; Gaelic *fàilte*, 'welcome'; there was at one time an old house
in Evie named 'Welcome'; Map Page VI.

**Fairhaven** St. Margaret's Hope; occupied; fanciful name; built on the site of the
*Black Smiddy*; Map Page IV.

**Fairview** St. Margaret's Hope; occupied; fanciful name; Map Page IV.

**Fairview** Hoxa; derelict; fanciful name; 434942; Map Page IV.

**Fairwinds** Ontoft Road, St. Margaret's Hope; occupied; fanciful name; Map Page
IV.

**Falls** Grimness 1871; vanished; origin uncertain; perhaps the same as *Fold*; see
also *Fauld*.

**Far Ouse** field name, *Roeberry Farm*; the 'Ouse' referred to is the *Oyce o Quindry*; 437929; Map Page IV.

**Farewell** Ronsvoe 1841; occupied; the name is much older than this; a James Fairwell lived in South Ronaldsay in 1641; ON *faer* sheep; ON *völlr* field; compare Faravel in Birsay; 440932; Map Page IV.

**Fauld** St. Margaret's Hope 1861; vanished; Sc. *fauld*, a pen for animals.

**Faulds** Burray; empty; see above for derivation; 466965; Map Page II.

**Fey** see *Fea* below.

**Fea** Burray; 1750, 1821; vanished; ON *fjall* hill; it must have stood near the *Hillock of Fea*; there are at least six dwellings in Orkney with the name Fea, all deriving their name from the hill on which they stand; Fea is a very common hill name often appearing in disguised forms such as *Keefa Hill* in *Swona*, Cuiffie Hill in Firth or Ravie Hill in Birsay.

**Fedi Geo** Mod. Ice. *feygya* to let decay, a reference to seaweed; ON *gjá* ravine; there is a Fay Geo in Marwick derived in a similar way; compare *Denni Geo*; 403928; Map Page V.

**Felipress** Burray, 1821; derelict; also known as *Tillydelph*: origin unknown; 478968; Map Page II.

**Felli Geo** Burray; probably ON *füll* stinking, referring here to rotting seaweed; compare *Fedi Geo* above; 489953; Map Page VII.

**Fernleigh** Burray; occupied; 475958, Map Page VI.

**Ferry House** Grimness 1821, 1861; vanished but position is known; see *Cara Ferry*; 471948; Map Page VI.

**Fiddler's** Burray, 1821; vanished; from the surname 'Fiddler'; this surname was recorded in South Parish, South Ronaldsay in the 17th century; see below.

**Fiddler's Green** *Windwick*; the Fiddlers presumably lived near here; see above; 460875; Map Page XIII.

**Filiber Burn** a stream; named after the adjacent reef; see below; 431862; Map Page X.

**Filiber Fishing Rock** see below for derivation; 432863.

**Filiber Skerries** ON *füll* stinking, referring here to bird dung; *berg* rock; *sker* reef; 429864; Map Page X.

**Fillibery** Swona; see *Filiber Skerries* above; 393846; Map Page XII.

**Fish Farm** Burray; see *Weddell Fish Farm*.

**Flaits/Flettis/Fletty** Hoxa 1821, 1851, 1871; vanished; probably derived from the family name Flett which is long established in South Ronaldsay; compare the place-name Fletts in Stromness Parish.

**Flaws** 1. Holland 1653, 1821; occupied; also known as *Mid Flaws;* there are several *Flaws* place-names in Orkney; ON *flag* a spot where turf has been cut with Eng. plural; turfs were removed from certain types of soil and used for thatching, the operation being called *pauning* or *poning,* a word related to Nor. dialect *panna* a roof tile; this thin soil was also stripped to make a kind of compost to improve areas with deeper soils; there are other Flaws place-names in Birsay, Harray and Holm; this Flaws was one of a number of Flaws place-names in Orkney which provided an Orkney surname; John Flaws lived in

**Flaws**, South Ronaldsay in 1695; a searchlight, one of at least twenty on the island was positioned here during World War II; the new kirkyard is sited at this location; 456855; Map Page XIII.

**Flaws** 2. St. Margaret's Hope; occupied; Map Page IV.

**Flaws** 3. field-name; 450862; Map Page XIII.

**Flaws** 4. field-name; 458836; Map Page XII.

**Fleece (The)** coastal feature; no connection with *Grey Ewe* on Swona! ON *fles* skerry; compare *Lace Skerry*; 393847; Map Page XII.

**Flood Crag** Burray; 502966; Map Page III.

**Floor (The)** coastal feature, referring to flat rocks here; see *Slates* for explanation of name; 468895; Map Page XI.

**Flower Cott** Herston; see *Craigflower Cott.*

**Fort** (site of) see *Mound*; 473913; Map Page XI.

*Viewforth, Burray, location of the Fossil Museum and Vintage Centre.*

**Fossil Museum and Vintage Centre** contains a magnificent collection of fossil fish from the Devonian Period extracted from Cruaday Quarry in Sandwick, West Mainland forming a basis for a display of fossils from all over the world; the museum also houses separately items which reflect the social history of the islands; see also *Viewforth*; 475971; Map Page II.

**Fogralea** Burray village; occupied; Map Page VI.

**Fold** Grimness 1851; vanished; Eng. 'fold' pen for animals.

**Forbes' School** see *Brandyquoy.*

**Forbes' Brae** the name applied to the hill slope on which *Forbes' School* stands; 457928; Map Page VI.

**Frithillie** ON *freyða* to froth; *hella*, flat rock; 422903; Map Page IX.
**Front Road** St. Margaret's Hope; Map Page IV.
**Front Road** 1. a house; occupied; St. Margaret's Hope; Map Page IV.
**Front Road** 2. a house; occupied; St. Margaret's Hope; Map Page IV.

**Gables (The )** a popular British house name; 474945; Map Page VI.
**Gairy/Gaira** Sandwick; 1557, 1595, 1821, 1841; occupied; it was called Garaye in 1557 and Cara in 1595; see *Garay* below for origin of the name; 445889; Map Page VIII.
**Gairy Hill** see *Garay* below for origin of the name; 465856; Map Page XIII.
**Gairy Lochs** on *Gairy Hill* above; 467855; Map Page XIII.
**Galley Inn/Galley** see *Anchorage*.
**Gallowha/Gallahill/Gallowshill** Burray; 1821; occupied; there are Gallow Hill place-names in Sanday and Westray, all believed to be the sites of former Gallows; at one time a cottage named Gallowha stood at the top of the Clay Loan in Kirkwall; 477969; Map Page II.
**Gammons/Gamon Park** Eastside 1841; occupied; ON *gaman* game or sport; old folk say that a ball game used to be played here, corroborating the origin of the name; compare *Ballgreen*; the presence of several standing stones in this area and the site of *St. Ninian's Chapel* suggests that this was an important assembly area in the middle of the island; see *East Links* for a reference to such a ball game; 460890; Map Page XI.
**Gamse** 1821; in all likelihood the same place as *Gimps*.
**Garages** before World War II there were several garages and two separate petrol pumps on Burray and South Ronaldsay; now there is only *Widewall Garage* in St. Margaret's Hope and two garages in Burray village.
**Garay** Grimness 1492, 1500, 1595; vanished; it seemingly lay near *Cara* and is probably a variant of that name; ON *garðr*, an enclosed piece of land; one of a number of Orkney place-names which provided a surname; Andrew Garay lived in South Ronaldsay in 1534; this surname apparently changed later to Gray and Gorie.
**Garaye** Sandwick, South Ronaldsay; see *Gairy*.
**Garden Field** 465895; Map Page XI.
**Gariel Hole (The)** coastal feature; a puzzling name; in Flotta we find a coastal feature by the name 'The Giral's Hoose'; the definite article attached to both these suggest the name of the ogress ON *grýla*; compare Da Gruila, a small hill on Burra Isle in Shetland; it was believed that this fiercesome spirit inhabited such wild places; compare *Carlan Geo*; 459873; Map Page XIII.
**Garisle** Burray village; occupied; Map Page VI.
**Garleton** St. Margaret's Hope, holiday home; fanciful name; Map Page IV.
**Garrickquoy** see *Gerraquoy*.
**Garsnya Geo** Swona; coastal feature; ON *garð-s(taðr)-ný gjá* new wall ravine; 393847; Map Page XII.

**Garth** 1595, 1696; St. Margaret's Hope; ON *garðr* farm; the original farm has vanished; only the name remains and is applied to a district; this has happened in many cases in Orkney; there are at least seven other farms in Orkney called Garth; Walter Garth lived in South Ronaldsay in 1623; the name *Garth* is now applied to the dwelling formerly known as *Binniewindows*; 457935; Map Page IV.

**Garthingrock** coastal feature; ON *garðr-inn*; the wall; perhaps Eng. 'rock'; 462868; Map Page XIII.

**Gasader** coastal place-name; probably a corrupt form of *Gasander* below; 433885; Map Page X.

**Gasander/Gasender** coastal feature ON *garðs-endir* wall-end; (compare this name with Gorsendi Geo, the termination of a massive dyke, on Papa Stour in Shetland); such a place-name usually takes the form Garson in Orkney; *Dykend* lies in the vicinity; 475918; Map Page XI.

**Gatehouse** Grimness 1851; vanished.

**Geddesta** 1750; vanished; it lay near *Garth*; first element is the Scots surname 'Geddes'; this surname was well established in Kirkwall by the 17th century where the Geddes were merchants but there is no record of them in South Ronaldsay at this time; second element seems to be a rare usage of Nor. *tåg* a small enclosure for cattle, a word also found in Shetland.

**Geo Back** ON *gjá* ravine, *bakki* bank of a ravine etc; 463875; Map Page XIII.

**Geo Hest** ON *gjá* ravine; named from the nearby *Hesta Rock*; 464878; Map Page XIII.

**Geo Longo** Swona; coastal feature; ON *gjá* ravine; ON *langr* long; 391853; Map Page XII.

**Geo o the Hall** Swona; ON *hallr*, rocky shelf; ON *gjá* ravine; 386837; Map Page XII.

**Geordie Ross** field-name; named most probably from the site of a vanished house which lay here; it was common for simple houses and turf hovels to be named after the occupier; Ross is an old established South Ronaldsay and Burray surname; 465896; Map Page XI.

**Geo Ritch** coastal feature; ON *gjá* ravine; the element 'ritch' suggests ON *rettr* sheepfold but this geo can only be approached by sea; the name probably derives from ON *hrytr* snoring, a reference to the sound of the sea in the geo; compare the *Gloup o Root*; 463876; Map Page XIII.

**Gemps** see *Gimps*.

**Gerraquoy** Grimness 1821, 1861; occupied; earlier Garrickquoy; from the family name Garrick; there were Garokes (sic) in Burray in the 17th century, originally a merchant family from Holm; in 1821 they were in *Cableton/Cavelton* in the Eastside; Gerraquoy is now a privately run centre for the study of wildlife and local archaeology; ON *kví*, enclosure; 479931; Map Page VI.

**Giddesta** see *Geddesta*.

**Gill** Hoxa 1861; occupied; ON *gil* stream running in a narrow channel; there is a Gill in Westray and an Ottergill in Stenness; 441943; Map Page IV.

**Gill Bay** see *Gill* above for derivation; 440945; Map Page IV.

**Gillbreck** Widewall; occupied; see *Redhouse (The)*; 438912; Map Page IV.

**Gilbroch** Burray; 1492, 1500; vanished; ON *gil* stream running in a narrow channel; ON *borg*, normally applied to a broch, but it could also mean merely an enclosure.

**Gillieselly** see *Gill* above for derivation; ON *selr* seal; 429854; Map Page X.

**Gillietrang** Burray; 1821; occupied; see *Gill* above for derivation; ON *þröngr* narrow; 475977; Map Page II.

**Gimps** Grimness; derelict; probably an old dialect word for 'mud' or 'mire' as in Nynorsk *gympa*; 482935; Map Page VI.

**Girsay Schottis** 1492, 1500; Burray; vanished; second element seems to represent the surname 'Scottie' as in Quoyscottie, Birsay; Robert Kincaid from South Ronaldsay married Barbara Scotty (sic) of Burray in 1664; the first element Girsay is probably a corruption of the personal name 'Kirsie' = 'Kristie'; compare the place-name Quoykirsay in Harray; the place-name therefore means 'Christie Scottie's' (place); see *May Scottie's*.

**Glebe (The)** Burwick 1841; empty; a glebe was originally land attached to a parish church, in this case, *St. Mary's Kirk*; a place-name found throughout Scotland and England; there is a Glebe farm in Harray; 445846; Map Page X.

**Glebe land** land attached to *St. Peter's Kirk*; 474914; Map Page XI.

**Glendoran** occupied; formerly *Manse 1*; fanciful name.

**Glenfield** Quindry and Ronsvoe district; 1891; vanished; fanciful name.

**Glen Haven** St. Margaret's Hope; occupied; Map Page IV.

**Glims/Glimps/Glums Holm** pronounced 'Glimps'; *glim/glum* appears to be a lost word for phosphorescence—the common old dialect word was *limro* also recorded in the form *glimro*; *Glim* seems to have been a Will o the Wisp type spirit; the name also appears in Glims Moss, a boggy tract near Dounby; Lucifer Moss is the name given to a stretch of moor near Dunnett in Caithness; ON *holmr*, small island; the Burray ferry foundered east of this island in 1775 with the loss of four lives; 473990; Map Page II.

**Glims Holm Skerry** *Glims Holm*; 483995; Map Page III.

**Gloup (The)** Swona; a blow-hole on the east coast of the island; see above for derivation; see also *The Smoo*; 397844; Map Page XII.

**Gloup (The) o Halcro** a blow-hole near the cliff face which, when approached from the sea, is impressive but from above is an insignificant and dangerous grass covered depression; in former times old and lame horses were disposed of by backing them over the edge of this gloup; it was common practice in Orkney (and Iceland) to back such horses over cliffs; ON *gloppa* a big hole; see *Halcro* and *Gloup o Root* below; 474856; Map Page XIII.

**Gloup (The) o Root** an old name for the *Gloup of Halcro*; ON *rjóta* to roar; in his *Orkneys and Shetland* published in 1883, Tudor said of this gloup, 'even in the calmest weather the much resounding sea sends a deep boom through this tunnel'.

**Golden Bowl** South Parish 1851; vanished; fanciful name; compare the former Golden Slipper at the Brig o Waithe in Stenness!

**Golf Course** see *Blanster*; see also *Old Golf Course*.

**Golt (The)** coastal feature; ON *göltr* boar, but usually 'pig' in Ork. dial.; such names were frequently applied figuratively to rocks and promontories in Orkney; Golta in Flotta is the site of the oil industry; 445947; Map Page IV.

**Goosie Geo** coastal feature; ON *gás* goose, a reference to wild geese; ON *gjá* ravine; 433879; Map Page VIII.

**Gospel Hall** St. Margaret's Hope; meeting hall of the Plymouth Brethern; Map Page IV.

**Gossigar/Gossigair/Gossakir** South Parish 1492, 1500, 1595, 1750, 1821, 1841; occupied; ON personal name *Gási*; ON *akr* arable field; compare *Thurrigar*; 439854; Map Page X.

**Gossigar Cott** occupied; see above; 441853; Map Page X.

**Gowan Brae** Burray village; occupied; fanciful name; Map Page VI.

**Gow's** see *Sunnybank*.

**Gow's Corner** a Gow family lived in the adjacent house of *Sunnybank*; 'Gow' is a surname associated with South Ronaldsay but it is not recorded here before 1700; 442902; Map Page VIII.

**Grahamstone** 1. St. Margaret's Hope; occupied; Map Page IV.

**Grahamstone** 2. South Parish; occupied; 443849; Map Page X.

**Graemston** Burwick; 1821; vanished mansion house; after surname 'Graeme'; on 18th July, 1690, George Graeme of Gramstoun (sic), husband to the Lady Halcro, depairted this lyfe'; at the beginning of the 20th century the ruins of this house could still be seen; ON *tún* enclosure; 449849; Map Page X.

**Graemston Loch** see *Graemston* above for derivation; 449845; Map Page X.

**Graemston Laik** a stream; see *Graemston* above; ON *laekr* stream; this is one of the few examples known to the writer of the use of the ON word *laekr* in Orkney place-names; see also *Leoquoy*; 443847; Map Page X.

**Grannie's Well** coastal feature; origin of name uncertain; first element may be a corruption of 'Cra Ness', a common Orkney coastal place-name; 483927; Map Page VII.

**Grass** South Parish 1871; vanished.

**Great Auk Cottage** Burray; empty; 463957; Map Page VI.

**Great Head** not a significant headland as the name would suggest; perhaps a corruption of ON *grjót*, rough stones; 464862; Map Page XIII.

**Great House of Cara** see *Cara*.

**Green Clivvie** ON *klufðr* cleft; a marked gash in the hill near the Mill of Firth has long been known as The Clivvie; 434865; Map Page X.

**Greenhall** Widewall, 1821; vanished.

**Green Head** 432848; Map Page X.

**Greenhead Bay** 432849; Map Page X.

**Greenhouse** Grimness 1861; vanished but position is known; 487939; Map Page VII.

**Greenhow** Quindry, Ronsvoe and St. Margaret's Hope district; 1851, 1881; vanished; ON *haugr* mound.

**Greenhowe** coastal feature; a common name in Orkney for a green (usually prehistoric) mound; sometimes the Norse adjective is at the end as in Howana Gruna on Burgar Hill in Evie; ON *haugr* mound; ON *graenn* green; 488940; Map Page VI.

**Greenquoy** 1. Widewall; occupied; ON *kví* enclosure; 426906; Map Page IX.

**Greenquoy** 2. South Parish; also referred to as *Hillhouse*; occupied; see above; 439865; Map Page X.

**Green Sleigh** Burray; a small winter stream which drains *Northtown Moss*; ON *slý* slime; 454964; Map Page I.

**Greenvale** 1. Barswick 1841; empty; fanciful name; it is intriguing to think that it may have been on this site where Sveinn Asleifarson had his meals! (see *Barswick Bay*); 435867; Map Page X.

**Greenvale** 2. Burray; occupied; 469966; Map Page II.

**Greenwell** Burray; holiday home; origin uncertain; there is (or was) a well nearby; 457972; Map Page II.

**Greesback** St. Margaret's Hope 1861; vanished; unlikely to be a Norse name despite its appearance; Sc. *grice*, pig, Eng.'back', which makes the name the equivalent of Eng. 'hog's back'; probably a reference to the shape of a turf house; compare Ork. dial. *gilt* a long-shaped haystack from ON *gyltr*, a young sow; see the *Griceback* place-names below.

**Greslet** coastal feature; ON *grár* grey; see *Slett*.

**Grey Chair** a chair-like rock; compare *Chair (The)*; 495926; Map Page VII.

**Grey Ewe** Swona, coastal feature; apparently a 'sheep-like' rock; compare French *roches moutonneés*, 'sheep like rocks'; 393851; Map Page XII.

**Greystone** occupied; 445845; Map Page X.

**Grey Stones** Burray; a flat rock, a noted place for rock fishing, a short distance from *Burray Ness;* 505963; Map Page III.

**Griceback** 1. Eastside 1821, 1841; now *Upper Lythes*; see *Greesback* above for explanation of the name.

**Griceback** 2. vanished; see above; 465914; Map Page XI.

**Griceback** 3. vanished; see above; 466915; Map Page XI.

**Gricegarth** near *Grindley*; occupied; ON *gríss* young pig, *garðr*, yard; 445855; Map Page X.

**Grieveshouse** empty; Sc. *grieve* farm overseer; 444854; Map Page X.

**Grimsalie** Swona; coastal feature; perhaps the ON personal name *Grímr* but unlikely to be *Grímr* who, according to the *Orkneyinga Saga* was resident in Swona in the 12th century; ON *hjalli* ledge of rock; 393853; Map Page XII.

**Grim Ness (Head)** ON *nes* point; many such peninsulas carried the names of old gods; in this case the reference is to *Grímr*, a by-name of the god Odin; compare Odin Ness, Gairsay or the many Tor (Thor) Ness place-names on the Orkney coast; a number of vessels have been wrecked in this locality; 1. the sloop *Lady Charlotte* of Kirkwall with a cargo of salt in 1794. 2. the *Orion* in 1825 (other details not known but see *Lippa*). 3. the SS *Giralda* of 2178 tons and with a cargo of coal was set ablaze by enemy aircraft 4 miles SE of Grimness in 1940; the crew of 23, mostly Shetlanders, abandoned ship but their lifeboat capsized ¼ mile from the shore and all were lost. 4. the *Irene*, a Liberian registered steamer in ballast ran aground near to the *Stack o Kame* in 1969; it was on this occasion that the Longhope Lifeboat, which had responded to a distress call, was lost with all hands; 495926; Map Page VII.

**Grimness** 1492, 1500, 1595; a district name; see *Grim Ness* above for derivation; 483935; Map Pages VI and VII.

**Grimness Common** an old name for *Alma*.

**Grimness Head Wireless Station** vanished; a R.A.F (Royal Air Force) Wireless Station operated from here for part of the war; 456886; Map Page XI.

**Grin** 1881, St. Margaret's Hope, vanished; perhaps same as *House of Grun*; origin unknown.

**Grind** 1750; vanished; it lay near *Flaws 1*; apparently the 17th century South Ronaldsay surname Grind/Grim originated here; ON *grind* a lattice gate.

**Grindley/Grindalla** Burwick 1492, 1500, 1595, 1736, 1750; derelict; there are, or were at least six other similar place-names throughout Orkney; ON *grind-hlið*, a gate made of spars of wood; see *Quoygrindla*; 448855; Map Page X.

**Grinds** Burray; a shoal to the west of Hunda; ON *grunn* a shallow (with English plural); in Sanday this Norse word takes the form 'green' in the Baa Green o Rinnabreck.; 425966; (N.B. lies off the maps supplied).

**Groat Head** ON *grjót* rough stones; 466862; Map Page XIII.

**Gropenally** coastal feature; both elements mean 'ditch'; ON *gröfin* the ditch, (Nor. *grop*); ON *áll* channel; 409926; Map Page V.

**Groot Fa** coastal feature; ON *grjót* rough stones; 'fa' is probably Eng. 'fall', hence a 'scree'; 445845; Map Page X.

**Grud (The)** coastal feature; ON *grjót* rough stones; 473910; Map Page XI.

**Grutha** 1. St. Margaret's Hope; holiday home; probably a very early transferred name from *Grutha (Old)*; see below for derivation; 442938; Map Page IV.

**Grutha** 2. Grimness; occupied; see below; 475943; Map Page VI.

**Grutha (Old)** Grimness 1653; vanished but location is known; a very important, large house in its day; when inspected by the Royal Commission on Ancient Monuments in the 1930s, it was estimated that the extant structure then dated from the 17th century; its name and location suggests it took its name from the shore; one of a number of Orkney place-names which provided a surname; Robert Gruthay lived in Ronaldsvoe in 1601; ON *grjót* rough stones (compare *The Grud* above); ON *hallr* ledge; 486946; Map Page VII.

**Grutha Point** coastal feature; see *Grutha (Old)*; 487945; Map Page VII.

**Grutla** 1750; vanished; it lay near *Linklater*; ON *grjót* rough stones; ON *hlað* stepping stones.

**Grutla House** 1750; vanished; see above.

**Gunnerhill** Burwick 1750, 1841; occupied; a difficult name to interpret; apparently it has nothing to do with coastal defence; the Norse first name Gunnar existed in Deerness in the early 18th century which may be a pointer to its origin; the second element 'hill' may be ON *hóll*, mound, the combined elements meaning 'a mound on Gunnar's land'; see also *Gunnie's* below; 447843; Map Page X.

**Gunnie's** field name, *Kirkhouse*; the name suggests that it is called after the owner of a house, no trace of which remains; possibly after the first name Gunnar; compare Gunnista on Bressay in Shetland; see also *Gunnerhill* above; 438920; Map Page IV.

**Guttar** Grimness 1750, 1821, 1851; vanished; Ork. dial. *gutter* mud; compare Gutterquoy in Birsay.

**Gutter** St. Margaret's Hope 1861; vanished; Ork. dial *gutter* mud.

**Gutterhall/Gutteryhall/Guthriehall** near *Rockerskaill*, Eastside 1821, 1841; vanished; from the family name Guthrie which is locally pronounced 'Guttery'; Sc. *hall* cottage.

**Guthriehall** Herston; 1821; see above.

**Gutteryhools** 1821; near *Gossigar*; vanished; probably dialect 'guttery', muddy; Eng. 'holes'; compare *Hools*.

**Gylliosquoy** alias **Scushan** 1736; occupied; from Gilius/Geiles, a form of the personal name Giles; this first name for a girl is found in old South Ronaldsay records, e.g. Geiles Flaws married Donald McBeth in *St. Peter's Kirk* in 1660; ON *kví* enclosure; see *Schusan*.

**Haas Geo** Swona; ON *háls* neck, dialect *haas* where it also carries the meaning 'throat'; here it seems to relate to a narrow neck (or throat) of water as in Hassie a narrow stretch of water between Thieves' Holm and Carness in St. Ola; compare *Burray Hass*; 386847; Map Page XII.

**Habcarke** a farm recorded in North Parish, South Ronaldsay in the 17th century; possibly a corruption of *Hallbreck* which, as a surname, was written 'Habreck'.

**Haddock Ben** a nickname for the farm of *Isbister 2*; it clearly relates to a former occupant!

**Hailey** see *Hellie*.

**Halcro** Holland 1545, 1841; occupied; one of a number of Orkney place-names which provided a surname; David Haucrow (sic) lived in *Quoybrown*, South Ronaldsay in 1492; ON *hallr* slope or, more likely, *hár* high; *kró* small pen; the place-name Hackra in Marwick in Birsay probably had the same origin; 462854; Map Page XIII.

**Halcro Head** see *Halcro* above; 476856; Map Page XIII.

**Hall** 1. near *Blanster*, 1821; vanished.

**Hall** 2. see *Hall o Linkletter*.

**Hall/New Hall** near *Isbister* 1821; occupied; 463849; Map Page XIII.

**Hall (The)** Windwick; vanished; location known; Sc. *hall* cottage; 450870; Map Page XIII.

**Hall o Aikers** Eastside 1871; vanished; 'hall of . . .' usually refers to an important dwelling house in Orkney as in the case of the Hall of Rendall; the use of 'hall' on its own or attached to some other name (as in *Gutterhall* above) refers to a simple cottage; see *Aikers*.

**Hall o Cara** see *Cara*.

**Hall o Herston** occupied; see *Hall o Aikers* above and *Herston* for explanation name; 418908; Map Page V.

**Hall o Hoxa/Hall (The)** occupied; see *Hoxa*; 420940; Map Page V.

**Hall o Linkletter** 1750, 1821; derelict; 450870; Map Page XIII.

**Hall Cottage** Burray village; occupied; Map Page VI.

**Hall Geo** Swona: ON *hallr* ledge; 386838; Map Page XII.

**Hallbreck** 1. Grimness 1750, 1861; occupied; there is also a Hallbreck in Wyre; one of a number of Orkney place-names which provided a surname; Alexander Habreck (sic) lived in South Ronaldsay in 1552 which proves that the place-name *Hallbreck* goes back to the 16th century at least; a searchlight, one of at least twenty on the island, was positioned near here during World War II to spot incoming enemy aircraft attacking Scapa Flow Naval Base; see *Habcarke*; ON *hallr* ledge (compare *Gru<u>th</u>a* nearby); ON *brekka* slope; 487943; Map Page VII.

**Hallbreck** 2. Widewall; occupied; see *Hallbreck* above for explanation of name; 426900; Map Page IX.

**Hallbreck** 3. St. Margaret's Hope; a former workshop and store which may have been a dwelling house; Map Page IV.

**Halls (The)** area of flat rocks on the coast; probably ON *hallr* ledge, with English plural; 454830; Map Page XII.

**Hallstead Chapel** Burwick; an entry in archaeological records based on a 19th century traveller's account; it must be an error for *Halcro Chapel* (*Lady Chapel*) which lay some distance away.

**Ham Geo** also known as *Salt Geo*; ON *hamn* harbour; compare *Lammer Geo*; 468839; Map Page XII.

**Hameneuk** a house; occupied; fanciful name; 422906; Map Page IX.

**Hamisquoy/Hammarsquoy** field-name; from *Hamie* a diminutive of the Old Norse name *Hámundr*; a Magnus Hamie lived at Sebay in St. Andrews in 1614; 449869; Map Page X.

**Hammarshoorie** Swona; coastal feature; ON *hamarr*, rock, personal name 'Shurie', a form of ON *Sigurd*; compare *Taftshurrie*; these are very old names; there is no 'Shurie' recorded in South Ronaldsay, Burray or Swona even in the mid 17th century; 393852; Map Page XII.

**Hammarsquoy** South Parish 1851; vanished, now a field to the north of *Masseter*; see *Hamisquoy* above; ON *kví*, enclosure; 446867; Map Page X.

**Hammer (The)** ON *hag-mýrr* pasture marsh; 433863; Map Page X.

**Hammer How/Hammer House** South Parish 1851, 1871; vanished; there is also a Hammer place-name in Birsay; ON *hag-mýrr* pasture marsh; *haugr* mound.

**Handy** Eastside 1861; vanished; origin uncertain; perhaps a corruption of 'Hangi' used in place-names referring to a steep slope.

**Hang Geo** local tradition says that the ship *Edinburgh* of Leith ran aground here in 1799; a young boy, James Thomas, ran up the bowsprit to get ashore but fell into the water; when he tried to climb the cliff, he slipped, caught his head in a rock fissure and was hanged; he is buried in *St. Mary's* Kirkyard; 427859; Map Page X.

**Hang Rock** associated with the above feature.

**Hannipow/Hanni Pows** a large rock pool which never ebbs; the resting place of HMS *Opal* (see *Slates o Hest*); probably Eng. 'harn' flax (an 'r' in front of an 'n' was not pronounced in former times); flax was steeped in such pools as part of the process of producing linen; compare *Lint Pows*; 464877; Map Page XIII.

**Hanscone** Quindry, Ronsvoe and Hoxa district; 1861; vanished; origin unknown.

**Haap (The)** Swona; ON *hóp* small bay, which seems to relate to the stretch of water partially enclosed by *Selki Skerry*; The Hap is an old name of Sandside Bay in Graemsay; 383840; Map Page XII.

**Harbour View** 1. St. Margaret's Hope; occupied; Map Page IV.

**Harbour View** 2. St. Margaret's Hope; occupied; Map Page IV.

**Harrabrough** Widewall; occupied; a searchlight, one of at least twenty on the island, was positioned here during World War II; ON *harðr* hard, i.e. 'stony'; ON *borg* walled enclosure; 422903; Map Page IX.

**Harrabrough Head** coastal feature; 415904; Map Page IX.

**Hattaf** Burray; occupied; an old cottage at *Pole*; origin unknown; 487959; Map Page VII.

**Hattie's** also known as *Hillhouses*; the first name 'Hattie' is a familiar form of 'Harriet'; houses were frequently called after the first name of their occupants, particularly if the occupant were an elderly spinster; an old house (now vanished) in Marwick in Birsay was called 'Hannah's' and 'Babbie's' (Barbara's) was a house in Sanday; 474933/474934; Map Page VI.

**Havanah** Quindry, Ronsvoe and Hoxa district 1871; vanished; from Havana, Cuba; a name probably given by a sea-faring man; compare *Canton* etc.

**Haven** Grimness 1821; vanished.

*An old photograph of The Haven, Swona, the only suitable landing place on the island.*

**Haven (The)** 1. Swona; ON *hafn* harbour; this word usually took the form *hamn* in the isles as in Hamnavoe, Stromness but the form *hafn* was kept in South Ronaldsay where there are seven examples; *The Haven* is the only suitable landing place on Swona; 392850; Map Page XII.

**Haven (The)** 2. compare above; 433983; Map Page IV.

**Haven (The)** 3. Quindry, Ronsvoe and Hoxa district 1821, 1851; occupied; named after a nearby inlet; see *Haven (The), Swona* below for explanation.

**Haven (The) o Orally** compare above; 466862; Map Page XIII.

**Havlesquoy** Hoxa 1821; vanished; ON *há* high; *völlr* field; *kví* enclosure; compare Hawell (earlier Havell) in St. Andrews.

**Haw** 1. Grimness 1851; vanished; origin uncertain; perhaps Sc. *haugh* a stretch of flat land.

**Haw** 2. Widewall 1851; vanished; see above.

**Haybrake** St. Margaret's Hope; 1821; occupied; ON *hey-brekka* hay slope; there is also a Haybrake in Walls; 450931; Map Page IV.

**Head** 1. Grimness 1821, 1861; occupied; refers to the nearby prominent cliff or headland; 488929; Map Page VII.

**Head** 2. Windwick; 1821; occupied; see below for possible interpretation; 456875; Map Page XIII.

**Heads** Hoxa; occupied; origin uncertain; perhaps originally 'head rigs'; 439935; Map Page IV.

**Heather Brakes** Widewall 1851; vanished; see *Barebreck*.

**Heatherbell** 1. occupied; fanciful name; 443868; Map Page X.

**Heatherbell** 2. occupied; 433938; Map Page IV.

**Heatherbrae** Quindry, Ronsvoe and Hoxa district 1871, 1881; vanished; Sc. *brae* hillside.

**Heathercowspunk** Burray; it would be interesting to know how this house got its name which means, 'a spark flying from a piece of burning heather bush'; perhaps it was a phrase used by a former inhabitant when a spark flew from the open fire, the phrase becoming a nickname of the inhabitant then subsequently applied to the house; Clankvengeance in Rendall may be explained in the same way; 468969; Map Page II.

**Heatherhall** Burray; occupied; 463969; Map Page II.

**Heatherhill** Burray; occupied; 459968; Map Page II.

**Heathervale** Burray; occupied; fanciful name; 464967; Map Page II.

**Heatherum/Hetherum** St. Margaret's Hope; occupied; if the place-name is old it may represent ON *heiðar-hvamm* heath-slope; see *Vamh* for a comparison; 434929; Map Page IV.

**Heddle's Quarry** the Heddle family previously owned much land in South Ronaldsay; there were Heddles in Hoxa in the 17th century; 461924; Map Page VI.

**Heights** 1. field-name, *Burwick*; this field lies close to the coast, the highest elevation being over 30 metres; 437846; Map Page X.

**Heights** 2. field-name, *Cletts*; it is not the highest field here by any means; the fields below *England* in the Eastside were also referred to as Heights, even though there were higher fields on the farm; 460906; Map Page XI.

**Heights of Alma** see *Alma*.

**Helenlea** St. Margaret's Hope; occupied; fanciful name; Map Page IV.

**Helliar/Hellie** coastal feature; ON *hella* flat rock; 468884; Map Page XI.

**Hellie** South Parish 1861, 1871; derelict; named after the above feature which lies to the north-east; 463883; Map Page XI.

**Henderson's** derelict house; named after a previous occupant; there were Hendersons in South Ronaldsay as early as the 17th century; a common Caithness surname; 443903; Map Page IV.

**Herston/Harthstath** 1492, 1500, 1595, 1821; now a district; ON *Harðar-staðir*, the farm of a man *Hörðr*; 418917; Map Page V.

**Herston Battery** 178 Battery, 63 Anti-Aircraft Regiment R.A (Royal Artillery) protected Scapa Flow Naval Anchorage from this point; during an air-raid on the night of 10th April 1941 when this battery was in action, a shell exploded in the breech of one of the guns killing Gunner Thomas Cockburn and Gunner Alfred Sayers whose bodies are interred in *St. Peter's* Kirkyard; 415915; Map Page V.

**Herston Head** see *Herston* above; 411915; Map Page V.

**Herston Hall** formerly *Mission Hall*; it belongs to Church of Scotland; empty; 423915; Map Page V.

**Herston Taing** see *Herston* above; ON *tangi* point; 417923; Map Page V.

**Hesta 1.** Burray, small headland to the west of the old jetty at *Westshore*; see below for derivation; 468954; Map Page VI.

**Hesta 2.** Burray; a house, occupied; name derived from the above; 475970; Map Page II.

**Hesta Head** ON *hestr* stallion or horse generally; animal names such as 'pig', 'horse', 'calf', 'hen' were used for coastal features; there is a Hesta Geo in Birsay; compare also the Horse o Copinsay; 467878; Map Page XI.

**Hesta Rock** coastal feature; see above; 464878; Map Page XIII.

**Hestily** occupied; ON *hestr* stallion; ON *hlíf,* Nor. *live* shelter; there is a Hestwall in Sandwick, West Mainland; 452869; Map Page XIII.

**Hetap** Swona; a cliff; nearby lies *Peedie Hetap*; ON *haed* height, ON *toppr* top; compare Het, a small cliff on the coast of Orphir; 393851; Map Page XII.

**Hetherum** see *Heatherum*.

**Hill 1.** field name, *Kirkhouse*; a large field to the west of *Vensilly Hill*; 448915; Map Page IV.

**Hill 2.** Midtown, South Parish 1871; vanished.

**Hillbanks** Burray; occupied; 467970; Map Page II.

**Hillcrest** Burray village; occupied; Map Page VI.

**Hill Dam** this dam was filled in in the 1980s; 472936; Map Page VI.

**Hill Dyke 1.** Widewall; see below; 422916; Map Page V.

**Hill Dyke 2.** Grimness; normally an Ork. dial. term for the turf wall which enclosed a tunship; the common Norse term was *garð-staðr* which appears in Ork. place-names as Gersty; see *Gasender*; 482926; Map Page VI.

**Hillfield 1.** Burray, occupied; 465958; Map Page VI.

**Hillfield 2.** field-name; 446868; Map Page X.

**Hillfield 3.** field-name; 455838; Map Page XII.

**Hillhead** Burray; empty; 469964; Map Page II.

**Hillhouse 1.** Burray; 468969; Map Page II.

**Hillhouse 2.** Quindry, Ronsvoe and Hoxa district 1851; vanished; there is also a Hillhouse in Graemsay.

**Hillhouse 3.** see *Greenquoy.*

**Hillhouses** vanished; but the position is known; there were two houses here close together by this name, one of which was known as *Hattie's*; 474934; Map Page VI.

**Hillock o Fea** Burray; a prominent man made hillock, the origin of which has not been determined; the vanished farm of *Fea* lay nearby; 494955; Map Page VII.

**Hill o Snebb** there is only one recording of this place-name (see reference under *Newark*; see also *Snebb*); location unknown.

**Hill Park** St. Margaret's Hope 1851; vanished.

**Hilltoft** Burray occupied; there is also a Hilltoft in Holm; 466967; Map Page II.

**Hilltop** St. Margaret's Hope 1861; vanished.

**Hillside** 1. Widewall 1851; vanished but location is known; Hillside is a name also applied to districts in Birsay and Stenness; 433929; Map Page IV.

**Hillside** 2. Burray; a district name; 465965; Map II.

**Hillside Camp** vanished; during World War II this large camp was at different times home to R.E. (Royal Engineers), Royal Signals, Pioneer Corps and various Infantry Regiments, e.g. K.O.S.B. (King's Own Scottish Borderers), Gordon Highlanders, Argyll and Sutherland Highlanders, South Wales Borderers; after the war a detachment of the 25th Infantry Battalion, Polish Army, was based here temporarily; in the early 20th century Hillside Camp was the site of the old *Golf Course*; 436930; Map Page IV.

**Hivills** Windwick 1861; vanished; see *Havlesquoy* for derivation.

**Hoghouse** 1. South Parish 1746, 1851; vanished. Sc. *hog* yearling sheep.

**Hoghouse** 2. Grimness 1746; vanished; see above.

**Hoghouse** 3. 1736; vanished; see above.

**Hogs' Hole** coastal place-name; probably a place where sheep sheltered when they had access to the shore; Sc. *hog* yearling sheep; 424897; Map Page IX.

**Hole** Grimness, 1821; vanished; probably ON *hóll*, a mound.

**Hole o Sagill** a narrow sea cave and a haunt of seals; in those days when seals were hunted for their meat, blubber and hides, a narrow purpose-built boat was used to enter this cave; ON *sae* sea; ON *gil* stream running in a narrow channel; 472848; Map Page XIII.

**Hole o the Altar** Swona; a cave; see *Slates o the Altar* and *The Bishop*; 391841; Map Page XII.

**Holhouse** Grimness 1851; vanished.

**Hollocast** 1821; vanished; it lay near *Cletts*; apparently Eng. 'holocaust', an extraordinary name for a house; perhaps a variation of 'Hell', the name of several houses in Orkney; on the other hand it could point to the possibility of a previous house on the this site being burnt down and its inhabitants dying in the conflagration.

**Holland** mentioned in all the Rentals of Orkney; occupied; *há-land* high land or *hóll-land* a hillock; there are at least eight Holland place-names in Orkney; the South Ronaldsay place-name 'Holland' is one of a number of Orkney place-names which provided an Orkney surname; Sir Richard Holland was canon of St. Magnus Cathedral in 1457 and probably came from here; he is considered to be Scotland's earliest poet though Orkney was Danish at the time of his birth! He lived the latter part of his life in England, having a price on his head as a subversive!; 458851; Map Page XIII.

**Holyrood Chapel** see *Rood/Ruid Kirk/Chapel*.

**Holm House** Grimness 1851; vanished; reason for name unknown.

**Home of Kirk** Eastside 1891; vanished; ON *hvamm*, valley.

**Homes** Burray; 1750; vanished; see *Home of Kirk* above for derivation.

**Honeysgeo** ON *húnn*, a young bear; *gjá*, a ravine; the Norse frequently used animal names to describe coastal features; it seems strange to use a 'bear' name in Orkney yet we find a similar usage in Walls on the island of Hoy in the place-name Bersi Geo, where *bersi* is a bear; see also *Barni Taing*; 487933; Map Page VII.

**Honeysgeo/Honesgow/ Hanisgeo** Grimness 1821, 1851, 1861, 1881; occupied; it took its name from the nearby ravine; see above; also known as *Haven*; 487933; Map Page VII.

**Hools** Widewall 1821, 1861; occupied; local dialect *hools* 'holes'; compare *Gutteryhools*; 427904; Map Page IX.

**Hope Cottage** St. Margaret' Hope, holiday home; Map Page IV.

**Hope (The)** 1. a commonly used name for *St. Margaret's Hope*; it was referred to in this way by Tudor in his *The Orkneys and Shetlands* published in 1883 and he suggests that the name had long been in use.

**Hope (The)** 2. Hunda, Burray; ON *hóp* bay; compare *The Haap* on Swona; 433963; Map Page I.

**Hopeness** St. Margaret's Hope; occupied; Map Page IV.

**Horns o Mouster** coastal feature referring to prominent horn shaped rocks; see *Mouster Head* for interpretation of name; 466883; Map Page XI.

**Horse Binks** coastal feature; a depression on the cliff top here suggesting stone quarrying at one time; compare *Birbinks*; significance of the name 'Horse' not understood unless it applied at one time to the cliff itself; compare *Hesta Head*; 459873; Map Page XIII.

**Horse Geo** 1. may have the same explanation as below but more likely ON *hross* horse; *gjá* ravine; see *Hesta Head* for explanation of name; 432852; Map Page X.

**Horse Geo** 2. its location in *Burwick Bay* suggests an inlet where horses could be shipped; see reference in Introduction to this; it is said locally that Cromwell's troops landed their horses here; 438839; Map Page X.

**Horse Park** field-name; 441847; Map Page X.

**Horse Rock** coastal feature, the Norse settlers frequently applied animal names to coastal features; in this instance 'horse' is a corruption of ON *hross*; 468905; Map Page XI.

**Hoston Bay** see *Hoston Head* below; 430873; Map Page VIII.

**Hoston Head** 'Hoston' may represent ON *haesti-tún* highest field/enclosure; 434874; Map Page VIII.

**Hotel** see *Murray Arms Hotel*.

**Hottit** Grimness 1595; occupied; the element *tit* represents ON *topt*, ancient house site; Howcost (sic), the earliest recording of this name suggests that the first element is ON *haugr* mound and it is therefore an identical place-name to *Howatoft*; one of a number of Orkney place-names which provided a surname; Henry Hottite (sic) lived in South Ronaldsay in 1601; 475939; Map Page VI.

**Hottit Rock** coastal feature; see *Hottit* above; may refer to a fishing rock used by *Hottit*; 488943; Map Page VII.

**Houny Cletts** St. Margaret's Hope 1861; vanished; ON *haugrinn* mound; see *Cleat* for origin of 'cletts' element.

**Housebreck** Burray; 1627, 1750; occupied; ON *hus*, house; *brekka* slope; 485959; Map Page VII.

**House Geo** Swona; 393852; Map Page XII.

**House of Burn** 1. St. Margaret's Hope 1821; derelict; at the time of the 1821

Census it was a shop operated by a Laughton family; the form 'House of . . .'
in place-names seems to be unique to South Ronaldsay and must have been seen
as giving status to the dwelling; notice how many of these have disappeared; see
examples below; 455938; Map Page IV.

**House of Burn** 2. Burwick 1821; occupied; 457837; Map Page XII.

**House of Cleat** South Parish 1851; vanished; see *Cleat.*

**House of Grun** St. Margaret's Hope 1821; vanished; same name as *Grin.*

**House of Hest** South Parish 1851; vanished; origin uncertain.

**House of Park** Widewall and Herston 1821; vanished; 'park' is used here in the Sc.
sense of 'field enclosed by a wall'.

**Hoxa Tapestry Gallery** see *Craft Centre 3.*

**How** Grimness, a new house said to be on the site of a former house with this name;
488940; Map Page VI.

**Howe** Hoxa 1861; occupied; ON *haugr* mound; 425939; Map Page V.

**Howatoft/Howtoft** 1821, 1841; empty; apparently named after the small mound near
the shore; ON *haugr* mound, *topt* ancient house site; there is a Howatoft in North
Ronaldsay and there was formerly a Howatoft in Rousay; 467917; Map Page XI.

**How o Hoxa** a broch on *Hoxa*; ON *haugr* mound; see *Hoxa*; 425939; Map Page V.

**Howe** Burray; occupied; there are at least six other How(e) dwellings in Orkney;
ON *haugr* mound; 472962; Map Page II.

**Howe Taing** Hoxa; ON *haugr* mound; ON *tangi* point; 426939; Map Page V.

**Hoxa** 1329 (*Haugs æði*), 1492, 1500, 1595, 1861; now a district; ON *haugs,*
genitive case of *haugr* mound; *eið* isthmus; supposedly the burial place of Earl
Thorfinn Skullsplitter; the Welsh brigantine *Hugh Roberts* of Caernarvon with
a cargo of coal was wrecked on Hoxa in 1890; 423938; Map Page V.

**Hoxa Bay** see *Dam o Hoxa.*

**Hoxa Head** see *Hoxa* above for derivation and *Hoxa Sound* below; the brigantine
*Industry* of Liverpool was wrecked here in 1781 and the brigantine *Bristol
Merchant* of Perth suffered the same fate in 1807; 403927; Map Page V.

**Hoxa Head Lighthouse** a small automatic light; 404927; Map Page V.

**Hoxa Hill** see *Hoxa* above; 433936; Map Page IV.

**Hoxa Sound** see *Hoxa* above for derivation; ON *sund* strait; the most important
entrance to the Naval Base of Scapa Flow and heavily defended with boom nets
during two world wars; in World War I, gun emplacements known as the Hoxa
Battery were established at Hoxa Head; these consisted of four 4 inch quick
firing guns overlooking the boom and two 6 inch quick firing guns mounted to
the east of these with an arc of fire which covered the entrance to Swltha Sound;
supporting these were two 24 inch searchlights; in 1940, during World War II,
the so-called Balfour Battery was established here, named in honour of Thomas
Balfour; the first commanding officer of the Orkney and Shetland Fencibles in
1793; two 12 pounder quick-firing guns were mounted here, later replaced by 2
twin 6 pounder quick-firing guns supported by two 24 inch searchlights; almost
on the site of the old Hoxa Battery, two 6 inch breech-loading MK7 guns were
positioned, again supported by two 24 inch searchlights; at 419937 and at
315934 two anti-aircraft batteries were set up which formed part of the curtain
of gunfire known as the 'Scapa Barrage' which was triggered at the approach of

enemy aircraft; gun laying radar was also located here to assist these batteries; by 1950 all the armour had been removed but many of the buildings still remain; two vessels have been wrecked on the coast here; 1. the sloop *Harriet Helen* of Flotta in 1888. 2. *Alexandra II* of Liverpool, a tug, in 1915. 3. the German submarine UB116 was sunk here in October 1918 while attempting to penetrate the boom defences; 390930; Map Page V.

**Huddost** Eastside 1861; vanished; origin unknown.

**Huludale** Eastside 1861; vanished; ON *hol* hole, *ló* water hole; see *Dale* for interpretation of 'dale' element.

**Hummle (The)** coastal feature; a variant of Sc. *humple* a small mound; 432863; Map Page X.

**Hunda** Burray; no longer an island as the name suggests but linked to Burray by a shingle bar on which a military road was built in World War II; 1. the Norwegian brigantine *Haabets Anker* of Christiana (Oslo) with a cargo of hides, cotton and tobacco was wrecked here in 1850. 2. sailing vessel *Eva Potter* of Kirkwall with a cargo of coal suffered a similar fate in 1912; ON *hundr* dog; *ey* island; the application of animal names to coastal features was common in Norse times; 437967; Map Page I.

**Hunda Barrier** during World War II a boom net was placed between *Hunda* and the Calf of Flotta; the *Hunda Reef* below was also reinforced to form an inner defence and protection for the Home Fleet; 444905; Map Page I.

**Hunda Reef** Burray; a natural feature connecting the former island of *Hunda* to Burray; nine hundred yards of two feet gauge railway were laid across this reef during World War II to transport from a quarry here stone to reinforce this feature and contribute to the so-called *Hunda Barrier*; similar railways were built on Burray and Flotta; 443965; Map Page I.

**Hunda Sound** Burray; ON *sund* channel; 445967; Map Page I.

**Hune** coastal feature, Grimness; it was here where the lifeboat of the S.S. *Giralda* came ashore (see *Grimness Head*); name suggests ON *haugrinn*, the mound, as in Huant in Birsay; this name is also found at the other side of South Ronaldsay; see below; 490941; Map Page VII.

**Hune Bay** there are burnt mounds on the coast here; see above for derivation; 434882; Map Page VIII.

**Hune Taing** see above; ON *tangi* point; 433883; Map Page VIII.

**Hunni Geo** Muckle Skerry, Pentland Skerries; see *Honeygeo* for possible interpretation; 461781; Map Page XIV.

**Husenter Point** ON *haugs* genitive case of *haugr*, mound; *endir* end; compare *Gasander*; 433864; Map Page X.

**Husbay** Sandwick 1871; vanished; perhaps a transferred name from one of several Housebay place-names in Orkney; ON *húsa-baer*, buildings.

**Hykoch** Swona; coastal feature; Eng. 'high'; origin of 'koch' element unknown; Map Page XII.

**Hylack** Swona; coastal feature; Eng.'high'; 'lack' is probably a corruption of Sc. *lug* ear, in the sense of a projecting part of shore or cliff; compare *Meg's High Lug* in South Ronaldsay; 385837; Map Page XII.

**Inger Cottage** Burray; occupied; 467960; Map Page II.

**Ingland** see *England.*

**Ingleneuk 1.** Burray village; occupied; fanciful name; Map Page VI.

**Ingleneuk 2.** St. Margaret's Hope; occupied; Map Page IV.

**Ingma Clivvy** coastal feature; ON *klufðr* cleft; origin of first element uncertain; perhaps a corruption of ON *innra*, innermost; 414905; Map Page IX.

**Inkbottle 1.** Hoxa; occupied; several houses shaped in the form of the old style 'inkbottle' were built in Orkney during the late 19th century e.g Midbigging in Firth and Binscarth Cottages (Nos. 2 and 3), the original dwellings now demolished; 428927; Map Page IV.

**Inkbottle 2.** the field on *Roeberry Farm* on which the house of *Inkbottle* above stands.

**Inkerman** Grimness 1861; some remains may still be seen; named after the battle of that name fought in the Crimean War in 1854; there is also an Inkerman in Shapinsay; compare *Alma, Balaclava* and *Sebastopol*; 478923; Map Page VI.

**Inn** it lay at the junction above St. Margaret's Hope but ceased operating before the war; it is now a dwelling house divided into four flats, all occupied; Map Page IV.

*The sale of a shipwreck, a common occurrence on the islands in olden days; in this case, the wreck of the Croma on Swona in 1899 (see Inverbiggings).*

**Inner Ganges** Swona; one of two channels in the rocky beach lying parallel to the coast; a corruption of ON *gang-stöð* 'where a boat may be berthed'; the place-name Gunstie on Noss in Shetland is derived in the same way; the Graemsay Pier was formerly (and appropriately) called the Gansti Pier; see also *Outer Ganges*; 386843; Map Page XII.

**Inner Scaw** coastal feature; ON *skagi* projecting point of land; compare *Skaifles*; 475906; Map Page XI.

**Innskerry** Swona; see *Outskerry*; 392850; Map Page XII.

**Instabely** a farm in the Flaws and Holland district of South Ronaldsay in the 17th century; vanished; ON *innsta-boeli*, innermost farm; there is an Instabillie in Sandwick and there was at one time a farm of Instabillie near Orquil in St. Ola; see also *Allibelly Geo*.

**Inverbiggings** Swona, 1821; empty; this house is unusual in that it is referred to at different periods by four names including *Upper Biggings, Ivor's Biggings*; and *Rose Cottage*; it was extended and heightened in 1900, the heavy roof timbers coming from the deck of the steamer *Croma* of Newcastle which was wrecked on the island in 1883 (see entry under *Swona* for details of other wrecks); see below for interpretation of 'inver'; apparently the name of the house was changed to *Rose Cottage* when it was occupied by the Rosies at the beginning of the 20th century; 389848; Map Page XII.

**Inverollit** Widewall 1821; 'inver' suggests Gaelic influence but the place-name is most probably a corrupt form of Ork. dial. 'iver', i.e.'over' as in *Iverattty* below; the name seems to mean 'the upper house of *Olad*'; see *Olad*.

**Inyequoy** 1492; see *Quoyinga*.

**Isbister** 1. 1492, 1500, 1595, 1627; derelict; there are Isbister place-names in Rendall, Harray and Birsay; this Isbister is first recorded as *Estirbister* and later as *Ystabustare* which suggests ON *yztr-bólstaðir*, outermost farm, a good description of its position; a Wireless Station was built here by the Admiralty during World War I with the purpose of communicating with ships at sea and with the Royal Naval Base at Lyness; 466846; Map Page XIII.

**Isbister** 2. empty; known locally by the nickname *Haddock Ben*; the most easterly of three farms set close together, the others being *Midbister* and *Wasbister*; ON *eystri-bólstaðir* the eastern farm; 448902; Map Page VIII.

**Issy Gutcher's** an alternative name for *Alma*, now *West Cara*; the family name 'Gutcher' has existed in South Ronaldsay since 1594 at least and, remarkably, has not been recorded elsewhere in Orkney.

**Italian Prisoner of War Camp 34** Warebanks, Burray; vanished; see *Warebanks*.

**Iveratty** Sandwick 1871; Ork. dial. 'iver', over or 'upper'; almost certainly the same name as *Upper Attley*.

**Ivor's Biggings** see *Inverbiggings*.

**Ivydean** Burray village; occupied; formerly the old Post Office; Map Page VI.

**Jacky Flett's Hole** coastal feature; one of a number of Orkney coastal place-names which date from the time of the Napoleonic War and which are associated with Press Gang 'recruiting'; a local boy, Jackie Flett, (possibly from *Newbigging, Holland*) hid here but was eventually captured; it is said that he served his time in the navy and when he returned he flogged with cart chains the local constables who had apprehended him; 470836; Map Page XII.

**Jamie Green's** see *Mayfield (The)*.

**Jeanie Broon's** a house; vanished; 473942; Map Page VI.

**Jessie Budge's Field** field-name; Budge is a common South Ronaldsay surname, first recorded here in 1601; see *Tom Budge's Stone*; 448835; Map Page X.

**Jimmy Dick's** field-name, *Roeberry Farm*; the first 'Dick' recorded in South Ronaldsay was Alexander Dick, who was ordained minister of *St. Peter's Kirk* sometime before 1574; the field is apparently called after Jimmy Dick, the mason, who lived in a house at the *Quindry* Corner; 431927; Map Page IV.

**Jolly Farmers** field-name, *Roeberry Farm*; origin of this name is unknown; 436930; Map Page IV.

**Kail Yard** Burray; coastal area; enclosures built to grow 'kale' or cabbage were at one time common in Orkney; only the name remains here; 496966; Map Page III.

**Kaleyard and Long Kelp** a fishing mark below *Gill,* Hoxa, offshore; 438950; Map Page IV.

**Kame** coastal feature; ON *kambr* ridge; there are several such place-names in Orkney e.g. Kame o Hoy; 488925; Map Page VII.

**Kame o Stews** see *Kame* above and *Stews*; 468887; Map Page XI.

**Kammerbusk** St. Margaret's Hope; occupied; a name transferred from the coastal feature *Camberbosk/Kammerbusk*; Map Page IV.

**Karinya** Burray village; occupied; fanciful name; Map Page VI.

**Keefa Hill** a point near the summit of *Warbister Hill*, Swona; ON *kyr* cattle, *fjall* hill; Kierfea Hill in Rousay, Kier Fiold in Sandwick, West Mainland and Cuiffie Hill in Firth are identical place-names; 387843; Map Page XII.

**Kelda** St. Margaret's Hope; occupied; modern name modelled on ON *kelda* a well; Map Page IV.

**Kelso** Quindry, Ronsvoe and Hoxa district, 1871; vanished; a transferred place-name from Kelso in the Scottish borders.

**Kennedy's** St. Margaret' Hope; empty; one of the most striking houses in the village has no name; the upper floor of this house was used as a hospital in World War I; the name 'Kennedy's' refers to the name of the last proprietor; Map Page IV.

**Kennisquoy** Hoxa 1821, 1851; vanished but position is known; perhaps the surname Kennedy rather than the personal name Kenneth which is extremely rare in old Orkney records; in 1821 Alexander Kennedy lived in *Braehead* and his daughter Margaret is recorded living at *Roeberry* in *Hoxa*; see also *Wilfred Kennedy's*; ON *kví* enclosure; 421937; Map Page V.

**Kenzie's Field** from the surname MacKenzie; Helen Mackenzie lived at *Fletty* in Hoxa in 1821 and Barbara Mackenzie in *Purgatory* at that time; compare Kenzie's Tower on Flotta; the prefix 'Mac' of Scottish surnames tended to be omitted in place-names in the South Isles; compare *Cullocks* for a similar reference; 462934; Map Page VI.

**Kettle (The)** coastal feature, *Pentland Skerries*; ON *ketill* a cauldron, but used here metaphorically of a hollow; sometimes such features were used for evaporating sea water to make salt; 468779; Map Page XIV.

**Keys (The)** coastal feature; ON *kös* heap of stones; see *Quoycous*; 494928; Map Page VII.

**Kiln (The)** Muckle Skerry, Pentland Skerries; coastal feature and relates to persistent sea spray in the air here which suggests a smoking, grain drying kiln; there is a similar feature known as The Kiln on Swaitha; see *Sinilie* for another example; 465785; Map Page XIV.

**Kingshouse** Burwick 1821, 1841; built in an extremely exposed position so it is not surprising that it has vanished; a fanciful name applied originally to a poor dwelling to give it status; there are Kingshouse place-names in Harray and Firth; 433849; Map Page X.

**Kirk** Eastside 1601; holiday home; one of a number of Orkney place-names which provided a surname; Hucheon Kirk lived in South Ronaldsay in 1601; 455893; Map Page VIII.

**Kirkbrake** Eastside 1871; vanished; see *Barebreck* for origin of 'brake' element.

**Kirk Cottage** 1871; empty; the 'kirk' in question was the so called *Secession Church* built at *Garth*; 463926; Map Page VI.

**Kirk Geo** 1. also known as *Chapel Geo*; ON *gjá*, ravine; the ruins of *St. Colm's Chapel* are nearby; 488935; Map Page VII.

**Kirk Geo** 2. Swona; nearby lies the remains of the *Twinly Kirk*; 383846.

**Kirkhouse** 1. a large farm, Widewall; occupied; *St. Ola's Chapel* was situated here; 436914; Map Page IV.

**Kirkhouse** 2. Widewall; numbered field-names on this farm include; 1. 435915; 2. 435917; 3. (now combined with 5) 442915; 4. 438918; 5. (now combined with 3) 438915; Map Page IV.

**Kirkhouse** 3. Paplay 1841; occupied; private house adjacent to *St. Peter's Kirk*; 469905; Map Page XI.

**Kirkhouse Mill** occupied; formerly *Corn Mill 2*; now restored as a private house.

**Kirkhouse Point** see *Kirk Taing*; 473906; Map Page XI.

**Kirkie Hill** Sandwick; 436902; Map Page VIII.

**Kirkiehill** a house, occupied; 436898; Map Page VIII.

**Kirklea** Burray; occupied; 477965; Map Page II.

**Kirk Ness** ON *nes* point; 476912; Map Page XI.

**Kirk Taing** 1. Burray, a rocky point of land near the ruin of *St. Lawrence's Kirk*; ON *tangi* point; 493965; Map Page III.

**Kirk Taing** 2. also known as *Kirkhouse Point*; ON *tangi* point; the Norwegian brigantine *Argo* of Tonsberg with a cargo of wood and bricks was wrecked here in 1901 and the Norwegian barkentine *Adele* of Brevik with a cargo of pit props suffered the same fate at this point in 1912; the *Adele* was the last sailing ship to be wrecked on South Ronaldsay; 473906; Map Page XI.

**Kirkyard** 1. field-name; 458838; Map Page XII.

**Kirkyard** 2. see *Flaws 1*.

**Kirn** 1. coastal feature, Grimness; see below for explanation; 483925; Map Page VII.

**Kirn** 2. coastal feature, Hoxa; Sc. *kirn*, churn, relating to the churning movement of the sea 409926; Map Page V.

**Kirona** Burray; occupied; a new house; 476967; Map Page II.

**Kist (The)** ON *kista* a chest, the reference is to a box-like rock; 432872; Map Page VIII.

**Kist Skerry** see *Kist* above; *sker* reef; 432871; Map Page VIII.

**Klaete (í)** see *Cleat* (*Thurrigar*).

**Klondyke** Burray; occupied; recorded as *Cloddyhall* in 1821; renamed presumably by a gold prospector who took part in the Klondike (sic) gold rush in Yukon, Canada in 1896 and for some short years afterwards; however there was also a silver and lead mine by the name Klondyke (sic) in Arizona and therefore the ultimate origin of the house name is in doubt; compare the house name *Balarat*; 463967; Map Page II.

**Knockday/Knockdry** St. Margaret's Hope; 1851, 1861; vanished but location is known; the suffixes 'day/dry' suggest that this is an old name adopted from a local feature; the 'day' element is ON *dý* marsh and 'dry' suggests ON *drit* filth; Sc. *knock* a knoll; compare *Knockhall* below; 444943; Map Page IV.

**Knockhall** 1578, 1750, 1861; St. Margaret's Hope; occupied; usually a house/farm name which ends in 'hall' is to be interpreted as Ork. dial. 'simple cottage', usually of late origin, paralleling the Knockhall place-names of Shetland, Aberdeenshire and Ireland; Sc. *knock* a knoll; *Knockhall* in Stromness Parish is situated beside a very prominent knoll; a searchlight, one of at least twenty on the island, was positioned here during World War II; 453942; Map Page IV.

**Knockhall Point**; see *Knockhall* above; 454944; Map Page IV.

**Knockhall Taing** also called *Taing o Knockhall*; 455946; Map Page IV.

**Knoll** see *Knowe 2*.

**Know** St. Margaret's Hope 1821; vanished; Sc. *knowe* mound.

**Knowe** 1. Quindry; Sc. *knowe* mound; 434925; Map Page IV.

**Knowe** 2. Holland; 1821, 1841, 1871; vanished; Sc. *knowe* mound.

**Knowe (The)** Swona; Sc. *knowe* mound; 393854; Map Page XII.

**Knowe o Quindry** occupied; see above for derivation; 429924; Map Page IV.

**Kuikobba** 1329; vanished; the location is unknown; referred to in a document written in Kirkwall in the Norse language; ON *kví* enclosure; the element 'Kobba' suggests a diminutive of the feminine personal name 'Jakoba'.

**Kyelittle** see *Ryelittle*.

**Lace Skerry** ON *fles* skerry with loss of initial 'f'; other instances of the loss of the initial 'f' are found in coastal place-names which usually take the form 'Lash' as in The Lash, a skerry in the north of Graemsay; in Flashes, a coastal name to the north of Braebuster in Hoy, the 'f' is retained as it is in the case of *The Fleece* on Swona; 438839. Map Page X.

**Lady Bank** Eastside 1891; vanished; refers to the *Our Lady's Chapel*, Halcro.

**Ladybreak** South Parish 1891; vanished; see above.

**Ladypark** Windwick 1891; formerly *Bersiedale*; some remains may yet be seen; see above; 456879; Map Page XIII.

**Ladyhaven** Burray; occupied; 460956; Map Page II.

**Ladywater** Burray; occupied; this house was badly damaged in August 1940 when a parachute mine landed nearby; fortunately the occupants were only slightly injured; 459956; Map Page II.

**Lady Weem's Castle** see *Weems Castle*.

**Laftlie Point** ON *lopta* to lift, used in the Shetland sense of 'rising up'; ON *hlíð* slope but also used in Orkney in the sense 'cliff; nearby is *Stromlie Point*; 410913; Map Page V.

**Lairdene House** St. Margaret's Hope; see *Waterside*.

**Lally/Lawley** Grimness 1821, 1841, 1881; vanished; spelt *Laley* in a 17th century document; this name is also found in Fetlar in Shetland; ON *hlað* stepping stones, probably over a marsh; compare *Grutla*; ON *hlíð* slope; see *Commonty o Lally*.

**Lammer Geo** ON *hlað-hamarr* a natural rock jetty, compare the *Lober/s* place-names; 412939; Map Page V.

**Lands End** Widewall 1901; vanished; 426907; Map Page IX.

**Lang Ayre** 1. coastal feature; ON *langr* long; *eyrr* sand or shingle spit; 485933; Map Page VII.

**Lang Ayre** 2. coastal feature; see above for derivation; 435922; Map Page IV.

**Lang Ayre Road** leads westwards from *Lang Ayre 1*; 485933; Map Page VII.

**Langa Clivvy** coastal feature; see *Clivvy*; 469892; Map Page XI.

**Langa Taing** 1. Eastside; scene of the wreck of the Norwegian barkentine *Georges Ville* of Sandefjord with a load of coal in 1902; ON *tangi* point; 468904; Map Page XI.

**Langa Taing** 2. Burray; see above for derivation; 462953; Map Page VI.

**La Plata Hole** Swona; coastal feature; the Norwegian brigantine *La Plata* of Frederikstad was wrecked here in 1886; 383835; Map Page XII.

**Laxigar** coastal feature, Hunda, Burray; probably the equivalent of Norw. *laksedam*, a pool in which wild salmon are trapped; ON *lax* salmon; *garðr* fence; compare Laxfirth in Shetland; 439964; Map Page I.

**Lawley** see *Lally*.

**Lawrona** Burray village; occupied; fanciful name; Map Page VI.

**Lay Burn** Burray; northern course of *Burn of Sutherland* draining *Etna Loch*; 476965; Map Page II.

**Lay Skerry** a derivative of the ON verb *leggja* to lie, a reference to where seals lie; *sker* reef; 435838; Map Page X.

**Lay Taing** see above; ON *tangi* point; 467862; Map Page XIII.

**Leaburn** Burray; there are fourteen houses in this development, thirteen of which are occupied; 475959; Map Page VI.

**Lead Mine** see *Old Shaft*; 477922; Map Page VI.

**Lee Geo** suggests Eng. 'lee' sheltered, since it stands next to *Blow Geo* but most likely *lee* here has the same meaning as in *Bratlee Ber*; ON *gjá* ravine; 403926; Map Page V.

**Leekum** coastal feature to west of *White Beach*, Windwick; seems to contain the Norse words *hlíð*, cliff and *kambr* ridge but origin is uncertain; 463864; Map Page XIII.

**Leggit's** an alternative name for *Quoynethes*; apparently from the surname 'Leggat'.

**Legion (The)** St. Margaret's Hope; former branch of the British Legion; this branch is now closed; Map Page IV.

**Leika kwi** see *Leoquoy*.

**Leirvoe** St. Margaret's Hope; occupied; modern name based on a Norse form; Map Page IV.

**Leith** Burray; 1627; empty; perhaps ON *hlíð* gate, i.e., a gate on the *Ness Road*; 493960; Map Page III.

**Leiths** St. Margaret's Hope; occupied; from the family name 'Leith'; it was at one time a shop; Map Page IV.

**Lerdie** see *Lurdy*.

**Leyni Geo** ON *hlein* rock projecting like a pier into the sea; *gjá* ravine; 403933; Map Page V.

**Leoquoy** Brough 1329, 1500, 1584, 1627; vanished; one of the earliest recorded Orkney farm names, originally *Leika kwi* in a 14th century document written in Norse; ON *laekr* stream, *kví* enclosure; compare *Graemston Laik*.

**Liddel(l)** 1492, 1500, 1595; occupied; also known as *North Liddel*; earlier recorded as Luddale which is also one of the recorded forms of Lidda in St. Andrews; probably related to Ork. dial. *lubba* coarse hill grass and ON *loðinn* shaggy; ON *dý* marsh; compare *Lobady* and *Ludenhill* in Birsay; 463838; Map Page XII.

**Liddel(l)** district name for the area around *Liddel(l)* above; 460836; Map Page XII.

**Liddel(l) Head** coastal feature also known as *Banks Head*; in former times the sandstone strata lent itself to the quarrying here of roofing slates; 460832; Map Page XII.

**Liddel(l) Loch** see above; 455835; Map Page XII.

**Liddel(l) Ayre** see *Liddel(l)* above; ON *eyrr*, sand or shingle spit; the Norwegian brigantine *Svalen* of Drammen with a cargo of pit props was wrecked here in 1877; 454832; Map Page XII.

**Limbo** Grimness 1861; occupied; a pejorative name; Eng. *limbo*, the borderland of Hell, referring to some negative aspect of the house or situation, usually the land; compare the sprinkling of Hell and Purgatory house names found throughout Orkney; 486937; Map Page VII.

**Lime Banks** coastal feature; so called from the calcareous secretions on the rock face here; 478923; Map Page VI.

**Lime Kiln** coastal feature, Hoxa; turf kilns, using peat as a fuel to burn lime for mortar, are recorded in Orkney; 403933; Map Page V.

**Limes Geo** Swona; origin of 'limes' uncertain; ON *gjá* ravine; 393852; Map Page XII.

**Linburn** St. Margaret's Hope; occupied; fanciful name; Map Page IV.

**Lindale** St. Margaret's Hope; occupied; fanciful name; Map Page IV.

**Linegar/Lynegar** Hoxa; a ruin; suggests ON *hlíð-inn* slope; *garðr* enclosure or wall; 410935; Map Page V.

**Link** Widewall 1851; vanished.

**Linklater** 1492, 1500, 1595, 1627; now a district; there is also a Linklater in Sandwick, West Mainland; ON *lyng* heather; for *klater* element see *Cleat*; the Orkney surname Linklater originated here and in the West Mainland; Andrew Linkletter (sic) lived in Garth in 1695; 451872; Map Page XIII.

**Links** 1. field-name on *Roeberry Farm*; see below for derivation; 425935; Map Page V.

**Links** 2. Sandwick 1821, 1861, 1881; vanished; Sc. *links* stretch of sandy ground near a shore; 435892; Map Page VIII.

**Linkshouse** Burray 1750; vanished.

**Linley** field-name; probably a variant of North Ronaldsay 'Lint-lues', Sc *lint* flax, ON *ló* marsh; flax was grown in this area; compare *Lint Pows* below; 458853; Map Page XIII.

**Linnview** Burray; occupied; fanciful name; 469966; Map Page II.

**Lint Pows** pools in which 'lint' or flax was steeped; the name dates from the end of the 18th/ beginning of the 19th centuries when linen was produced in Orkney in considerable quantities; see *Hanni Pow*; 485929; Map Page VII.

**Lippa** Blaeu's (1654) map and Mackenzie's *Orcades* map (1750), record a rock, or possibly a sandbar, off the eastern entrance to *Water Sound*, between Burray and South Ronaldsay and called by this name; there are two references to this feature in local tradition today, 1. it was here where the *Orion* went aground (see under *Grim Ness Head*); 2. there is a tale that an Orkneyman in Norway met a woman from Burray there and asked her how big the trees on Lippa were (a similar tale is told about Otterswick in Sanday and the 'woods o Skaill' in Eday; see also *Sand o Wright* in this connection); the name Lippa suggests ON *hlið* gate, used in the sense of passageway between reefs; 'pa' is probably a corruption of Ork. dial. *ba* = ON *boði*, reef; compare *Baaes*; 485948; Map Page VII.

**Lið** see *Lythe*.

**Little Ayre** coastal feature; see *Ayre* for derivation; 438926; Map Page IV.

**Little Berriedale** Grimness; see *Upper Berriedale*.

**Little Gillieselly/Lower Gillieselly** vanished but the location is known; see *Gillieselly*; 432851; Map Page X.

**Little House** Sandwick 1861; vanished.

**Little Howe** ON *haugr* mound; 434908; Map Page VIII.

**Little Howe/Knowe** Hoxa; an insignificant mound near the north shore of *Howe Taing*; 425940; Map Page V.

**Little Mire** Widewall; see *Mire* for derivation; 435910; Map Page IV.

**Little Ness** Burray; occupied; 495959; Map Page III.

**Little Ore** see *Big Ore* for derivation; 467893; Map Page XI.

**Little Quoy** Burray; occupied; 448964; Map Page I.

**Little Skerry** 1. one of the *Pentland Skerries*; ON *sker* reef; 472765; Map Page XIV.

**Little Skerry** 2. see above for derivation; 433915; Map Page IV.

**Little Stews** Eastside; also known as *Crowsnest/Craw's Nest* and *Egypt*; originally a house; now a farm building not used as such now but could be renovated and used as a dwelling house again; see *Stews*; 464893; Map Page XI.

**Little Wart** Burray; occupied; see *Wart*; 467960; Map Page VI.

**Little Wart Cottage** Burray; occupied; see *Wart*; 466960; Map Page VI.

**Lober Rock** ON *hlað-berg* a natural rock jetty; compare *Lammer Geo*; 433944; Map Page IV.

**Lober/s** Hoxa; holiday home; named after nearby *Lober Rock*; 433942; Map Page IV.

**Lobers** 1. coastal feature see above for derivation; 491931; Map Page VII.

**Lobers** 2. coastal feature; see *Lober Rock* above for derivation; 433878; Map Page VIII.

**Loch House** Burray; see *Lower Loch House*.

**Loch o Lythe** see *Lythe*; 444858; Map Page X.

**Loch o the Tarf** Swona; see *Outra Loch*.

**Lochmailing/Lochmellon** Burwick 1736, 1821; Sc. *loch* lake; it lay very near *Burwick Loch* which was almost certainly larger than it is today; Sc. *mailing* a tenanted farm; 443843; Map Page X.

**Lochmellan** Burray; 1821; vanished; apparently a transferred name from *Lochmailing/Lochmellon* above.

**Loch Sheen** field-name, Burwick; a most interesting field-name; it seems that the nearby *Burwick Loch* was originally called *Sheen*, dialect pronunciation of ON *tjörn* little lake; when, at a later date, this Norse word was not understood, the word 'loch' was attached to it; subsequently the loch came to be called Burwick Loch and the name 'Loch Sheen' was given to the nearby field; 438844; Map Page X.

**Lochside** 1. Brough; derelict; 455845; Map Page X.

**Lochside** 2. Burray; empty; 477968; Map Page II.

**Lodgicks** Burray 1750; vanished; seems to mean Sc. *ludge* in the sense of fisherman's hut with dialect diminutive.

**Loft Gallery** St. Margaret's Hope; art exhibitions are held here each summer; on the floor below is the *Workshop*; Map Page IV.

**London** Grimness 1861; derelict; there are also London place-names in Harray and Eday; 484945; Map Page VI.

**Longhouse** Hoxa 1821; vanished.

**Look Out** Garth district; occupied; Map Page IV.

**Lookout** Burray occupied; 463972; Map Page II.

**Loordie** see *Lurdy*.

**Loppack** coastal feature; *Little Skerry*; ON *hlaup,* literally 'a leaping out' used metaphorically in Orkney of a point of land; compare Lopness in Sanday; the suffix 'ack' is a diminutive; 476767; Map Page XIV.

**Lostquoy** Quindry, Ronsvoe and Hoxa district 1861; vanished; ON *kví* enclosure; origin of *lost* uncertain; if the name is genuinely old it may derive from ON *losa* to fall loose and refer to a loosely built structure; compare Tuiltry in Sanday and Rickla in Harray.

**Lother Rock** off Burwick; several vessels have been wrecked on this treacherous reef; 1 the brig *Columbus* in 1862; a poem called 'The Wreck of the Columbus' records that the sole survivor, David Huntie, registered the death of the carpenter, the only body to come ashore; 2. the Norwegian steamer *Ansgarius* of Tonsberg with a cargo of coal was wrecked in 1895; 3. the schooner *Mary Roberts* of Caernarvon with a cargo of coal suffered a similar fate in 1903; see below for derivation of Lother; 435830; Map Page X.

**Louther Skerry** *Pentland Skerries*; ON *hljóðaðr* sounding; compare Loth in Sanday; *sker* reef; 480773; Map Page XIV.

**Lovers' Lane** a track between two fields along the *Quindry* road; it was used by tinkers as a camping area; now ploughed over; 436928; Map Page IV.

**Lower Barswick** (see *Barswick*); occupied; 433856; Map Page X.

**Lower Bigging** Widewall; vanished.

**Lower Braehead** vanished; 450902; Map Page VIII.

**Lower Collie** vanished; now a field-name on *Kirkhouse*; see *Collie*; 444914; Map Page IV.

**Lower Crook** 1. 1821; Herston; vanished.

**Lower Crook** 2. Eastside; 1821; vanished but location is known; 460912; Map Page XI.

**Lower Dam** 1821; it lay near *Oback* Widewall.

**Lower Faulds** Burray, 1821; see *Netherfaulds*.

**Lower Gillieselly** see *Little Gillieselly*.

**Lower Hamisquoy** field-name; see *Hamisquoy*; 449868; Map Page X.

**Lower Haven** Grimness 1871; vanished; (see *Haven*).

**Lower Holland** see *Holland*; 457848; Map Page XIII.

**Lowerhouse** Burray; occupied; 465969; Map Page II.

**Lower Kirk Geo** 435847; Map Page X.

**Lower Links** Sandwick 1881; vanished; see *Links*.

**Lower Loch House/Loch House** Burray; 473966; Map Page II.

**Lower Midtown** Herston; occupied; 421914; Map Page V.

**Lower New Bigging** vanished; 428908; Map Page IX.

**Lower Ollad** Sandwick 1821, 1861; vanished though location is known; also known as *Nether Ollits*; see *Olad* Sandwick; 446885; Map Page VIII.

**Lower Quoydam** Widewall; vanished; see *Quoydam*.

**Lower Stone** Windwick 1861; vanished; see *Stone*.

**Lower Tarland** 1. Burwick; see *Tarland*; 443841; Map Page X.

**Lower Tarland** 2. Brough; see *Tarland*; 443838; Map Page X.

**Lowertown** Hoxa; it lies below *Hoxa Hill*; 435942; Map Page IV.

**Lower Yarpha** St. Margaret's Hope 1861; vanished; see *Yarpha*.

**Loxley** Burray; occupied; 466966; Map Page VI.

**Lug** Swona; Sc. *lug* a projecting part, referring to a cliff in this instance; 393845; Map Page XII.

**Lurdy** Burray; occupied; known as *Lerdie* in 1627 and *Loordie* in 1750, 1821; there is also a Lurdy on Flotta; ON *ler* clay, *dý* marsh; 485956; Map Page VII.

**Lyall** fieldname on *Kirkhouse*; some unknown association with the surname Lyall which was recorded in South Ronaldsay as early as the 17th century; 440914; Map Page IV.

**Lynburn** Burray; occupied; fanciful name; 478959; Map Page VI.

**Lyndale** Burray village; occupied; Map Page VI.

**Lynnview** Burray; occupied; 467967; Map Page II.

**Lyra House** Herston village; occupied; named by Capt. Cromarty, a previous owner, from the small constellation Lyra with its dominant star Vega, brightest of the summer stars; 423918; Map Page V.

**Lyrawall** Widewall; occupied; perhaps takes its name from Lyrawa Bay in Walls; 438924; Map Page IV.

**Lyre Back Falls** a stream which runs over the cliff after heavy rain but which is usually blown back on the land again; ON *líri* shearwater; ON *bakki* slope; 468893; Map Page II.

**Lythe** Barswick; 1821; occupied; one of the earliest recorded Orkney farm names; it appears in a document written in Norn in 1329 as *Lið* and later as *Quoyleith*; in this instance most likely ON *hlíð* slope; one of a number of Orkney place-names which provided a surname; John Leith who lived in Campston, Toab in 1546 was son of John Leith married to Margaret Cromarty both of whom were clearly from South Ronaldsay; significantly John (younger) had a sister called Eden; see *Quoyleith* and *Quoyeden*; 443863; Map Page X.

**Lythes** 1821; this, the original *Lythes,* is empty; *Nether Lythes* is now called *Lythes*; ON *hlíðar* slopes with Eng. plural; compare *Stews* for such a changed plural; 456897; Map Page VIII.

**Lythe Tail** Swona; coastal feature; see *Lythe* above for derivation; Eng. 'tail' is used in the sense of 'projecting part'; compare *Tarf Tail*; 391840; Map Page XII.

**Maggie Broon's** field-name near *Grindley*; the site of a vanished house; see an illustration of this house on p. 49; 449853; Map Page X.

**Manitoba** fields to the east of *Gaira*; such fields are normally called after a vanished house which lay at one time in the vicinity and which have been named after a returned emigrant; compare *Canada* etc; 458853; Map Page VIII.

**Manse** 1. Barswick; occupied; originally manse of Free Church of Scotland, now private house renamed *Glendoran*; 442856; Map Page X.

**Manse** 2. St. Margaret's Hope; serves *St. Margaret's Kirk*; occupied; 449934; Map Page IV.

**Manse** 3. served *St. Peter's Kirk, Paplay*; occupied; 474915; Map Page XI.

**Manse** 4. served *St. Mary's Kirk*; now renamed *Tanglin*.

**Manse** 5. Burray village; also known as *South Manse*; see also *Stoodley Pike*; 472955; Map Page VI.

**Manse** 6. Burray; formerly *North Manse*; now *Summerton*; 472962; Map Page II.

**Manse Bay** the brigantine *Emma* of Dundee with general cargo was wrecked here in 1850; 476917; Map Page XI.

**Manse Cott** also known as *Willie Kirkness's*; he was employed at the Manse; 475917; Map Page XI.

**Manse Road** the road to the Manse in *Paplay*; 473914; Map Page XI.

**Manse Taing** ON *tangi* point of land; 478915; Map Page XI.

**Mardale** Windwick; occupied; 458868; Map Page XIII.

**Marengo Road** St. Margaret's Hope; houses numbered 1-10 are all occupied; a name adopted in the 1970s/80s from *Marengo Square*.

**Marengo Square** St. Margaret's Hope; one of the oldest parts of the village; named after the American barkentine *Marengo* which, with a cargo of coal and glass, was wrecked in Widewall Bay in 1840; in the village, a small shop in the square used a deck house from the wreck of the *Marengo* as a store and the name was eventually passed on to Marengo Road; the barkentine *Marengo* was named after a place of that name in Austria where Napoleon defeated the Austrian army in 1800; 448936; Map Page IV.

**Mariner's Cottage** 1939; also known as *Mrs. Allan's*; empty; 433926; Map Page IV.

**Marshburn**, St. Margaret's Hope; occupied; Map Page IV.

**Masser Rock** coastal feature; origin unknown; 422903; Map Page IX.

**Masseter/Mossater** Windwick 1492, 1500, 1595, 1627, 1821; occupied; the earliest recording is Morsetter which suggests that the name is derived from *mór* moorland; the 's' which immediately follows the 'r' has eclipsed the 'r'; *saetr* seasonally used hut; 446865; Map Page X.

**Mathi's Glen** a small valley near *Upper Serrigar* supposedly haunted by an old man and woman; the tale would seem to have its origin in the 17th century when several instances of the first name 'Matthew' are recorded (there are no instances of this first name in the 1821 Census); at any rate the place-name points to an old couple who met a sad fate here; Sc. *glen* valley; 444877; Map Page VIII.

**Mayfield** Hoxa; occupied; fanciful name; there are Mayfield place-names in St. Ola, Stromness Parish and Westray; 432942; Map Page IV.

**Mayfield (The)** now field-name and site of a house by that name; also known as *Jamie Green's*; Jamie Green was captain of the *Dunbar*, a full-rigged ship, which foundered at the entrance to Sydney Harbour on 20th August 1857 with the loss of 63 passengers and all but one of the 59 crew; 446842; Map Page X.

**Maygreen** South Parish 1851; vanished; fanciful name.

**May Scottie's** a vanished house; May lived at *Haven* in Grimness in 1821 when she was aged 39 and she is remembered for her remarkable 'second sight' in later life; as an instance of this, in 1848 she heard a sound which she said predicted that a vessel had struck the cliffs on *Stews Head*—even though her house was ¾ mile from the coastline; her prediction proved to be correct; the vessel was the *Penang*; 'Scottie/Scotty' is a Burray and South Ronaldsay surname first recorded in 1566; it has now died out; Robert Kincaid from South Ronaldsay married Barbara Scotty from Burray in 1664; 456893; Map Page XI.

**Meall** Quindry, Ronsvoe and Hoxa district 1851; vanished; site unknown; this was also the original name of Graemeshall in Holm and Newark in Deerness; ON *melr* sand, see *Moill*.

**Megs Highlug** coastal feature; Sc. *lug* used in the sense 'projecting', describing a

128

*The Place-Names of South Ronaldsay and Burray*

cliff in this instance; the use of the woman's name 'Meg' is not understood; 488932; Map Page VII.

**Melhaven** Windwick; occupied; 459866; Map Page XIII.

**Merchants Geo** records the wreck of a merchant's vessel; 468888; Map Page XI.

**Merle Haven** Herston village; named after the first resident which was a blackbird! (French *merle*, blackbird); 421917; Map Page V.

**Merrybank/Merrybraes** Grimness 1821, 1881; vanished; fanciful name.

**Midbanks** coastal feature; 423903; Map Page IX.

**Midbister** derelict; the middle farm, from ON *bólstaðir* farm; it lies between *Isbister* and *Wasbister*; 447901; Map Page VIII.

**Middle Hill** field-name, *Roeberry Farm*; 432932; Map Page IV.

**Middle Field 1.** field-name, *Cletts*; 462908; Map Page XI.

**Middle Field 2.** field-name, *Roeberry Farm*; 428934; Map Page V.

**Middle Park** Quindry, Ronsvoe and Hoxa district 1851; vanished.

**Middle Windi/Wini Skerry** Swona; one of three reefs here; see *West Windi/Wini Skerry*; 385836; Map Page XIII.

**Mid Flaws** see *Flaws*.

**Midhouse 1.** St. Margaret's Hope; occupied; Map Page V.

**Midhouse 2.** Burray, occupied; now renamed *Saorsa*; 465965; Map Page II.

**Midhouse 3.** Eastside; 456907; Map Page VIII.

**Midtown 1.** Herston; occupied; 1821; 417914; Map Page V.

**Midtown 2.** Hoxa; occupied; 417940; Map Page V.

**Military Hospital** vanished; it was built behind St. Margaret's Cottage during World War II for the R.A.M.C. (Royal Army Medical Corps) and served also as a Dental Clinic; 449934; Map Page IV.

**Mill (The)** Burray; see *Corn Mill 1*.

**Mill 1.** Sandwick; 438896; Map Page VIII.

**Mill 2.** 1821; near Stews; vanished.

**Milldam 1.** Eastside 1891; vanished.

**Milldam 2.** Burray, 1750; see *Tumol o Milldam*.

**Mill Dam 1.** 457878; Map Page XIII.

**Mill Dam 2.** 468943; Map Page VI.

**Mill Dam 3.** 471941; Map Page VI.

**Mill Dam 4.** 472931; Map Page VI.

**Mill Dam 5.** 469934; Map Page VI.

**Mill Dam 6.** 467892; Map Page XI.

**Mill Dam 7.** 448889; Map Page VIII.

**Millennium Stone** see *Standing Stone 4*.

**Millfield 1.** Brough; field-name; 445843; Map Page X.

**Millfield 2.** Burray; occupied; 465963; Map Page II.

**Millhouse 1.** Burray; 470967; Map Page II.

**Millhouse 2.** Eastside 1841; derelict; 472908; Map Page XI.

**Millhouse 3.** Widewall 1851; vanished.

**Millhouse 4.** Windwick; occupied; 459866; Map Page XIII.

**Mill o Clappag** a click mill, the best example of which is preserved near Dounby in the West Mainland; the name 'clappag' suggests a local word for the 'clapper', a feature of such a mill; it took the form of a wooden tongue which struck a knob of wood on the upper mill stone, making a clicking sound; the stream on which this mill stood has been diverted; 445843; Map Page X.

**Mill Pond** 453912; Map Page IV.

**Millquoy** Burray; 472967; Map Page II.

**Millstone Geo** ON *gjá* ravine; millstones were quarried here just as they were at Yesnaby in Sandwick, West Mainland; 410914; Map Page V.

**Mire** St. Margaret's Hope, 1821; vanished; ON *mýrr* moor; 431909; Map Page VIII.

**Mires/Myres** Grimness; empty; ON *mýrar* swamps, with English plural; there is a Mires in Sanday and a Myres in Birsay; 485930; Map Page VII.

**Mission Hall** a church hall; now *Herston Hall*; 421907; Map Page IX.

**Miugar/Moygare** see *Mugar.*

**Moi Geo** 1. related to Sh. dial *mui* a sandy/stony stretch (of shore), a word related to ON *mór* (stony) moor; compare *Mugar* below and Moi Fea, a hill in Walls in Orkney; ON *gjá*, ravine; 403935; Map Page V.

**Moi Geo** 2. see above; 414919; Map Page V.

**Moi Geo** 3. see above; 429854; Map Page X.

**Moill** 1736; vanished; see *Meall.*

**Mon** St. Margaret's Hope; vanished; usually spelt Moan in Orkney; there are Moan place-names in Harray, Firth and Graemsay; ON *mó(r)-inn*, the moorland.

**Morris Geo** origin of first element uncertain; ON *gjá* ravine; 446828; Map Page X.

**Morsetter** see *Masseter.*

**Moss Battery** Burray, there are still some traces of this camp where 4 heavy ack-ack guns and gun-laying radar were sited during World War II; 457968; Map Page I.

**Moss** field-name, *Roeberry Farm*; ON *mosi* moorland; 427935; Map Page V.

**Moss o Cletts** Eastside; see below.

**Moss o Dale** see *Dale Moss.*

**Mossater** see *Masseter.*

**Mossbank** Burray; occupied; 459968; Map Page II.

**Moss Edge/Moss House/Moss o Cletts** Eastside; occupied; 458913; Map Page XI.

**Mosshouse** Burray; 448959; Map Page I.

**Moss House** 1. St. Margaret's Hope 1861; vanished; ON *mosi* moorland.

**Moss House** 2. vanished but location is known; 450898; Map Page VIII.

**Mound** described in the 19th century O.S. map as a 'Fort'; 473913; Map Page XI.

**Mount Hooly** St. Margaret's Hope 1861; vanished; fanciful name; there are several Mounthoolie (sic) place-names in Orkney; Mounthoolie Lane in Kirkwall is named after a house which stood near the Albert Street end of this lane; the Kirkwall Mounthoolie existed as early as the 1600s; 453924; Map Page IV.

**Mount Pleasant** 1. 1861; occupied; fanciful name; there are Mount Pleasant place-names in Birsay, Stromness, Sandwick, Westray and Stronsay; Mount Pleasant in Harray is a transferred name from the Mount Pleasant Goldfields in Australia; see *Pleasant*; 458926; Map Page VI.

**Mount Pleasant** 2. see above for explanation of name; 478928; Map Page VI.

**Mouster Head** a headland; recalls the name of a lost enclosure with same derivation as *Masseter*; it is said that the last sea eagle to nest in South Ronaldsay nested on the cliffs here; men from *Stews* climbed down the cliff and destroyed its eggs and the bird did not return; 466881; Map Page XI.

**Moyer** Burray, 1821; vanished.

**Mrs. Allan's** field-name, *Roeberry Farm*; named after the former occupant of a house known now as *Mariner's Cott* in this field; this field is also known as *Near Ouse Field*; Allans have been recorded in South Ronaldsay since the 17<sup>th</sup> century; 435927; Map Page IV.

**Mrs. Miller's** see *West Flaws*; the Miller/Millar surname has been recorded in South Ronaldsay since the 17<sup>th</sup> century; it is very likely that the surname is local, adopted by one (or more) of the millers of the original five water mills in South Ronaldsay—at Cara, Widewall, Sandwick, Windwick and Brough.

**Muckle Geo** Burray; 497966; Map Page III.

**Mucklehouse** 1. Sandwick; empty; there were several Mucklehouse place-names in Orkney; Sc. *muckle* large, which may be a reference in this case to the 'palace' which at one time stood here; see *Rood Chapel* and *Weems Castle* for interesting related references; 435890; Map Page VIII.

**Muckle House** 2. Eastside; occupied; Sc. *muckle* large; 455897; Map Page VIII.

**Mucklejocks** Herston; empty; a small dwelling based on a former store; the name was given by the last inhabitant; 419920; Map Page V.

**Muckle Mire** a house; occupied; see *Mire* for derivation; 433910; Map Page IV.

**Muckle Skerry** 1. the largest of the *Pentland Skerries* approximately 70 acres in size; ON *mikill* great; *sker* reef; 465785; Map Page XIV.

**Muckle Skerry** 2. Widewall; see above for derivation; 432918; Map Page IV.

**Muckquoy** Eastside 1841; occupied; just as *Suckquoy* was sometimes called *Surquoy*, Muckquoy was sometimes referred to as *Murquoy,* the 'r' being lost before the 'qu/k' sound; there is little doubt that the original form is Murquoy as the surname Murquoy suggests; Magnus Murquoy lived in South Ronaldsay in 1663; 457899; ON *mór* moor; ON *kví* enclosure; Map Page VIII.

**Mugar** also spelt Miugar/Moygare; Sandwick; 1821, 1851, 1861; occupied; ON *mór* moor, ON *garðr* farm; 436896; Map Page VIII.

**Murder** field-name; a field difficult to work; compare *Limbo* etc; 445862; Map Page X.

**Murka Hole** a small gloup; ON *myrkr* dark; 416904; Map Page IX.

**Murquoy** see *Muckquoy.*

**Murray Arms Hotel** St. Margaret's Hope; occupied; formerly William Sinclair's draper shop; it became an hotel operated by a Murray family in 1934; Map Page IV.

**Murraybreak/Murybrake/Murrayfield** Grimness 1939; occupied; most likely the surname *Murray* which has been recorded in South Ronaldsay since the 17<sup>th</sup> century; for 'brake' element see *Barebreck*; see also *Berriedale*; the present Murrayfield was recently built; 425939; Map Page VI.

**Musland Quoy** Quindry, Ronsvoe and Hoxa district 1851; vanished; there is a Musland in Westray and a Mousland (sic) in Stromness Parish; ON *mosa-land* moorland.

**Myre/Mire** Widewall 1736, 1861; occupied; see *Mire*; there is a Mire in Orphir; 434909; Map Page VIII.

**Myre House** St. Margaret's Hope; occupied; Map Page IV.

**Myrtledene** Burray village; occupied; Map Page VI.

**Myrtle Villa** Hoxa; occupied; 417937; Map Page V.

**Naeroy** St. Margaret's Hope; occupied; the adjacent house is named *Vikna* after an island in Norway; when Naeroy was built it was given the name of an island close to *Vikna*!; Map Page IV.

**Nap (The)** Burray; empty; name suggests Sc. *knap* used in the Orkney sense of 'hillock' as in Knap o Howar, the Neolithic settlement in Papa Westray; 466958; Map Page VI.

**Navigation Beacon** Swona; 393854; Map Page XII.

**Near Hill** field-name, *Roeberry Farm*; 431930; Map Page IV.

**Nearhouse** Burray; 465970; Map Page II.

**Near Ouse** another name for *Mrs. Allan's*, a field-name on *Roeberry Farm*; the 'Ouse' in question is the *Oyce o Quindry*; 434927; Map Page IV.

**Needle Point** 446946; Map Page IV.

**Ness** 1. Burray; 1821; occupied; lies on a prominent point which forms the most easterly part of the island; ON *nes* a point of land; 496961; Map Page III.

**Ness** 2. Swona; 390853; Map Page XII.

**Ness Road** Burray, the road to *Ness* above; a large military camp, incorporating a cinema straddled both sides of this road during World War II; 494960; Map Page III.

**Nether Braehead** occupied; see *Braehead*; 453904; Map Page VIII.

**Netherfaulds** Burray; Sc. *fauld* a small, enclosed piece of land, usually for penning animals; 478964; Map Page II.

**Nether Gaira** Sandwick; occupied; see *Gaira*; 446891; Map Page VIII.

**Nether Lythes** Eastside; occupied; now known as *Lythes*; the original *Lythes* is empty; 455898; Map Page VIII.

**Nether Ollits** see *Lower Ollad*.

**Nether Schusan** Widewall; occupied; see *Schusan*; 442907; Map Page VIII.

**Nev (The)** coastal feature; ON *nef* nose in the sense of a protruding part; 428893; Map Page IX.

**Nev Hill** see above for derivation; 428895; Map Page IX.

**Neviholm** the *Hoxa Tapestry Gallery*; 414937; Map Page V.

**Nevi Skerry** a reef which lies between *Croo Taing*, Hoxa, South Ronaldsay and Roan Head on Flotta; the schooner *Magnet* of Stromness was wrecked here in 1847; 398958; Map Page V.

**Newark** vanished—or almost; the bulk of the foundation is sand covered but parts of the walls may yet be seen; built some time before the middle of the 17th century, apparently by Pitcairn, a merchant family, it was described then as a 'mansion house'; it must have been an imposing residence since it gave its name to the whole bay and the stream which flowed into it; by the middle of the 18th century a shop was attached to the premises and Craven reports that a break-in to this shop led to a terrible miscarriage of justice; the thieves planted some of the stolen goods at a nearby farm owned by an elderly man, Hucheon Voy, and the ransellman, believing Voy to be the culprit, both he and his wife were strapped to harrows with the threat that their tongues would be cut out if they did not confess to stealing everything; fortunately in the nick of time the remainder of the stolen goods were found at the home of the Bruces in Aikers who, it is said, fled across the Pentland Firth, never to return but another version of the story says that they were caught and killed on the *Hill o Sneb*; the mansion house was apparently occupied (though not owned) latterly by Matthew Mowbray, a wealthy man and Chamberlain of Orkney, who is buried in *St. Peter's* Kirkyard; his daughter is said to have lived and died at Newark and since she married Rev. Walter Stewart, the local minister, it seems that this building became the manse for a short time; its ultimate fate is not known; by 1821 there was little trace of it; there are four Newark farms in Orkney; Sc. *new wark* new work.

**Newark Bay** see above; 465898; Map Page XI.

**Newark Burn** see above; 463895; Map Page XI.

**Newbanks** Burray; occupied; 464955; Map Page VI.

**New Bigging** 1. Burray 1750; holiday home; 453962; Map Page II.

**Newbigging** 2. Holland, 1821; occupied; see also *Dettinton*; 455850; Map Page XIII.

**Newbigging** 3. Widewall, 1821; occupied; Sc. *bigging* building; there are six other Newbigging place-names in Orkney; see *Betty Omand's* for an interesting reference to Newbigging; 429909; Map Page V.

**Newcastle** South Parish 1881; vanished; transferred place-name from Newcastle, England.

**Newcommon** Widewall; 422903; Map Page IX.

**Newhall** South Parish; occupied; there are Newhall place-names in Stromness Parish and Deerness; 463848; Map Page XIII.

**Newhouse** 1. Sandwick; 1821, 1861; vanished; there are at least nine other Newhouse place-names in Orkney in addition to those listed below; 449904; Map Page VIII.

**Newhouse** 2. Swona; 1821; empty; an alternative name for one of the *North Houses*; Map Page XII.

**Newhouse** 3. *Sandy Hill*; occupied; 443871; Map Page VIII.

**Newhouse** 4. 438896; Map Page VIII.

**Newhouse** 5. (*Norton*) Burray; occupied; 479978; Map Page III.

**Newhouse of Kirkiehill** Sandwick; occupied; 433898; Map Page VIII.

**New Quoys** 1861; vanished; ON *kvíar* enclosures, with English plural; 449886; Map Page VIII.

**New London** see *London*; vanished; 481945; Map Page VI.

**New Scews** Grimness 1871; vanished; see *Scews*.

**Newton** Eastside 1841; empty; 456894; Map Page VIII.

**New Zealand** Widewall 1851; vanished; transferred place-name; compare *Canada*.

**Nickle Head** Far. *hnikil* a knoll; there is a Nichol Point on Boardhouse Loch in Birsay; compare *Tafnichill/Taftnickie;* 435881; Map Page VIII.

**Niggle Point** Herston; see above for derivation; 414922; Map Page V.

**Niggles** Quindry and Ronsvoe district 1901; vanished; see above for derivation.

**Nile (The)** see *Egypt.*

**Nona** see *Whitelums.*

**Norhead** see *North House 1.*

**Nortaing** Swona; coastal feature; dialect 'nort' = 'north'; ON *tangi* point; 393854; Map Page XII.

**North Barth Clivvy** ON *klufðr* cleft; 427857; Map Page X.

**North Barswick Geo** 428858; Map Page X.

**North Bigging** Swona 1841; apparently an alternative name for one of the *North Houses*; see *Bigging*; for derivation.

**North Cara** Grimness; occupied; see *Cara*; 474946; Map Page VI.

**North Clett** Swona; coastal feature; ON *klettr* rock; 392854; Map Page XII.

**North Crook** Herston, 1821; vanished.

**North Dam** near *Oback*, Widewall; vanished; 1821.

**Northfield** Burray; a farm; occupied; because of the strategic position of this area, a coastal battery was established here during the early years of World War II; 487986; Map Page III.

**Northfield Cottage** Burray; occupied; 479980; Map Page II.

**North Flaws** occupied; see *Flaws* for definition; 458856; Map Page XIII.

**North Geo** 435843; Map Page X.

**North Head** Swona; the name given to that area of the island to the north of the *North Houses*; 394853; Map Page XII.

*Norhead, Swona; in the foreground two ruinous North Houses.*

**North House** 1. Swona, later *Norhead*; 1821, 1841; empty; 392849; Map Page XII.
**North House** 2. Swona; a ruin; 391849; Map Page XII.
**North House** 3. Swona; a ruin; 391849; Map Page XII.
**North House** 4. Swona; a ruin; 391849; Map Page XII.
**North Liddel** see *Liddel*.
**North Links** Burray; a district; 486978; Map Page III.
**North Lobers** coastal feature; see *Lobers* for derivation; 425894; Map Page IX.
**North Mires** field-name, *Cletts*; probably the site of a vanished house; 463908; Map Page XI.
**North Parish** one of two divisions of South Ronaldsay, originally called *St. Peter's;* the southern boundary of the parish lies on a line drawn approximately from *Mucklehouse* in *Sandwick* to a point in the middle of *Newark Bay*.
**North Parish School** St. Margaret's Hope, pre 1821; Map Page IV.
**North Taing** ON *tangi* point; 471842; Map Page XIII.
**Northtown** in common with many parts of Orkney, Burray was at one time divided into three areas; the three original divisions were *Northtown, Southtown* and *The Bu*; 475975; Map Page II.
**Northtown Moss** Burray; mentioned only in several archaeological reports detailing the discovery in 1899 of a hoard of Viking silver which included torcs and 10th/11th century Anglo-Saxon coinage; it suggests that in this case 'Northtown' was an enclosure to the north of *Mosshouse* and is an alternative name for what is now *Ourequoy*; ON *mosi* moor; 455965; Map Page I.
**Norton** Burray; occupied; there is also a Norton near Dounby; see also *Newhouse*; 478977; Map Page II.
**Noust** St. Margaret's Hope; formerly stores for merchants J. Spence and Son, now refurbished as three dwellings; 1. occupied. 2. occupied. 3. occupied; Map Page IV.

**Oback** 1. Widewall; 1821, 1841, 1861; empty; ON *ár-bakki* stream bank; there are also Oback place-names in Orphir, Deerness and Harray; 437910; Map Page IV.
**Oback** 2. vanished house Windwick, now only a field-name north of *Masseter*; see above for derivation; 449867; Map Page X.
**Oback Burn** 1. named after the house of *Oback* in Widewall; 449867; Map Page X.
**Oback Burn** 2. named after the vanished house of *Oback* in Windwick: 436915; Map Page IV.
**Observation Tower** in private ownership; this building, built by Brigadier Malcolm Dennison, offers a panoramic view from its position on *Wart Hill*, Hoxa; 434936; Map Page IV.
**Odinsay** a house; the name is a composite of 'Odin(stone)' Shapinsay and '(Ing)say', Birsay; 462942; Map Page VI.
**Olad** 1. Widewall; occupied; other forms of this name are *Quoyolla, Oula* and *Alla*; ON *á* stream; *hlað* something built up or a natural elevation of stone; Nor. *lad* a layer of stone; in this case the name refers to stepping stones originally

crossing the *Oback Burn 1*; compare Cubby Roo's Lade in Stronsay, the equivalent of the Giant's Causeway of Northern Ireland; a house built in the middle of the village of Finstown in the 1920s is called Olath and occupied by Cursiters, the house name perhaps being transferred from South Ronaldsay where Cursiters have been recorded since the early 19th century; there is also an Olad field-name in Harray; 423907; Map Page IX.

**Olad** 2. Sandwick; occupied; 447884; Map Page VIII.

**Olad Brae** there is a viewpoint at the top of this hill; see *Olad* Widewall above; 446879; Map Page VIII.

**Olad Burn** 1. named after the house of *Olad*; see *Olad* Widewall for derivation; 446879; Map Page VIII.

**Olad Burn** 2. a house; occupied; believed originally to have been a mill; 425905; Map Page IX.

**Old Bakehouse (The)** St. Margaret's Hope; occupied; it was formerly the *Temperance Hall* where the Good Templars met; plans to develop it as a bakehouse did not come to fruition but the name was subsequently applied to the house nevertheless; Map Page IV.

**Old Bank House** St. Margaret's Hope; occupied; Map Page IV.

**Old Ferry** see *Cara Ferry*.

**Old Golf Course** see *Hillside Camp*; 436930; Map Page IV.

**Old Grutha** see *Grutha*.

**Old Head** see *Old Skerries* below for interpretation of 'old'; the steamer *Duna* of Liverpool with a cargo of wood pulp was wrecked here in 1912; 471834; Map Page XII.

**Old House (The)** Rinibar, St. Margaret's Hope; occupied; Map Page IV.

**Old Scews** Grimness 1871; vanished; see *Scews*.

**Old School** St. Margaret's Hope; used presently as a store; Map Page IV.

**Old Schoolhouse** occupied; see *Brandyquoy*; 457928; Map Page IV.

**Old Shaft** as the name suggests, an old mine-shaft on the coast; lead was mined here but extraction did not prove economic; it is believed locally that the shaft was worked by Norwegians; 477922; Map Page VI.

**Old Skerries** 1. ON *alda* wave, probably with the sense 'breaking wave' as in ON *bára* wave, which gives Ork. dial, 'bore' in the Bore o Papay; ON *sker* reef; 473837; Map Page XII.

**Old Skerries** 2. see above; 473855; Map Page XIII.

**Onich** St. Margaret's Hope; derelict; origin unknown; Map Page IV.

**Ontoft** Hoxa; vanished; ON personal name *Örn; topt* ancient house site.

**Ontoft Road** the road which leads to the northern part of *Hoxa*; 443937; Map Page IV.

**Oralie/Orally** 1664, 1736, 1821; vanished but position is assumed from location of *Quoyorally*; ON *ár-hlíð* slope of the streams (draining *Blows Moss*); see also *Quoyorally*.

**Ore Lee** coastal feature; ON *eyar*; islands, (reefs in this case); ON *hlíð* slope but also used in the East Mainland in the sense 'cliff'; 493925; Map Page VII.

**Orkadee** occupied; formerly *Brain*; this new name telescopes 'Orkney' and 'Dundee' the place of origin of the present owners; there are houses by the name

Orcadee in Finstown and Orcadee in Westray where the name is a romanticised form of 'Orcades' the Latin name of Orkney.

**Orkney House** Herston; occupied; 421918; Map Page V.

**Orkney Seal Rescue Centre** see *Dyke End 1.*

**Ossi Taing** ON *áss* a rocky ridge; compare Little Osi, a skerry in Northmavine, Shetland; ON *tangi* point of land; 464866; Map Page XIII.

**Ossquoy** earlier *Ossaquoy*; Barthwick 1492, 1500, 1595, 1821, 1841; occupied; first element suggests ON female personal name *Ásleif* which still existed in the 19th century in the form Ossylla or more commonly Osla; ON *kví* enclosure; 447857; Map Page X.

**Otterhole** Quindry and Ronsvoe district 1891; vanished; compare the house of *Ottersgill* in Ireland in Stenness.

**Ourigair** St. Margaret's Hope, 1821; occupied; ON *aurr* clay; *garðr* farm; Map Page IV.

**Ourigar** Burray; 1750, 1821; occupied; see above for derivation; see also *Tumol o Ourigar*; 468956; Map Page VI.

**Ourequoy** Burray; ON *aurr* clay, ON *kví* enclosure; 452963; Map Page I.

**Our Lady's Chapel** Halcro; vanished; 461855; Map Page XIII.

**Oula/Alla** 1736; listed as being in South Widewall; perhaps same as *Olad.*

**Ourie Head** perhaps ON *aurr* clay but more likely ON *eyar* islands, referring to offshore reefs; compare *Ours o Stews* below; 433866; Map Page X.

**Ours o Stews** coastal feature, also known as *Rough o Kame*; small reefs off the coast; ON *eyjar* islands; compare Ire, a group of islands/reefs off Burness in Sanday; 474888; Map Page XI.

**Out Hillock** coastal feature; 494926; Map Page VII.

**Outer Ganges** Swona; see *Inner Ganges* for explanation of name; 386844; Map Page XII.

**Outer Scaws** see *Inner Scaws* for derivation; 475906; Map Page XI.

**Outlook** South Parish 1841, 1851; vanished; so named from its high position; 462838; Map Page XII.

**Outra Loch** Swona; also known as *Loch o the Tarf*; ON *ytri* outer; 384838; Map Page XII.

**Out Skerries** ON *sker* reef; 470837; Map Page XII.

**Out Skerry** the outer reef; ON *sker* reef; 426892; Map Page IX.

**Outskerry** Swona; nearby lies the *Innskerry*; see above; 392851; Map Page XII.

**Ovarburn** Grimness 1851; vanished; 'ovar' = 'upper'; see *Burn.*

**Overfaulds** Burray; also known as *Eastlynn*; 'over' = 'upper'; Sc. *fauld*, animal pen.

**Over Quoyolla** 1736; 'ovar' = 'upper'; see *Olla/Quoyolla.*

**Overvome** see *Vamh.*

**Oyce o Herston** ON *óss* mouth of a stream but in Orkney usually refers to a small lake dammed by a sand or shingle spit at the mouth of a stream as in the Oyce of Firth; see *Herston*; 423910; Map Page V.

**Oyce o Quindry** see *Oyce o Herston* above for derivation; see also *Quindry*; 435925; Map Page IV.

**Pairish (The)** a name used familiarly by those in the North Parish to refer to the South Parish! 'I think Ah'll go doon tae the pairish.'

**Papley/Paplay** a district; ON *Papýli* = *Papa-býli*; ON *papi* priest; *býli* place of residence; compare Papdale in Kirkwall and Papa Westray; *St. Peter's Kirk* was established in Papley and gave the name 'St. Peter's' to the whole of what is now North Parish; 468912; Map Page XI.

**Park** 1. field-name; 448866; Map Page X.

**Park** 2. field-name, *Roeberry Farm*; 431938; Map Page IV.

**Park Head** 433869; Map Page X.

**Park House** Grimness 1861; occupied; 469944; Map Page VI.

**Parklea** St. Margaret's Hope; occupied; Map Page IV.

**Park o Cara** 1821; Sc. *park*; in place-names, usually a large field enclosed by a wall which gave farm names such as Park of Heddle in Firth or Park in Rendall; this South Ronaldsay farm was owned by Sir James Stewart, Laird of Burray; in the inventory of his estate made in 1747, it was stated that there were in this park twenty oxen, four bulls, two cows, ten calves, three stallions and two mares; it was from this 'park' that much of *Berriedale* farm evolved, a very early example of agricultural improvement in Orkney.

**Park o Sootan** Swona; an isolated square-shaped area enclosed by drains; see *Sootan*; 390840; Map Page XII.

**Parliament Square** where the 'parliament' of cormorants met; compare *Tennis Court* and *Scartan Point*; 470782; Map Page XIV.

**Pealisquoy/Peeblesquoy** South Parish 1871, 1939; vanished but location is known; there was a Peebles family living in *North House* on *Swona* in 1821; the family name Peebles was established in Orkney at an early date since a Peiblis Cot is recorded in Birsay in 1595; the name originated in this case most likely from the lands of Peblis in Angus; the current family name Peebles has been recently introduced; 463847; Map Page XIII.

**Peat Geo** suggests an inlet from where peats were brought in by boat (probably from *Glims Holm*) since South Ronaldsay, unlike most of the other islands, was comparatively short of fuel; compare Peat Bay on Fara from where peat was exported; 495930; Map Page VII.

**Peedie Clett** 1. coastal feature; dialect 'peedie', small; ON *klettr* rock; 393855; Map Page XII.

**Peedie Clett** 2. Swona; coastal feature; see above; 388838; Map Page XII.

**Peedie Cott** St. Margaret's Hope; occupied; Ork. dial. *peedie*, small; Map Page IV.

**Peedie Hetap** Swona; a cliff; dialect 'peedie', small; see *Hetap*; 393851; Map Page XII.

**Peedie Hylack** Swona; see *Hylack* which lies nearby; 386837; Map Page XII.

**Peedie Kirk Geo** Swona; nearby lies *Kirk Geo 2*; 381836; Map Page XII.

**Pelt** field-name; Sc. *pelt* worthless, a reference to the quality of the field at one time; 452863; Map Page XIII.

**Penang** Northfield Burray; occupied; name transferred from Penang in Malaysia by a soldier who served there in World War II; compare Arnhem in Stenness; 481980; Map Page II.

**Penang Geo** marks location of wreck of a vessel by this name; 466884; Map Page XI.

**Penthouse** St. Margaret's Hope; occupied; Map Page IV.

**Pentland Firth** the stretch of strong tidal water between South Ronaldsay and Caithness; first recorded in the *Orkneyinga Saga* as *Péttlands Fjörðr* where *Péttland* was the old name of the north of Scotland, literally 'Pict land'; the name later became corrupted to 'Pentland'; it is commonly referred to today as 'The Pentland' or 'The Firth'.

**Pentland Skerries** first recorded in a Norn document of 1329 in the form *Petlandz skaer*; ON *Péttland* land of the Picts; *sker* reef; the largest, *Muckle Skerry*, which extends to approximately 70 acres in size was at one time inhabited; eight people were recorded living there in 1821; see below; Map Page XIV.

**Pentland Skerries Lighthouse** in 1794 two towers were erected here and modified in the 1820s, the lower tower later substituted by a foghorn; four families originally stayed on *Muckle Skerry* which was farmed by the lightkeepers; there was also a fine walled garden here; the light went automatic in 1994; 465785; Map Page XIV.

**Pentland View** empty; 434898; Map Page IX.

**Peterhead** Burray, 1821; transferred place-name; now known as *Echna View*.

**Peterkirk** the local name for *St. Peter's Kirk.*

**Peter Wylie's** Burray; empty; the only house on *Hunda*; apparently this house never had a name; 441968; Map Page I.

**Petrie House** see *West Flaws.*

**Petrie's Shed** only the foundations of this boat-building house remain on the frontage in St. Margaret's Hope; Map Page IV.

**Pickling Skerries** Swona; extensive rock shelf on west of the island; here fish would have been placed in barrels and 'pickled' with salt; this activity was commonly carried out on the shore; 385845; Map Page XII.

**Pier** 1. see *St. Margaret's Hope Pier.*

**Pier** 2. see *Smiddybanks.*

**Pier** 3. Hunda, Burray; 442967; Map Page I.

**Pier** 4. Burwick; 442839; Map Page X.

**Pier Road** St. Margaret's Hope; Map Page IV.

**Pinkie's Corner** named after 'Pink Pills', the nickname of John Sinclair, a resident of nearby *Suthergill*, who was prescribed pink pills for some ailment!; 447898; Map Page VIII.

**Place (The)** Burray; an old name applied to *The Bu*; Sc. 'place' = 'palace'; compare Earl's Palace in Birsay, also known locally as 'The Place'.

**Pleasant** Quindry, Ronsvoe and St. Margaret's Hope district 1881; (see *Mount Pleasant*)

**Ploverbrake** St. Margaret's Hope 1821, 1851; vanished; there were Ploverhall place-names in Wyre and Eday; pejorative name; Eng. 'plover'; compare *Tebrake*; see *Barebreck* for 'brake' element.

**Point (The)** a house; Burray village; occupied; Map Page VI.

**Point o Cara** see *Ayre o Cara.*

**Pole** Burray; called *Poolsherp* in 1627, 1821; occupied; ON *pollr* small loch or pool; normally written Pool or Pow in Orkney place-names; compare *Pool* below, Pool in Deerness, Pow in Sandwick (West Mainland) and Harray; for *sherp* element see *Quoysharps*; 487959; Map Page VII.

**Police Station (Old)** St. Margaret's Hope; now redeveloped into a small Council scheme known as *Sweyn Court*; Map Page IV.

**Police Station** formerly *Cot of Ronaldsvoe*; built as a teacher's house and occupied part-time today by a police officer based in Kirkwall; Map Page IV.

**Pond Field** field-name, *Roeberry Farm*; 427937; Map Page IV.

**Pool (The)** Swona; coastal feature; 380838; Map Page XII.

**Pool/Puile** Grimness 1595, 1750, 1821, 1861; occupied; there are Pool place-names in Deerness and Sanday; see *Pole* above; 475937; Map Page VI.

**Pool o Cletts** a sandy bay; it was here in 1937 that a lifeboat carrying thirteen passengers from the steamer *Johanna Thorden* was washed up; sadly five, including the captain were lost in the surf as the boat beached (see *Tarf Tail*); ON *pollr* pool, was used elsewhere in Orkney and Shetland in the sense 'small bay', e.g. Pool in Sanday; *Cletts* refers to the nearby farm; 468907; Map Page XI.

**Poolsherp** see *Pole*.

**Post Office** Burray; see *Westerlea*.

**Post Office** St. Margaret's Hope; in addition to normal Post Office business, it sells stationery and small gifts; Map Page IV.

**Post Road** 1. In former times mail from Burray was landed at *Cara* and brought by the postman along this old coastal road to *St. Margaret's Hope*; 452937; Map Page IV.

**Post Road** 2. Beginning in 1892, the S.S. *St. Ola* operated a mail and passenger carrying service on a triangular route between Stromness, Scapa and South Ronaldsay; the vessel hove to off *Hoxa Head* where mail and passengers were transferred to a small sailing vessel operated by Andrew Lennie and taken to a jetty at *Howe*; mail was then carried along this road to St. Margaret's Hope; 427938; Map Page V.

**Pow Park** field-name on *Cletts*; Sc. *pow* pool; 459911; Map Page XI.

**Priest's Loch** the significance of the name is not known; 450855; Map Page XIII.

**Purgator/Purgatory** on Vensilly Hill; 1821, 1851; vanished; Eng. 'purgatory', applied metaphorically to land which was originally difficult to work; there was a Purgatory in Birsay and a Purgator in Sanday; compare *Limbo*; 453918; Map Page IV.

**Purvis** field-name; a difficult name to interpret; there is a Scottish surname 'Purvis' but it has not been recorded in South Ronaldsay; it may be that the word has the original meaning of 'purvis', the courtyard in front of a cathedral, hence a holy place and applied in the first instance perhaps to give some dignity to a modest house which once existed here; compare *Mount Hooly*; 447843; Map Page X.

**Pyramid** Quindry, Ronsvoe and Hoxa district; 1851; vanished; origin uncertain; probably a nickname.

**Quarrel Geo** 'quarrel' is an old dialect word for 'quarry'; thin flagstones for roofing *St. Peter's Kirk* were extracted from here in the 17th century; there was a Quarrelhouse in Orphir; 464831; Map Page XII.

**Quarry** 1. disused; 452907; Map Page VIII.

**Quarry** 2. disused; 449878; Map Page VIII.

**Quarry** 3. Hoxa; 439942; Map Page IV.

**Quarry** 4. Burray, Hunda; disused; this quarry was used to construct part of the *Hunda Barrier* during World War II; the others below supplied material for the *Churchill Barriers*; 438966; Map Page I.

**Quarry** 5. Burray; *Northfield*; 962983; Map Page III.

**Quarry** 6. Burray; *Warebanks*; 473979; Map Page II.

**Quarry** 7. Burray; *Pole*; 488958; Map Page VII.

**Quarry** 8. Burray; *Links*; 483988; Map Page II.

**Quarry Field** field-name; 453862; Map Page XIII.

**Quarryhouse/Quarry (The)/Quarry/ies** Hoxa 1861; occupied; 415942; Map Page V.

**Quarries** Hoxa; disused; 435935; Map Page IV.

**Quindry/Quindrie** a district; ON *kví-in* the enclosure; *drit* filth, referring most likely to marsh in this instance; compare Drit Ness in Stronsay; 429924; Map Page IV.

**Quindrie House** occupied; 427926; Map Page IV.

**Quindrie Bank** Widewall 1861; vanished; see above.

**Quoy** Widewall 1851; vanished though location is known; ON *kví* enclosure; one of the most common Orkney place-names; 424904; Map Page IX.

**Quoyangry** 1. St. Margaret's Hope 1861; occupied; there are or were Quoy-angry/Quoyanger place-names in Stronsay, Westray, Orphir, Stromness Parish and even Kirkwall; ON *kví* enclosure; *vangr* field; the initial 'v' is lost; 445927; Map Page IV.

**Quoyangry** 2. Burwick 1595; vanished; see above for derivation.

**Quoyball** Barthwick; 1821; vanished but position is known; Ice. *kvía-ból* a place where cattle and sheep are penned; 455896: Map Page XI.

**Quoybanks** 1. Grimness; occupied; ON *kví* enclosure; *bakkar*, banks; 481947; Map Page VI.

**Quoybanks** 2./**Quoybank** 1595; occupied; see above; 425907; Map Page V.

**Quoybirse** Grimness 1746; vanished; ON *kví* enclosure; ON personal name *Bersi*.

**Quoybond/Quoyboon** Sandwick; occupied; ON *kví* enclosure; second element difficult to interpret; probably ON *búð-in* the hut, which usually gives the form Bewan; such buildings were used seasonally as in the case of Netherbooth high in the Stenness hills; the Stone o Quoybune is a large standing stone in Birsay; 442882; Map Page VIII.

**Quoybreck** Burray; ON *kví* enclosure; ON *brekka* slope; 467967; Map Page II.

**Quoybrown** vanished; ON *kví* enclosure; an alternative name Quoybrownaris suggests the first name Bernard rather than the surname Brown; there was a Quoybernardis in Holm in 1492.

**Quoybutton** Hoxa 1492, 1500, 1595, 1736; vanished; ON *kví* enclosure; see *Button*.

**Quoycous/Quoycouse/Quoycuise** Eastside 1595, 1736, 1841; vanished; ON *kví* enclosure; *kös* a heap of stones; compare *Coss*.

**Quoydam** Widewall 1861; occupied; ON *kví* enclosure, Eng. 'dam'; 431903; Map Page IX.

**Quoydoun** 1595, 1736; vanished; ON *kví* enclosure; 'doun' may mean 'lower' in this context; compare Doonatoon in Stronsay.

**Quoy Dyke** Swona; one of two walls which divide the island into three; ON *kví* enclosure; 386839; Map Page XII.

**Quoyeden** Eastside 1750, 1841; occupied; ON *kví* enclosure; *Eden* is a rare English female personal name, a diminutive of Old English *Eadu*; the name was used by the Leith family in South Ronaldsay in the mid 16th century; several South Ronaldsay place-names carry the name of a woman; compare for example *Cathysquoy, Gylliosquoy, Quoyinga* and *Kwikobba*; see also *Lythe* for a separate reference; 454902; Map Page VIII.

**Quoyenis** 1821, Herston; probably a form of *Quoyinga*.

**Quoygreen** Herston; occupied; ON *kví* enclosure; *graenn* green; 414918; Map Page V.

**Quoygrindla** Grimness 1746; vanished; ON *kví* enclosure; see *Grindalla*.

**Quoyhall** St. Margaret's Hope 1821; vanished; ON *kví* enclosure; see *Hall*.

**Quoyhorsetter** see *Quoyschorsetter*.

**Quoyinga** 1746, 1750; St. Margaret's Hope; vanished; probably same place as *Inyequoy* and *Quoyenis*; ON personal name *Inga*; *kví*, enclosure.

**Quoyleith** 1492, 1500, 1595; ON *kví* enclosure; see *Lythe*.

**Quoy Liray** 1736; vanished; ON *leira* a clay field; compare Leary in Birsay; *kví* enclosure.

**Quoyloo** 1. also recorded as **Quoylieu** and **Quoylue** Barthwick 1841, 1871; occupied; ON *kví* enclosure; *ló* marsh; there is also a Quoyloo in Sandwick, West Mainland; 439861; Map Page X.

**Quoyloo** 2. St. Margaret's Hope; undoubtedly named after the above.

**Quoyloo Cottage** occupied; 439861; Map Page X.

**Quoynethes/Quoynathues** Grimness, 1821; occupied; also referred to as *Leggit's*; ON *kví* enclosure; *nethes* etc. seems to be a contraction of *neðra-hús* lower house; 481946; Map Page VI.

**Quoy o Herston** see *Quoygreen*.

**Quoyoback** South Parish 1746; vanished; ON *kví* enclosure; see *Oback*.

**Quoyolet** ON *kví* enclosure; see *Olad,* Sandwick.

**Quoyolla** 1736, 1750; ON *kví* enclosure; see *Olad 1*; ON *kví* enclosure.

**Quoyorally** Windwick; 1750; holiday home; ON *kví* enclosure; see *Oralie*; 456863; Map Page XIII.

**Quoys** 1. Burray; 1492, 1500; derelict; 'Quoy/Quoys' is one of the most common place-names in Orkney; ON *kvíar* enclosures with English plural; the Norse plural is retained in such Orkney placenames as Quoyer and Queer; 455958; Map Page VI.

**Quoys** 2. Grimness; 1750, 1821; may be the same place as *Quoybanks 1*; see above for derivation.

**Quoys** 3. Holland 1492, 1500, 1562, 1595; occupied; see above for derivation; 452849; Map Page XIII.

**Quoys** 4. St. Margaret's Hope 1750, 1821; derelict; see above for derivation; 455932; Map Page IV.

**Quoys o Berriedale** occupied; 463926; Map Page VI.

**Quoys o Herston** see *Quoygreen*.

**Quoyschorsetter/Quoyhorsetter** Widewall; 1595, 1750; occupied; ON *kví* enclosure; Nynorsk *skur* hut; *saetr* seasonally used hut; see *Sossater*; 453922; Map Page IV.

**Quoysharps** 1497, 1500, 1595; vanished but possibly near *Cara*; ON *kví* enclosure; *skarpr* dry and barren (soil); see *Pole*, Burray.

**Quoysmiddie** see *Smiddy*

**Radar Station** 442873; Map Page VIII.

**Rami Geo** 1. ON *hramn* raven; there is a Ramna Geo in Birsay which was the haunt of ravens until they were recently driven out by fulmars; ON *gjá* ravine; 473851; Map Page XXIII.

**Rami Geo** 2. Muckle Skerry, Pentland Skerries; see above for derivation; 464780; Map Page XIV.

**Ramsquoy** South Parish 1584, 1627, 1881; vanished; there is also a Ramsquoy in Stenness; from the ON personal name *Hramn*; ON *kví* enclosure.

**Ravenscraig** St. Margaret's Hope; occupied; suggests a transferred name from Ravenscraig in Lanarkshire; Map Page IV.

**Red Bank** Quindry, Ronsvoe and Hoxa district 1851; vanished.

**Redbanks** Burray; 453959; Map Page I.

**Redd (The)** Swona; coastal feature; the nearby place-name *The Brook* which means a 'heap of rubbish' suggests that 'The Redd' here carries the same meaning, hence; ON *hroði* rubbish; 392849; Map Page XII.

**Redhouse (The)** the name is said to have been given because of the red roof tiles which were distinctive in an Orkney setting (compare 'Redroof' in Stromness); these tiles are alleged to have been part of the cargo of a vessel which stranded at Clestrain in Orphir; this house is now known as *Gillbreck*.

**Red Park** field-name; 448853; Map Page X.

**Reed Mine** land mentioned in *Fea's Rental*, 1750; location and meaning not known.

**Reef Point** Burray; 445965; Map Page I.

**Reefs o Turriegeo** ON *þari* seaweed; *gjá* ravine; 432848; Map Page X.

**Remuera** Burray; a house; occupied; 473965; Map Page II

**Rendalls** Quindry and Ronsvoe district 1901; vanished but position is known; name derives from the Orkney family name 'Rendall'; 433940; Map Page IV.

**Rennis** Quindry, Ronsvoe and Hoxa district 1861; vanished; from the surname 'Rainy' which was recorded in South Ronaldsay in the 17th and 18th centuries;

Theodore Rainy was the teacher in *South Parish School* (i.e. Tomison's first school) in 1821.

**Rensas** vanished; a house recorded in South Ronaldsay in the 17th century; origin unknown.

**Rental (The)** Swona; coastal feature but the name almost certainly relates to an inland feature; it suggests the location of an ancient shared field system known in Orkney and Shetland as 'rental' or 'rendal', the Scots equivalent of run-rig; the word seems to be Gaelic *rinndeal*, a piece of land; 391849; Map Page XII.

**Reservoir** 468923; Map Page VI.

**Richmond Villa** St. Margaret's Hope; occupied; fanciful name; Map Page IV.

**Retreat** Quindry and Ronsvoe district 1901; vanished; fanciful name; there is also a house named Retreat in Finstown.

**Rifle Range** 1. operated on the Links, Eastside during World War II; 462900; Map Page XI.

**Rifle Range** 2. this range lay above *Hillside Camp* and was in operation during World War II; 433930; Map Page IV.

**Rifonda Hole** Swona; the site of a shipwreck as in *La Plata Hole*; see *Tarf Tail*; 379836; Map Page XII.

**Rigbister** *Little Skerry*, Pentland Skerries; ON *hryggr* ridge; the *bister* element is usually interpreted as ON *bólstaðir* farm, but that would make no sense here; perhaps it was a temporary pen for sheep during the summer season; 470775; Map Page XIV.

**Rigini** Burray; holiday home; pronounced 'Ridginee'; formerly *Roslin*; so named by the current owner 'Rab' who, in the common Orkney naming pattern, may now call himself 'Rab o Rigini' (a pun on 'aborigine'!); 473955; Map Page VI.

**Rigs** field name; Sc. *rig* a longish shaped field; 463895; Map Page XI.

**Rigs o Lint** *Halcro Head*; position unknown; Map Page XIII.

**Rigg** vanished; it lay near *Masseter*; ON *hryggr* ridge.

**Riggin** coastal feature; ON *hryggr-inn* the ridge; 429853; Map Page X.

**Rinibar** Hoxa; occupied; takes its name from the coastal feature below; 410931; Map Page V.

**Riniber/Rinebir** Hoxa; ON *hraun* stony ground; *berg* rock; 412929; Map Page V.

**Riv** coastal feature; ON *rif* reef; 490933; Map Page VII.

**Riv House** vanished but position is known; 489932; Map Page VII.

**Rivin (The)** coastal feature; ON *rifan* the cleft; 413907; Map Page IX.

**Roadside Cottage** Quindry; occupied; there is a Roadside Cottage in Firth and in Sanday; 433925; Map Page IV.

**Roadside** occupied; 444906; Map Page VIII.

**Rob o the Hill's Reef** such a reef was usually named after a local man whose boat foundered on it; in this case a Robert Annal of *Hillhouse*, *Masseter* was stranded on it while rock fishing; 464864; Map Page XIII.

**Rock o Rinibar** coastal feature; an alternative name for *The Chair*; see *Rinibar* above and *The Chair*; 412929; Map Page V.

**Roeberry Bungalow** occupied; 427930; Map Page V.

**Roeberry Castle** see *Roeberry House*.

**Roeberry Cottage** occupied; 427931; Map Page V.

**Roeberry Farm** Hoxa 1750; ON *rauða-berg* red rock a reference to the iron-stained rocks on the coast; compare *Red Bank*; the farm was once owned by the Grays of Roeberry House; 426931; Map Page V.

**Roeberry House**, occupied; locally known as *Roeberry Castle*; it is separate from *Roeberry Farm (House)*; during World War II it was requisitioned as headquarters of 64 H.A.A. (Heavy Anti-Aircraft) Regiment and Headquarters of 279 Field Company R.E. (Royal Engineers); it was also a Military Detention Barracks; 429930; Map Page IV.

**Roeberry Taing** see *Roeberry* above; ON *tangi* point; 419932; Map Page V.

**Rockarry** Quindry, Ronsvoe and Hoxa district 1861; vanished; origin unknown.

**Rockerskaill** Eastside; 1821; occupied; ON personal name *Hrókr*; ON *skáli* a seasonal dwelling in this case; 454906; Map Page VIII.

**Rögnvaldsey** see below.

**Ronaldsay/*Rögnvaldsey*,** Rognvald's island, the first mention of which is in the *Orkneyinga Saga*; later styled South Ronaldsay to distinguish it from Ronaldsay (earlier Rinansey) in the North Isles; John Ronaldsa, captain of a vessel, is recorded in Ryfylke in Norway in 1568 and later appears in Kirkwall records.

**Ronaldsdale** Quindry, Ronsvoe and Hoxa district 1871; vanished; probably based on *Ronaldsvoe* etc. form; see *Dale* for derivation.

**Ronaldsvoe/Ronsvoe/Ronsa** 1500, 1595, 1750, 1841; *Rögnvalds-vágr* in *Orkneyinga Saga*; the name applies to a large district to the west of the bay of St. Margaret's Hope including *Heads, Hetherum, Grutha* etc. and extending down to, but not including, Quindry; originally it was the name of the bay in which King Hakon's fleet of ships lay in August 1263 on its way to the fatal encounter at the Battle of Largs; the district is now pronounced 'Ronsa' but is used only by older local residents; ON personal name *Rögnvaldr*; ON *vágr* bay; 442931; Map Page IV.

**Ronaldsvoe** occupied; a house which has adopted the above name; 438926; Map Page IV.

**Ronsa** see *Ronaldsvoe/Ronsvoe*.

**Rood/Ruid Kirk/Chapel** Sandwick 1736; originally *Holyrood Chapel*; this was one of three important chapels in South Ronaldsay, the others being *St. Peter's* and *St. Mary's*; it lay in what is now the farm yard of *Mucklehouse*; 436890; Map Page VIII.

**Root** 1. vanished house, the site of which is known; ON *rjóðr* a clearing; 442847; Map Page X.

**Root** 2. see *Gloup o Root*.

**Rose Bank** 1. Burray; occupied; fanciful name; there are at least six other Rosebank place-names in Orkney; 465954; Map Page VI.

**Rosebank** 2. Quindry, Ronsvoe and Hoxa district; 1861, 1871; vanished.

**Rosebank** 3. St. Margaret' Hope; occupied; Map Page IV.

**Rose Cottage** 1. Quindry; occupied; fanciful name; 'Rose Cottage' is the second most popular British house name (the most popular name is 'The Cottage'!); 433926; Map Page IV.

**Rose Cottage** 2. Swona; formerly *Inverbiggings*; *Iverbiggings*, *Upper Biggings*; it is said that it was named 'Rose Cottage' when the Rosie family occupied it; 389848; Map Page XII.

**Rosehaven** Eastside; occupied; named by a Rosie family; 465984; Map Page XI.

**Roselea** 1. St. Margaret's Hope; occupied; fanciful name; Map Page IV.

**Roselea** 2. Herston village; occupied; Map Page V.

**Roslin** Burray; see *Rigini*.

**Rossmyre** St. Margaret's Hope; occupied; perhaps transferred from Rossmyre in Firth; Map Page IV.

**Rotterdam** St. Margaret's Hope 1861; vanished; a name probably introduced by a seaman; compare *Canton*.

**Rough o Kame** a fishing spot; ON *rif* reef; see *Ours o Stews*; 474888; Map Page XI.

**Royston** St. Margaret's Hope; empty and in a ruinous condition; a transferred name from Royston in Glasgow; Map Page IV.

**Ruff (The)** 1. ON *rif* reef; there is a farm in Rendall called The Riff after a nearby coastal feature; 448946; Map Page IV.

**Ruff (The)** 2. a house near the above feature; occupied; Map Page IV.

**Ruff (The)** 3. Burray; derelict; formerly *Sheepquoy*; ON *rif* reef; 451967; Map Page I.

**Rufford** Burray; occupied; fanciful name; 473964; Map Page II.

**Ryelittle** a small green mound near *Taftnica* Burray, believed to be of archaeological interest; the name seems to be related to Roy, the name of a farm in Holm and Ryo, a cairn in Evie, both deriving their name from ON *reyrr* a cairn; see *Rur* below; 485953; Map Page VII.

**Rumley/Rumly Point** there are several 'Rumly' place-names on the Orkney coast; all relate to the rumbling noise made by small boulders as wave action rolls them too and fro; dialect *rumle* to rumble; 488945; Map Page VII.

**Rur** Grimness, 1821; vanished; ON *reyrr* a cairn.

**Ruthie** name of a field bordering the shore, *Kirkhouse*; probably at the time of naming, a field full of corn spurrey, locally known as 'ruithy girse'; 433913; Map Page IV.

**Sacquoy** Burray village; occupied; a new house; Map Page IV.

**Salmon Rock** in the 1700s a vessel with a cargo of salted salmon was wrecked on this reef; 464864; Map Page XIII.

**Saltwater Geo** Muckle Skerry, Pentland Skerries; 488785; Map Page XIV.

**Samaria** Widewall 1871; vanished; Biblical place-name; ancient capital of Israel; there were several such old house names in Orkney; compare Jericho in Dounby and Babylon in Stenness (both vanished).

**Salt Geo** an alternative name for *Ham Geo*; in those days when salt was not freely available, there were several salt pans round the coast of Orkney which provided a coarse salt for local use; there is a Salt Pan place-name on the coast of Orphir; see also below; 468839; Map Page XII.

**Salt Taing** ON *tangi* point; suggests an area of the coast where sea salt was extracted; compare Salt Ness in Shapinsay and Walls; 467838; Map Page XII.

**Sand o Right/Wright** if the conditions are suitable, the Sand o Right is traditionally the preferred location for the Boys' Ploughing Match, now referred to as the 'Festival of the Horse'; at exceptionally low tides the stumps of fairly large trees may be seen here; (such relics may have given rise to tales of woods which existed in Orkney at one time, often in exposed places—see *Lippa* for an illustration of this); during World War II units of R.E.M.E. (Royal Electrical and Mechanical Engineers) and R.A.O.C. (Royal Army Ordnance Corps) had workshops on the coast here where military vehicles and heavy artillery pieces were repaired; ON *sandr* sand; *rettr* sheepfold; compare North Right on Fara and Ritquoy in Birsay; 423935; Map Page V.

*Lower: Boys' Ploughing Match on the Sand o Right.*

*Upper: A gaily decorated 'Horse'.*

**Sand Geo** 1. coastal feature ON *sandr* sand; *gjá* ravine; ON *sandr* is a very common element in Orkney place-names; 483945; Map Page VII.

**Sand Geo** 2. coastal feature; see above; 419923; Map Page V.

**Sand House** Grimness 1851; vanished.
**Sand Pit** 1. North Links, Burray; this locality has long been prized for its high quality sand; 487973; Map Page III.
**Sand Pit** 2. 465881; Map Page XI.

*The Sands Hotel, Burray.*

**Sands Hotel** Burray; 474954; Map Page VI.
**Sand Taing** 435890; Map Page VIII.
**Sand Wick** ON *sandr* sand; *vík* bay; two vessels have come to grief in this bay; 1. the brigantine *Agnes* of Fraserburgh with a cargo of wheat in 1877. 2. the schooner *Isabella* of Alloa in 1872; a searchlight, one of at least twenty on the island was positioned here during World War II; 428890; Map Page VIII.
**Sandwick** 1492, 1500, 1595; now a district; Sandwick is also the name of a parish in the West Mainland; see above; 434887; Map Page VIII.
**Sandwick Burn** 440896; Map Page VIII.
**Sandwick House** empty; 439896; Map Page VIII.
**Sandy Brown's** vanished house; but position is known; 433943; Map Page IV.
**Sandy Field** field-name, *Cletts*; 462905; Map Page XI.
**Sandy Hill** 1. a searchlight, one of at least twenty on the island was positioned here during World War II; 442874; Map Page VIII.
**Sandyhill** 2. South Parish; a private house; occupied; 443871; Map Page VIII.
**Sandyhook** Burray village; occupied; 476958; Map Page VI.
**Sandy Riddles** sea-bed area south-east of *Pentland Skerries*; origin of 'riddle' uncertain; probably related to Ork. dial, *rittle* to make a furrow; approximately 490760; N.B. off the maps supplied.
**Sandy's Toon Lands** field-name, *Stews*; the personal name 'Sandy' may refer to

Alex (Sandy) Norquoy who farmed at *Stews*; the name *toon lands* here probably means 'arable land'; in the old system of land holding the *tún* field or *toomal* as it was usually called, was an arable field close to the farm and not shared by others in the tunship; compare *Bill's Toonlands*; 464896; Map Page XI.

**Sangar** Burray; occupied; there were at one time farms by this name in Stronsay and Westray, the latter now known as Sanquhar; 477958; Map Page VI.

**Saorsa** see *Midhouse*, Burray.

**Savona** St. Margaret's Hope; occupied; fanciful name; Map Page IV.

**Savi Geo** ON *saevar* (of the) sea; *gjá*, ravine; 420904; Map Page IX.

**Scaesgar** Sandwick, 1665; vanished; perhaps ON *skíð(s)-garðr* a fence made of wooden staves; compare *Timmer Dykes*.

**Scapa Flow** usually referred to as 'The Flow'; the sheltered harbour and deep anchorage to the west of South Ronaldsay and Burray which has played such an important part in the history of the British Navy; it was also valued by the Norsemen but strangely was not given a specific name by them; they referred more to the bays within Scapa Flow such as *Barðsvik* i.e. Bars Wick in South Ronaldsay or *Ásmundarvágr*, now Kirk Hope in Walls; the name Scapa appears in the *Orkneyinga Saga* as *Skalpeið à Hrossey* i.e. Scapa on the Orkney Mainland; although there are several examples in Iceland, the word 'flow' in 'Scapa Flow' is the only recording in Orkney and Shetland of the Norse word *flói* with the meaning 'deep bay'; it is however recorded in Caithness in 'Flow (Country)' where it has the alternative meaning 'marshy moor'.

**Scapa View** occupied; 464945; Map Page VI.

**Scarf Skerry** 1. ON *skarfr* cormorant; *sker* reef; a common coastal name in Orkney; the cormorant rested on such skerries to dry its wings; 496931; Map Page VII.

**Scarf Skerry** 2. see above; 433870; Map Page VIII.

**Scarf Skerry** 3. see above; 404933; Map Page V.

**Scarf Skerry** 4. see above; 468893; Map Page XI.

**Scarf Taing** coastal feature; ON *skarfr* cormorant; *tangi* point; 495930; Map Page VII.

**Scartan Bay** Muckle Skerry, Pentland Skerries; named after *Scartan Point* below; see below for derivation; 469783; Map Page XIV.

**Scartan Point** Muckle Skerry, Pentland Skerries; ON *skarfa tangi* a peninsula favoured by cormorants; there is a Scartan in Sanday and a Scarataing in Sandwick, West Mainland; see also *Parliament Square* and *Tennis Court*; 470782; Map Page XIV.

**Scews** Grimness; occupied; Ice. *skjár* hut made of slatted wood, with English plural; in Orkney some of these houses were built of stone in such a way that the air passed through them since they were frequently used for drying meat and fish; in the 1980s this word was still known in dialect and took a variety of forms such as *skyo, skeo, skio* and *skoo*; see *Schusan* below, *Scows* and *Sk-yeos*; 466944; Map Page VI.

**Scholt (The)** earlier *Windbrake*; now *South Liddel*; origin of 'The Scholt' nickname uncertain; connected somehow with a Shetland pony or a Shetlander!

**School** 1. former subscription school, Burray, near *Chapel Cottage*; 479966; Map Page II.

**School** 2. Burray; 474957; Map Page VI.

**School** 3. see *Cullocks*; 444939; Map Page IV.

**School** 4. Grimness; it closed in 1965/1966; now a private house named *Skyran*; 473937; Map Page VI.

**School** 5. St. Margaret's Hope; opened 1990, replacing *Old School*; 443934; Map Page IV.

**School** 6. Widewall; it closed in 1968; now a private house named *Widewall View*; a searchlight, one of at least twenty on the island was positioned here during World War II; 447909; Map Page VIII.

**School** 7. Herston; no longer exists; a searchlight, one of at least twenty on the island was positioned here during World War II; 420916; Map Page V.

**School** 8. see *Viggie*.

**School** 9. see *Tomison's Academy*.

**School** 10. see *Brandyquoy*.

**School** 11. Swona, opened 1878 with 14 pupils; closed 1927; derelict; 391849; Map Page XII.

**School** 12. Burray village; a new school; Map Page VI.

**Schoolbrae** Sc. *brae* hillside; 437907; Map Page VIII.

**School Field** field in which Grimness School stands; 472938; Map Page VI.

**School House** 1. St. Margaret's Hope; empty; Map Page IV.

**School House** 2. South Parish; occupied; was formerly *South Parish School* until *Tomison's Academy* was opened in 1851 when it became the head teacher's house; now a private dwelling; see *Tomison's Academy*; 444854; Map Page X.

**School House** 3. Grimness; occupied; 473938; Map Page VI.

**School House** 4. Swona; derelict; the teacher's accommodation and the school occupied the same building; compare *Forbes' School*; 391849; Map Page XII.

**Schusan** pronounced 'Skoosan'; Widewall; occupied; Ice. *skjár* hut, with Eng. plural and definite article; see *Scows* below and *Scews*; also known as *Gylliosquoy*; 442909; Map Page VIII.

**Sco Taing** ON *scagi* point of land; *tangi* point; 490925; Map Page VII.

**Scows (o Cara)** 1750; occupied; there is also a Scows in Orphir; Ice. *skjár* hut; Nynorsk *skjaa*, a hut of loose boards in which things are dried; Ork. dial. *skoo* etc; see *Scews* above, *Cara* and *Berriedale*; 466946; Map Page VI.

**Seaforth** Burray; occupied; 473955; Map Page VI.

**Sea Geo** Burray; 497956; Map Page VII.

**Sea Taing** Burray 488952; Map Page VII.

**Sea View** 1. Burray village; occupied; also operates as a shop and garage; Map Page VI.

**Seaview** 2. St. Margaret's Hope; occupied; it is built on the site of the former *Café*; Map Page IV.

**Sebay** 1. Herston, 1821, 1901; vanished; possibly a transferred name from Sebay in St. Andrews; ON *saer* sea; *baer* farm; 413912; Map Page V.

**Sebay** 2. Back Road, St. Margaret's Hope; occupied; transferred name; Map Page IV.

**Sebay Geo** near the vanished house of Sebay; ON *gjá* ravine; 413907; Map Page IX.

**Sebastapol** (sic) St. Margaret's Hope 1861, 1871; vanished; named after the fall of the Russian fortress at Sebastopol in 1855 which brought the Crimean War to an end; compare *Alma, Balaclava* and *Inkerman*; there was a village by the name Sebastopol in Wales, now part of the town of Griffithstown in Gwent.

**Secession Church** vanished; *Kirk Cottage* stands on the site; the Session Church was a large building constructed in 1827; when the Scottish Secession Church united with the Free Church of Scotland; this quite new building was carefully demolished and all the stone and timber transported to build the United Presbyterian Church in St. Margaret's Hope in the 1840s; the rebuilt church was later renamed the United Free Church and when the bulk of the Scottish Presbyterian churches came together again, it was renamed Church of Scotland!; it is now *St. Margaret's Church*; see Introduction for an explanation of this confusion!

**Sedan** Quindry, Ronsvoe and Hoxa district 1871; vanished; transferred name from Sedan in France.

**Selkie Hole** see below; 493928; Map Page VII.

**Selkie Holes** Sc. *selkie* seal; 429852; Map Page X.

**Selki Skerry** Swona; see above; 384841; Map Page XII.

**Sellyland/Solyieland** Burray, 1627, 1750; ON *selja* willow; see *Vensilly.*

**Senoldies** Grimness 1851; vanished; if we assume that *Senoldies* is the correct form, the second element is ON *alda* breaking wave; see *Sinilie.*

**Serrigar 1.** Sandwick 1492, 1500, 1595, 1750; occupied; first recording of this name is *Southirgarth* and later as *Sougare*; ON *suðr-garðr,* south farm; this Norse farm name became corrupted to 'Sugarhouse' in North Ronaldsay! Serrigar is one of a number of Orkney place-names which produced an Orkney surname; John Serrigar lived in South Ronaldsay in 1601; 438879; Map Page VIII.

**Serrigar 2.** occupied; 440881; Map Page VIII.

**Settling** South Parish 1841; vanished; an offensive nickname; Sc. *settling(s)*, dregs.

**Sgoilamar/Skolimar** Swona; a rock face; despite the Gaelic appearance of the name, it is a corruption of ON *skjól* shelter and ON *hamarr* exposed rock face; there are several stone shelters in this exposed area; 384836; Map Page XII.

**Shaird** see *East Shaird* and *West Shaird.*

**Shannon** Grimness; occupied; suggests a transferred name from Shannon in the Irish Republic; 483943; Map Page VII.

**Sharnymire/Shurrymire** Eastside 1841, 1861; now known as *Wardhill*; ON *skarn* dung; ON *saur* dirt; *mýrr*, marsh; what would be described today as 'indelicate names' were frequently employed in former times; perhaps the reader can guess the meaning of Skiddy in Rendall and Skidbrook in Lincolnshire; 459890; Map Page XI.

**Sheep Dip** *Glims Holm*; as the name suggests, where the island sheep were dipped; 477993; Map Page II.

**Sheep Pens** *Glims Holm*; 473988; Map Page II.

**Sheepquoy**: Burray; see *Ruff (The) 3*; 449967; Map Page I.

**Sheep Bight** coastal feature; the name suggests 'sheep bay' but is more probably 'sheep pen', referring to a vanished enclosure which lay here; Sc. *bucht* sheep pen; 490925; Map Page VII.

**Shipshank** coastal feature; also known as *Sockersie*; perhaps a corruption of 'sheep shank'; origin unknown; 468888; Map Page XI.

**Shops** St. Margaret's Hope; at the beginning of the 20th century the village rivalled Stromness in its prosperity; there were 6 grocers, 4 general merchants, 3 bakers, 3 drapers, 3 blacksmiths, 2 butchers and 2 joiners in addition to an hotel, an inn, a post office, a saddler, a watchmaker and jeweller, a photographic studio, a branch of the Union Bank and a resident doctor; Laughton's, general merchant, had already been established for almost 100 years; now, in addition to the Post Office there are only four shops—Doull's, Robertson's, the Trading Post and The Workshop, the latter specialising in crafts; all provide a useful service to islanders and to tourists.

**Shore** Widewall 1851; vanished.

**Shorehouse** 1. Quindry, Ronsvoe and St. Margaret's Hope district 1881; vanished.

**Shorehouse** 2. Sandwick; there is also a Shorehouse in Westray; 435891; Map Page VIII.

**Shoreside** Grimness; occupied; 465945; Map Page IV.

**Shorewindows** Garth; holiday home; second element represents ON *vindr* wind; ON *hús* house with the meaning 'exposed to the wind'; compare *Windbrake*; see *Binniewindows*; 453937; Map Page VI.

**Short House** Quindry, Ronsvoe and Hoxa district; 1871; vanished.

**Shortie Geo** probably a variant of ON *svartr* black; the initial 's' in Ork. dialect was sometimes pronounced 'sh' and the 'v' was omitted; (see *Sortoquoy*); ON *gjá* ravine; 427863; Map Page X.

**Sightly** South Parish 1881; vanished; origin uncertain.

**Sillerdyke/Cellardyke** Windwick; occupied; see *Cellardyke* for an explanation of the name; 448866; Map Page VIII.

**Silvars Quoy** Quindry, Ronsvoe and Hoxa district 1851; vanished; suggests the surname 'Silver' but such a surname has not been recorded in South Ronaldsay; perhaps it is the nickname of an inhabitant; there are several long established houses in Sanday with the name Silverha but in those cases, the names were adopted at the time of building, seemingly to give dignity to what were quite modest houses; ON *kví* enclosure.

**Silverdyke** Burray, 1821; see *Cellardyke*.

**Sinclair Park** field-name; 436840; Map Page X.

**Single Taing** 417904; Map Page IX.

**Sinilie** Shet. dial. *sinna* a small drying kiln; the reference is to sea spray in the air here which gives the impression of a smoking, grain drying kiln; the word must have been in use in Orkney too since it is found applied to blow holes on the Rousay coast called *Sinyans o Cutclaws* which shows the definite article as a suffix; compare *Kiln (The)* in this respect; the final element 'lie' is ON *hlíð* slope, but used also in the sense 'cliff' in South Ronaldsay and Copinsay; see *Camberbosk* for an interesting reference to a Shetland example; 427858; Map Page X.

**Sinmire** a former marshy area on the north side of Ward Hill; it was dry even in Norse speaking times as the name suggests; Nor. *sine* to dry up, used today only in the sense of 'unable to produce milk'; compare *Sinilie* above; ON *mýrr* marsh.

**Skae** vanished; at a meeting of the Kirk Session of South Ronaldsay in 1668, it was agreed that money should be collected for John Cromarty of Skae 'for repairing of his houses which were burnt'; John Cromarty lived in Widewall but the exact location of his houses is unknown; ON *skeifr* which seems to have been used in Orkney in the sense of 'sloping land'.

**Skaifles/Skui Flaes** a reef off the *Taing o Knockhall*; ON *skagi* projecting point of land; ON *fles* flat reef in the sea (see *The Fleece*); normally in Orkney place-names the initial 'f' of *fles* is lost to give a name such as The Lash on Graemsay; 456946; Map Page VI.

**Skaigram** ON *skagi* projecting point of land; the final element 'ram' seems a corruption of ON *raun*, stony ground; compare *Riniber*; 468833; Map Page XII.

**Skaitherlie** coastal feature; ON *skiðgarðshlið* a lattice gate; 493931; Map Page VII.

**Skarp** see *Skerpie*.

**Skebigo** Grimness, 1746, 1750; vanished; near *Skipi Geo*; see *Skipi Geo* for explanation of name.

**Skeldro** Burray; occupied; 'skeldro' is the Orkney dialect word for the 'shelduck'; compare *Tammie Norie's Cottage*; 476958; Map Page VI.

**Skerloom** coastal feature; ON *sker* reef; *hljómr/hlamma* to resound, a reference to the breaking of the surf; 477919; Map Page VI.

**Skerpie** Burray; 1627; occupied; called *Scarpa* in 1750 and *Skarp* in 1821; there is a *Skerp* place-name in Walls; see *Quoysharps* for derivation; 488957; Map Page VII.

**Skerrilee** ON *sker* reef; 'lee/lie' is found in several coastal place-names and is difficult to interpret since there are several possible explanations; here it may represent ON *hlíð* slope, but also used in the East Mainland in the sense 'cliff'; 494930; Map Page VII.

**Skerry/Skerries o Skaigram** ON *sker* reef; see *Skaigram*; 468833; Map Page XII.

**Skerry Sound** separates *Glims Holm* and Lambholm, now spanned by *Churchill Barrier No. 2*; the skerry in question is *Glims Holm Skerry*; see *Blockships 1*; 483998; Map Page II.

**Skingum** a small knoll near *Kirk Ness*, Eastside; ON *skygni* a shelter; ON *holmr*, island—usually an island in the sea or in a loch but it can refer to an elevated piece of land in a low-lying area; compare Curcum in Birsay; 471913; Map Page XI.

**Skipi Geo** ON *skipa-gjá* a ravine which can be used by a vessel; there is also a Skipi Geo in Birsay; see *Skebigeo*; 486928; Map Page VII.

**Skolimar** see *Sgoilamar*.

**Skorags (The)** Swona; relates to jagged rocks on the west coast; ON *skor* a rift in a rocky wall; the suffix represents the South Isles diminutive 'ack/ag'; 387847; Map Page XII.

**Skowsetter** Grimness, 1562; vanished; for first element 'skow' see *Scews*; see *Blanster* for 'setter' element.

**Skui Flaes** see *Skaifles*.

**Sk-yeos** Swona; old stone buildings originally used for storing fish; see *Scews* for interpretation; 382838; Map Page XII.

**Skyran** a house; see *School 4.*

**Slap** 1. Burray, 1821; holiday home; Sc. *slap*, gate; 472963; Map Page II.

**Slap** 2. Burray; see above for derivation; 463958; Map Page VI.

**Slates** ON *slettr*, flat and smooth of stone etc.; 426886; Map Page IX.

**Slates o Hest/Hess** the destroyers HMS *Opal* and HMS *Narborough* returning to Scapa Flow in blizzard conditions on 12/13th January 1918 were wrecked here with the loss of 188 crew; there was only one survivor; see *Slates* above and *Hest* for derivation; see 465877; Map Page XIII.

**Slates o the Altar** Swona; coastal feature; see *Slates* above for derivation; nearby is *The Bishop*; 392842; Map Page XII.

**Slett Head** see *Slates* above for derivation of name; 410916; Map Page V.

**Slipway** 1. Herston; 422917; Map Page V.

**Slipway** 2. Grimness; 488933; Map Page VII.

**Sly Well** coastal feature; ON *slý* slime, referring to the green algae which forms at the outlet of such a well; 485927; Map Page VI.

**Smaa Goes** coastal feature; ON *smár* small; 488935; Map Page VI.

**Small Tails** coastal feature; see *Tarf Tail* for use of 'tail' here; 474909; Map Page XI.

**Smiddy** 1./**Smithy** Grimness; formerly *Quoysmiddie* 1595, 1750, 1861; occupied; Sc. *smiddy* smithy; 476935; Map Page VI.

**Smiddy** 2. see *Black Smiddy.*

**Smiddy** 3. now vanished but location is known; 460893; Map Page XI.

**Smiddybanks** St. Margaret's Hope, 1746, 1861; occupied; on this site in the 17th century stood a two storeyed mansion house occupied by David Sutherland of *Windbreck*; this was the site of the original St. Margaret's Hope pier; 445938; Map Page IV.

**Smiddy Cottage** occupied; see *Timmer Dykes*; 445935; Map Page IV.

**Smiddy Museum** St. Margaret's Hope; Map Page IV.

**Smiddy Park** it belonged to the nearby *Smiddy* above; 462894; Map Page XI.

**Smith House** Grimness 1851; vanished.

**Smithy** Burray; 473954; Map Page VI.

**Smithy** 1. St. Margaret's Hope; vanished but site is known; one of a number of South Ronaldsay place-names which provided a surname; Nicol Smyddie lived in Ronaldsvoe in 1601; 449933; Map Page IV.

**Smithy** 2. Widewall; 423907; Map Page IX.

**Smithy** 3. on coast, Grimness; 487933; Map Page VII.

**Smithy Museum** an old established smithy, now a museum; 446853; Map Page X.

**Smoo (The)** Swona; the name seems to have applied originally to the upper part of *The Gloup*; ON *smúga* a gap; this word was used in Orkney in the sense 'hole'; the dialect word *smoo* was, for example, a hole in a wall allowing sheep to pass through; Smoo Cave is an impressive feature on the coast of Sutherland; 391844; Map Page XII.

**Smugglers' Hole** coastal feature; 455843; Map Page XIII.

**Sneb** Widewall 1851; vanished; Sc. *snab* steep, short slope.

**Snebb** Eastside 1861; vanished; this entry and the above may refer to the same place possibly located on the boundary between *Widewall* and *Eastside..*

**Snuddies** St. Margaret's Hope 1861; vanished; suggests family name Snoddie; such a surname is recorded in Caithness in the 17th century.

**Somerset** Sandwick; holiday home; a name recorded before 1880; transferred name from Somerset, England; 430893; Map Page VIII.

**Soo Taing** coastal feature; ON *sauðr* sheep; ON *tangi* point; compare Sowie Geo on Flotta; 490925; Map Page VII.

**Sootan** see *Souton*.

**Sockersie** coastal feature; probably a fishing rock where the fisherman has to sit down on a wet rock; there is a similarly named fishing rock in Rousay where it is called Koldeross, ON *kaldi-rass* cold arse; 468888; Map Page XI.

**Sodger's Close** a lane in *St. Margaret's Hope* linking *Church Road* to *Marengo Square* named after George Sinclair who had been a regular soldier in the Seaforth Highlanders before World War I; Map Page IV.

**Sorquoy** Paplay 1492, 1500, 1595, 1841; occupied; ON *saur* used in the sense 'swampy land'; ON *kví* enclosure; one of a number of place-names which provided Orkney surnames; Bessie Surquoy (sic) lived in South Ronaldsay in 1633; 466913; Map Page XI.

**Sortoquoy** Quindry, Ronsvoe and St. Margaret's Hope district 1881; vanished; ON *svartr* black (see *Shortie Geo* for explanation); ON *kví* enclosure.

**Sossater** 1821; an abbreviated form of *Quoyhorsetter*.

**Sougare** see *Serrigar*.

**Sound o Hoxa** see *Hoxa Sound*.

**Sound o Selkie Skerry** Swona; stretch of water which separates *Selki Skerry* from the coast; 382839; Map Page XII.

**Sounds Geo** 467834; Map Page XII.

**Sounds Loch** 467835; Map Page XII.

**South Barth Clivvy** see *Barth*; ON *klufðr* cleft; 428855; Map Page X.

**South Barswick Geo** 428857; Map Page X.

**South Breck** Burray; occupied; 483962; Map Page II.

**South Cara** Grimness 1861; occupied; part of the original house still existed here in the 1930s when archaeologists determined that it dated back to the late 17th century; a searchlight, one of at least twenty on the island was positioned above South Cara during World War II; see *Cara*; 478929; Map Page VI.

**South Church** Burray; see *Church 2*.

**South Clett** Swona; see *The Clett*; 389837; Map Page XII.

**South Cletts** Eastside, 1821; vanished; see above.

**South Dykend** Burray, 1821; see *Dykend* Burray.

**Southfield** Burray; empty; 484960; Map Page III.

**South Flaws** occupied; see *Flaws* for derivation; 454856; Map Page XIII.

**South Geo** position unknown.

**South Grimness** 1750; vanished.

**South House** Burray; occupied; 472964; Map Page II.

**South Liddel** occupied; earliest recording was *Windbrake*; later *The Scholt*; site of small subscription school in 1840s/1850s; see *Liddel*; 463836; Map Page XII.

**South Links** Burray; 486969; Map Page III.

**South Manse** Burray village; occupied; Map Page VI.

**South Mire** near Stews, 1821; vanished.

**South Mires** field-name; probably relates to a vanished house; 463907; Map Page XI.

**South Parish** one of two divisions of South Ronaldsay, originally called *St. Mary's*; the northern boundary of the parish lies on a line drawn from *Mucklehouse* in Sandwick to a point in the middle of *Newark Bay*; see *Pairish (The)*.

**South Parish School** established in 1821 by Tomison; after Tomison's Charity School (*Tomison's Academy*) opened in 1851, the *South Parish School* became the School House and is still known as the *School House* today; 443853; Map Page X.

**South Ronaldsay** see *Ronaldsay*.

**South Sheed** 1939; vanished; Ork. dial. *sheed* a name for nine rigs of land in the old system of land-holding.

**South Slett** see *Slates*; 434885; Map Page VIII.

**Southtown** one of the original three divisions of Burray; the others were *Northtown* and *The Bu*; 488963; Map Page III.

**South United Free Church** see *Church 4*.

**Southview** Burray village; occupied; Map Page VI.

**South Windwick** occupied; see *Windwick*.

**Souton/Sootan** Swona; a rocky point; ON *sauðr* sheep; ON *tangi* point; compare *Soo Taing* above; 389839; Map Page XII.

**Spindrift** Burray; a house; 482979; Map Page II.

**Spoot Hoops** coastal feature; the name suggests Ork. dial. 'spoot' razor fish but there is no sand in this area; probably a corruption of ON *spóa* curlew and *tupt* knoll, suggesting an area of the beach favoured by 'whaups' at the end of the breeding season; 428858; Map Page X.

**Springbank** St. Margaret's Hope; occupied; 454930; Map Page IV.

**Springs** Burray; occupied; 467967; Map Page II.

**Stackabank** South Parish 1881; vanished; ON *stakkr*, rock stack; *bakki* slope; 434868; Map Page X.

**Stack o Kame** ON *stakkr* rock stack; see *Kame*; 489925; Map Page VII.

**Stainsby's Corner** Back Road, St. Margaret's Hope; named from the manager of the shop here which was a branch of Robertson's; Map Page IV.

**Standing Stone** 1. near *Sorquoy*; a block of red sandstone 4.5 metres high and 0.5 metres thick; 467914; Map Page XI.

**Standing Stone** 2. near *Cloudyhall* almost 3 metres high and 20 cms. thick; 435896; Map Page VIII.

**Standing Stone** 3. a former standing stone approximately 3m. high which lay for some time to the south of St. Peter's Kirk; to commemorate the Millennium it was sensitively sculpted by local man Willie Budge and erected by him in conjunction with Johnny Tomison and John Laird; 474907; Map Page XI.

**Standing Stone** 4. near *Stews*; a triangular block of red sandstone 2 metres high and 30 cms. thick; see *Stews* for its interesting related derivation; 467890; Map Page XI.

**Standing Stone** 5. Burray; a house; occupied; there is no record of a standing stone near this old house; perhaps a transferred name from Stannanstane, Flotta; 469968; Map Page II.

**Stane** Linklater 1841; derelict; see *Stone*; 454873; Map Page XIII.

**Staneisbul** coastal feature; ON *steinn* stone; *nes* point; *ból* animal pen; 483925; Map Page VII.

**Stanemora** Swona; relates to a stretch of rocks on the coast; ON *steinn* stone; the termination probably represents a remnant of ON *hamarr*, rock exposure, as in the nearby *Sgoilamar/Skolimar*; 384836; Map Page XII.

**Stansger** Windwick, 1634; vanished; see *Stensigar* for interpretation.

**Starilea/Starilie** Grimness 1821, 1861; occupied; ON *stíar* animal pens; a 'lie' element can be interpreted in a number of ways in Orkney place-names; here it may mean ON *hlið* gate; 462944; Map Page VI.

**Starilea/Starilie (New)** occupied; see also *Berriedale*; 465944; Map Page VI.

**Station (The)** only the steethe stones remain of this fish curing station in St. Margaret's Hope though The Station may be seen in old photographs; much of the stone of this building is now built into the wall above the shore road; see *Cara Flats*; 450935; Map Page IV.

**Stavanger** Northfield Road, Burray; occupied; a name transferred from Norway; 479978; Map Page II.

**St. Andrews Chapel** (remains of); Windwick; 458869; Map Page XIII.

**St. Clair House** St. Margaret's Hope; occupied; 446935; Map Page IV.

**St. Clair Villa** St. Margaret's Hope; occupied; despite being a two storeyed property, it was locally known as 'The Cottage'; a substantial house; though several houses in South Ronaldsay have external stone staircases this house has an internal stone staircase which is an unusual feature; the name St. Clair was given by a Sinclair family who at one time owned the property; in the early 20th century it was fashionable to add 'villa' to a house name; compare *Daisy Villa*, *Myrtle Villa*, *Richmond Villa*; there is an Edenmore Villa in Finstown; 444934; Map Page IV.

**St. Colm's Chapel** 1. Hoxa; 422936; Map Page V.

**St. Colm's Chapel** 2. Burwick 441842; Map Page X.

**St. Colm's Chapel** 3. Grimness; 488935; Map Page VII.

**St. John's Geo** ON *gjá* ravine; unlikely to have been an old chapel in the vicinity here; the name 'St. John' may relate to the old custom of lighting a Johnsmas Bonfire on the nearby headland; compare St. John's Head on Hoy; see also *Ball Hill*; 427861; Map Page X.

**St. Lawrence's Kirk** 1. Southtown, Burray; it fell into a ruinous condition about 1800; the date 1621 carved on the lowest stone of the skew probably records a rebuilding; Low in his *Tour through the Islands of Orkney and Shetland* stated that the boat of a 'Fin-man' had been kept in this church, presumably an Eskimo kayak; there were several reportings of such boats in the waters of Orkney, probably blown eastwards by strong gales; 492964; Map Page III.

**St. Lawrence's Kirk** 2. Burray; see *Church 2*.

**St. Margaret's Chapel** (site of) St. Margaret's Hope; before the Wards Park houses were built, a rescue dig revealed some of the walls; it is locally believed that the chapel is named after Margaret, the 'Maid of Norway', who died on the voyage from Norway to Orkney in 1290, but this is unlikely; the St. Margaret in question was born in Hungary, the second wife of Malcolm III of Scotland; the name *Danska Kirk/Danskirk,* i.e. 'Danes Church' applied to this chapel is interesting; 'Dane' seems to be used here in the Old Norse sense of 'troll' (as in *berg-danir,* hill trolls); the best example from Orkney is probably the coastal feature known as the Danes' Pier in Stronsay; the name *Danska Kirk* was probably applied when the chapel was an enigmatic heap of stones; 'Dane' seems to have been used in Shetland in the same sense; 445935; Map Page IV.

**St. Margaret's Church** St. Margaret's Hope; see *Secession Church.*

**St. Margaret's Cottage** Hope; occupied; during the war it served as Headquarters of 61, and later, 59 Searchlight Regiment; 449933; Map Page IV.

**St. Margaret's Hope** ON *hóp* bay; a number of vessels have been wrecked in this bay; 1. the sailing vessel *Duchess of Gordon* owned by William Garrioch of Stromness in 1883. 2. the sailing vessel *Christiana,* with a cargo of coal in 1890. 3. the brigantine *Findhorn* of Blyth in 1849; see *Ronaldsvoe/Ronsvoe,* the original name; 447938; Map Page IV.

**St. Margaret's Hope** village; named after *St. Margaret Chapel*; locally known as *The Hope*; 448934; Map Page IV.

**St. Margaret's Hope Camp** vanished; a R.A.S.C (Royal Army Service Corps) camp stood behind the present *St. Margaret's Hope School*; it provided rations and materials for the many units stationed on the island; 443934; Map Page IV.

**St. Margaret's Hope Pier** known by older people as the *New Pier* since it replaced the old pier at *Smiddybanks;* today it is the terminus of the short-sea crossing for vehicles and passengers; during the war, in addition to the normal island traffic of slag and coal boats, it was extremely busy with the movements of Royal Naval ration and ammunition ships and ferry boats which ran a two hour service to ships in Scapa Flow; a large brick building here served as the Royal Naval Base for the minefield in *Hoxa Sound* and a wooden hut was constructed nearby to house the servicemen; an associated brick-built magazine still remains at 446943; Map Page IV.

**St. Mary's** the original name of what is now *South Parish*; named after *St. Mary's Kirk*; see *South Parish.*

**St. Mary's (New) Church of Scotland** see *Church 4.*

**St. Mary's Kirk** Burwick; now rarely used; inside is stored the Ladykirk Stone, a Pictish inauguration stone of great interest upon which the outline of two feet have been carved; the stone has rested in this church for at least four hundred years when it was referred to by Jo Ben in his description of the islands; 440843; Map Page X.

**St. Ninian's Chapel** (site of) Eastside; 465888; Map Page XI.

**St. Ola's Chapel** Widewall; 434915; Map Page IV.

**St. Peter's** the original name of what is now called *North Parish*; named after St. Peter's Kirk, Eastside; see *North Parish.*

**St. Peter's Chapel** 1. Swona; vanished; a house was built on the site; 391851; Map Page XII.

**St. Peter's Chapel** 2. Muckle Skerry, Pentland Skerries; it stood on *Broti Ber*; 464785; Map Page XIV.

**St. Peter's Kirk** Eastside; this church which originally gave its name to the whole of the parish was one of three important chapels in South Ronaldsay, the others being *St. Mary's Chapel* and *Holyrood Chapel*; the antiquity of this site is demonstrated by the fact that it lies in the *Papley* district and a very fine Pictish stone was found here; it contained at one time a wooden image of St. Peter which was destroyed in 1643 after the Reformation; a searchlight, one of at least twenty on the island was positioned near here during World War II; 470907; Map Page XI.

*This beautifully carved Pictish stone at one time formed a window sill in St. Peter's Kirk; it is now in the Museum of Scotland; the back is also carved; regrettably only the left half survives.*

**Stella Maris** South Parish; occupied; *Latin* 'star of the sea.'; the old name of this house was *Broll*; 455875; Map Page VIII.

**Stensigar** Sandwick 1595, 1821, 1861; occupied; ON *steins-garðr* standing stone farm so called from the stone which is actually nearer to *Cloddyhall*; 434894; Map Page VIII.

**Stews** Eastside 1329, 1492, 1500, 1595; occupied; ON *stúfar* stumps (of nearby standing stones) with Eng. plural; one searchlight, (one of at least twenty on the island) were positioned here during World War II; 467894; Map Page XI.

**Stews Head** see *Stews* above; a number of vessels have been wrecked here; 1. the French brigantine *Adela* in 1847. 2. the *Penang* of Liverpool with a cargo of tallow, hemp and wheat in 1848; see *Penang Geo*; 468894; Map Page XI.

**Stews Taing** see *Stews* above; ON *tangi* point; 469896; Map Page XI.

**Stockhelly** ON *stakkr* rock stack; *hella* flat rock; 472860; Map Page XIII.

**Stone/Stane** Linklater/Windwick 1821; empty; probably relates to a nearby standing stone though none is recorded; there was a Stannanstane in Flotta; 453873; Map Page XIII.

**Stonebreck** Burray; occupied; 465954; Map Page II.

**Stonefield** Burray; occupied; 458956; Map Page VI.

**Stonehall** Burray; 459969; Map Page II.

**Stonehouse** Quindry, Ronsvoe and Hoxa district 1871; vanished.

**Stone Kists** 435844; Map Page X.

**Stonepark** St. Margaret's Hope; occupied; Map Page IV.

**Stonequoy/Steeny Quoy** Herston; 1736, 1750; vanished; ON *steinn* stone; *kví* enclosure.

**Stony Bight** 415923; Map Page V.

**Stony Geo** ON *gjá* ravine; 461874; Map Page XIII.

**Stony Mountain** Quindry, Ronsvoe and St. Margaret's Hope district 1881; vanished; fanciful name; perhaps so named by a returning emigrant.

**Stoodley Pike** for some time in the 1970s/1980s *Manse 5* in Burray village was known by this name; 472955; Map Page VI.

**Store (The)** St. Margaret's Hope; refurbished and soon to be occupied; Map Page IV.

**Strathlyn** Burray; occupied; 473955; Map Page VI.

**Strip (The)** coastal feature; 418904; Map Page IX.

**Stromspirl** a small stream; ON *straumr* stream; second element suggests Nor. *spir* to gush out, hence a 'spring'; 464907; Map Page XI.

**Stromlie Point** ON *straumr* tide; compare Stromness Taing on Wyre; see *Laftlie Point* for origin of 'lie' element; 410916; Map Page V.

**Strone (The)** an alternative name for *Ayre o Burwick*; ON *strönd* coast.

**Storehouse** Widewall 1851; vanished.

**Stovlia** Hoxa; occupied; 417937; Map Page V.

**Studio House** Front Road, St. Margaret's Hope; occupied; Map Page IV.

**Stursy** Burray; occupied; 458956; Map Page VI.

**Stufum (í)** see *Stews*.

**Suckquoy** Sandwick 1595, 1821; a working farm but the original house is almost derelict; also found in the form *Surquoy* which is likely to be the original form; compare *Muckquoy* in this respect; Margaret Suckquoy lived in South Ronaldsay in 1638; 443884; Map Page VIII.

**Summerlea** Burray; occupied; 471955; Map Page II.

**Summerton** Burray; occupied; formerly *Manse 6*; 474964; Map Page II.

**Sunfield** Burray village; a new housing development with eight properties, three of which are occupied; Map Page VI.

**Sunless Geo** Hunda, Burray; a north facing geo; contrast with *Sunny Geo* below; ON *gjá* ravine; 439973; Map Page I.

**Sunnybank** Sandwick; occupied; earlier known as *Gow's* from a family who lived here; 440906; Map PageVIII.

**Sunnydale** 1. Burray village; occupied; Map Page VI.

**Sunnydale** 2. St. Margaret's Hope; occupied; Map Page IV.

**Sunny/Sunni Geo** contrast with *Sunless Geo* above; 425895; Map Page IX.

**Sunnyside** Quindry, Ronsvoe and Hoxa district 1871; vanished; fanciful name.

**Sunnyvale** Burray; occupied; 472965; Map Page II.

**Surquoy** see *Suckquoy*.

**Suthergill** now renamed *Breck*; the house lies near *Sandwick Burn* and may suggest the original name of this stream; ON *suðr* south; ON *gil* stream running in a narrow channel; 448898; Map Page VIII.

**Sutherland House** Burray 1821; occupied; there is also a Sutherland on Flotta; ON *suðr* south, ON *land* land; 482955; Map Page VI.

**Sutherland Lodge** Burray; occupied; 480958; Map Page VI.

**Swan House** St. Margaret's Hope 1851; vanished; see *Swanson House*; Map Page IV.

**Swannays** 1736; vanished; from the family name 'Swannay/Swannie'; this surname has been recorded in South Ronaldsay since the 17th century when it took the form Swaine; in 1664, Nicoll Swaine's child, Alexander, was baptised at *St. Peter's Kirk*; the name derives from Norse *Sveinn*.

**Swannies** Burray; see *Waaness*.

**Swannie's Point** Burray; named after the above house; see above; 460975; Map Page II.

**Swanson House** St. Margaret's Hope; occupied; earlier *Swan House*; name derived from previous owner William Swanson, Registrar and Inspector of the Poor; Map Page IV.

**Swaquoy** Sandwick, 1640; vanished; ON *svað* a slippery rocks, ON *kví* enclosure; the indication is that this enclosure was near the coast.

**Swarback Falls** during periods of heavy rainfall, streams pour over the edge of the cliffs near *Stews*; ON *svartr* black; ON *bakki* slope; 488932; Map Page XI.

**Swarbeg Hall** South Parish 1851; vanished; a pejorative name; Ork. dial. *swartback* black-backed gull; 'hall' is used here in the sense of 'simple cottage'.

**Swartquoy** Hoxa 1861, 1871; vanished but location is known; ON *svartr* black; *kví* enclosure; there is a Swartaquoy in Shapinsay; compare *Sortoquoy* above; 431940; Map Page IV.

**Sweyn Court** St. Margaret's Hope; the former *Police Station (Old)*; now a development of four occupied houses; Map Page IV.

**Swinna's Land** Ronsvoe, 1750; vanished; ON *svín* pig.

**Swona** ON *svín* pig; *ey* island; the use of animal names for islands and coastal features is not always understood; first recorded in the *Orkneyinga Saga,* where we learn the names of three men who lived on the island; they were Grim, a poor farmer and his two sons Asbjorn and Margad; Margad was a powerful man, very much in the mould of Sveinn of Gairsay; when Sveinn was in the Hebrides he gave Margad the stewardship of Caithness; it was Margad who accompanied Sveinn after Sveinn had murdered his namesake Sveinn Breast-Rope and had fled to seek refuge with King David of Scotland; the island maintained a viable community until it was finally abandoned in 1974; today the island is unique in that, aside from the ravages of time, the houses capture much of the way of life of the people who lived there more than thirty years ago; of particular interest is the herd of cattle which was left behind, which have interbred, and which now, because of their unique history, are the subject of special scientific investigation; a number of vessels have been wrecked on the shores here; 1. the sloop *Mary* of Peterhead in 1783. 2. *Jussrow Henrietta* (other details unknown) in 1807. 3. the Swedish steamer *Gunnaren* with general cargo in 1935. 4. steamer *Pennsylvania* of Copenhagen in 1931. 5. brigantine *Tauris* of King's Lynn with a cargo of barley in 1806. 6. schooner *Betsy Davidson* of Dundee with a cargo of coal in 1861. 7. brigantine *Mount Etna* of Sunderland with a cargo of timber in 1849; the roof timber of Tomison's Academy came from this vessel. 8. *Patriot* (other details unknown) with cargo of timber in 1825. 9. vessel (no other details known) with cargo of flax and tallow in 1849; see also wrecks on *Tarf Tail,* Swona; 388845; Map Page XII.

**Sycamores (The)** St. Margaret's Hope; occupied; Map Page IV.

**Tabister** 1939; vanished; perhaps a name fashioned on an ON form; *Isbister* is the only recorded *bólstaðir* names in South Ronaldsay (if we exclude *Warbister* on *Swona* and *Rigbister* on the *Pentland Skerries*).

**Table (The)** coastal feature; *The Chair* lies close by!; 410928; Map Page V.

**Tack** South Parish 1841; vanished; Sc. *tack* a piece of land held on lease.

**Taftingus/Taftinga** St. Margaret's Hope 1821; occupied; it is locally believed that it was here where the 'ting' (ON *þing*, assembly) met and it certainly is an ideal situation; the 'ting' may indeed have met here but if we compare this name with the other *Taftshurrie* below it is likely that the name is derived from ON *topt* ancient house site and the personal name *Inga*, a familiar form of ON female names with the first element '*Ing*' as in *Ing-unn* etc.; see *Quoyenis*; see also *Gammons* for a reference to an assembly site.

**Tafnichill/Taftnickie** Widewall 1851; vanished; ON *topt* ancient house site; it is tempting to see the second element as ON personal name *Nikolas* but the fact that there are three places with similar names suggests the derivation is Far. *hnikil*, knoll; see *Nickle Head*.

**Taftnica/Taftnickie** Burray; 1627, 1821; occupied; see *Tafnichill* above for derivation; 484956; Map Page VII.

**Taftnickie** Sandwick 1821; vanished; see above for derivation.

**Tafts/Tofts** Burray; occupied; ON *toptir* ancient house sites with English plural; there is a Tafts in Sanday; the house name Tufter in Birsay shows the original Norse plural; 475972; Map Page II.

**Taftshurrie** Grimness 1821, 1851; occupied; ON *topt* ancient house site; the personal name/family name *Shurrie* derives from ON *Sigurð*; 485935; Map Page VII.

**Taftsshucky** Grimness 1821; vanished; may have a similar derivation to *Taftshurrie* above; *Siggi* is a Norse familiar form of *Sigurð* though not recorded in Orkney.

**Tails o Sgoilamar** Swona; near *Tarf Tail*; see *Tarf Tail* and *Sgoilamar* for derivation; 383836; Map Page XII.

**Tails o the Tarf** see *Tarf Tail*.

**Tain Park** South Parish 1891; vanished; transferred name from Tain in Ross-shire.

**Taing** 1. field-name on *Roeberry Farm* so named from *Roeberry Taing*, the point on which the field stands; 425931; Map Page V.

**Taing** 2. field-name, *Stews Taing*; 468896; Map Page XI.

**Tainga** ON *tangi* point; 428860; Map Page X.

**Taing o Knockhall** ON *tangi* point of land; also called *Knockhall Taing*; 455946; Map Page IV.

**Taing o the Hune** 433883; Map Page VIII.

**Tammie Norie Cottage** former name of *Dunroamin*; there is a house named Tammie Norie north of Dounby; Ork. dial. *Tammie Norie* a puffin.

**Tanglin** South Parish; occupied; new name of former old Manse of *St. Mary's Kirk*; 443856; Map Page X.

**Tapestry Gallery** see *Craft Centre 3*.

**Tappicks o the Hest** see *Toppicks o Hess*.

**Tarf (The)** Swona; the southern tip of the island; see below for details; 384837; Map Page XII.

**Tarf Tail/Tails o the Tarf** Swona; this reef has been the graveyard of a number of vessels; 1. Norwegian brigantine *La Plata* of Frederikstad in 1886 (the site of the stranding is still referred to as the *La Plata Hole*). 2. the schooner *Mary Grace* of Stromness in 1927. 3. the Norwegian barkentine *Rifondo* of Oslo with a cargo of coal in 1877; only the dog survived. 4. the Dutch schooner *Sia En Elizabeth* of Zuidbroek with a cargo of wheat in 1862. 5. the trawler *Ross Tern* of Grimsby in 1973. 6. the trawler *St. Clair* of Grimsby in 1949. 7. steamer *Johanna Thorden* of Brando (Finland) with general cargo and cars in 1937; the lifeboats were washed up in the *Pool o Cletts* on South Ronaldsay and in Deerness; see also *Swona* for other instances of wrecked vessels; a running together of ON *þari* seaweed and ON *rif* reef; ON *tagl* tail used as in Eng. 'tail of a bank'; 380836; Map Page XII.

**Tarland** 1. Grimness 1746; vanished; ON *þari* seaweed; suggesting land manured with seaweed.

**Tarland** 2. Brough 1492, 1500, 1595, 1627, 1821; now field-name; see above for derivation; 444839; Map Page X.

**Tarland's Geo** ON *gjá* ravine, near the old farm of *Tarland 2*; 443841; Map Page X.

**Tarri Clett** Glims Holm; ON *þari* seaweed; *klettr* rock; 470987; Map Page II.

**Task** Sandwick 1861; vanished; probably Eng. in the sense 'land difficult to work'; compare the field-name *Murder* in South Ronaldsay and the Hardhill places of Orkney.

**Teacher's House** *Tomison's Academy*; empty; 443857; Map Page X.

**Tebrake** St. Margaret's Hope 1851; vanished; pejorative name; Ork. dial. *teeo* lapwing; compare *Ploverbrake*; for *brake* element see *Barebreck*; see also *Tiu House*.

**Telephone Exchange** 1. disused; this Telephone Exchange which served Service Personnel during World War II lay below *Hillside Camp* on the so-called *Burma Road*; 438929; Map Page IV.

**Telephone Exchange** 2. Burray; 473964; Map Page II.

**Telephone Exchange** 3. St. Margaret's Hope; Map Page IV.

**Temperance Hall** see *Old Bakehouse (The)*.

**Tennis Court** 1. St. Margaret's Hope; Map Page IV.

**Tennis Court** 2. Muckle Skerry, Pentland Skerries; a rocky point; an extraordinary name to find in this exposed place! The name was recorded by the Ordnance Survey in the 1870s suggesting a corruption of 'taing's court' from ON *tangi* a point of land where the 'court' of cormorants met; compare *Parliament Square* and *Scartan Point*; 469785; Map Page XIV.

**Terra Cliv** coastal feature; ON *þari* seaweed; *klufðr* cleft; 488942; Map Page VII.

**Terra Point** coastal feature; see above; 488943; Map Page VII.

**Thomson's** field-name, *Roeberry Farm*; 'Thomson' is a long established South Ronaldsay surname often written in the form 'Tomison'; in September 1657, David Thomisone's child, Thomas, was baptised at *St. Peter's Kirk*; see *Tomison's Academy* below; 431933; Map Page IV.

**Thorfinn Place** St. Margaret's Hope; one of several housing developments in the village using the names of the Norse Earls of Orkney; there are ten occupied houses in this development; Map Page IV.

**Thorshaven** St. Margaret's Hope; occupied; Map Page IV.

**Thurrigair** Burwick 1329, 1500, 1509, 1595, 1627, 1821; occupied; one of the earliest recorded Orkney farm names; in a 14th century document it was written *í Þordar ekru*, a Norn variant of ON *Þórðar-ekra* Thord's arable field; 451843; Map Page XIII.

**Tillydelph** alternative name of *Felipress*, Burray; origin unknown; the 'tilly' element suggests a transferred Scottish place-name as in 'Tillicoultry' etc; but the place-name Tillydelph is not known; perhaps a corruption of Tullyduff in County Mayo, Irish Republic; 478968; Map Page II.

**Timbertoe** St. Margaret's Hope 1851; vanished; origin unknown.

**Timmer Dykes** Quindry, Ronsvoe and Hoxa district 1851; Ork. dial. 'timmer', timber; a wooden fence in this case; a 'Timmerhouse' was formerly recorded in Stronsay; Timmer Dykes is now known as *Smiddy Cottage*.

**Tirry Geo** see *Turrie Geo.*

**Tiu House** St. Margaret's Hope 1851; vanished; Ork. dial. *teeo* lapwing; compare *Tebrake.*

**Toddenton** Eastside, 1861; vanished; a transferred name from Toddinton in Bedfordshire.

**Tofts** 1. *Herston*; ON *toptir* ancient house sites, with English plural; compare *Tafts*; 415920; Map Page V.

**Tofts** 2./**Tafts**. Burray; see *Tafts/Tofts.*

**Tomb of the Eagles** Neolithic chambered tomb in *Isbister*, so called from the large number of sea-eagle remains; 467845; Map Page XIII.

**Tom Budge's Stone** a coastal feature in *Sandwick*; probably a fishing rock favoured by Tom whose identity is unknown; he may have been Thomas Budge who lived at *Newbigging, Widewall* in 1821 aged 20; see also *Jessie Budge's Field*; 435881; Map Page VIII.

**Tomison's Academy** founded in 1851 with an endowment of £12,000 which represented half the estate of William Tomison, a native of South Ronaldsay who died in 1829; he was an employee of Hudson's Bay Company and latterly Governor of North West Territories; he had already built a small school in South Ronaldsay in 1821; Tomison had joined Hudson's Bay Company as a mere labourer in 1760 and became one of Orkney's richest men ever; the value of the fortune he had accumulated in the service of the Hudson's Bay Company can be shown by the fact that, near the year of his death, a substantial two storey house was built in Stenness for £26; his total earnings would have been the equivalent of many millions of pounds in today's money; this school was closed in the 1960s and, sadly, remains unused today while its future is being decided; a searchlight, one of at least twenty on the island was positioned here during World War II; see *South Parish School*; see also *Dundas House*; 443856; Map Page X.

**Toppacks o Hess** coastal feature, Windwick; three rocks in the sea shaped liked small haystacks; Sc. *tap/top* a conical shape with diminutive 'ack' in this case; see Hesta Head; 466882; Map Page XI.

**Touerlum** coastal feature; Sc. *tooer lum* tower chimney, a rock stack feature; 486928; Map Page VII.

**Toung** 1595; vanished; a house situated near a point of land, from ON *tangi* point; compare the vanished house of Toung in the Ireland district of Stenness.

**Towie Hole** coastal feature; the name suggests a derivation from 'tow', flax, but unlike *Lint Pows* etc., it was impossible to steep flax here since the name refers to a deep-water sea cave; 'Towie' is probably a lost dialect word for some kind of ogress with an unkempt, matted coat; ON *þófi* felt; compare *Gariel Hole*; 493929; Map Page VII.

**Trae Geo** Muckle Skerry, Pentland Skerries; ON *tré* wood, the reference being to driftwood; compare Tresness in Sanday; *gjá* ravine; 467785; Map Page XIV.

**Trance (The)** St. Margaret's Hope; a lane connecting the Back Road with the Front Road; Scots *trance*, a passage, from Old French *trance*; compare 'The Vennel', the old name for St. Magnus Lane in Kirkwall from Old French *venelle*; these names show the influence of French on the Scots language; in the middle of the 16th century a Frenchman by the name Bonot was appointed governor of Orkney by Marie de Guise, Queen of Scotland and wife of James V!; Map Page IV.

**Trance House** located in *The Trance*; Map Page IV.

**Tray/Tre Geo** Swona; ON *tré* wood, the reference being to driftwood; compare *Trae Geo* above; 387837; Map Page XII.

**Trena Burn** see below; 464848; Map Page XIII.

**Trena Loch** *tren* and *tron* elements in Orkney and Shetland place-names are usually associated with lochs; there is a strong suspicion that such elements relate to some unrecorded evil spirit; compare *Echna Loch*; 465851; Map Page XIII.

**Trin Geo** Swona; name suggests ON *þröngr* narrow as in *Gillietrang* Burray and *Trinkie Geo* below; 384839; Map Page XII.

**Triton Bank** Swona; a fishing bank between Swona and Switha; it was found by HMS *Triton*, a survey ship; approximately 375875; N.B. off the maps supplied.

**Trocaire** South Parish; occupied; 456874; Map Page XIII.

**Trofer** Burray, 1750; vanished; compare Troffers in Evie; a difficult name to interpret; 'th' in dialect was sometime pronounced 'f', for example 'Thursday' sometimes appears as 'Fursday' in early documents; this could suggest that this place-name may represent ON *traðir*, literally 'trodden' places and is probably used in the Icelandic sense of 'lane'; the Troffers in Evie is such a lane.

**Trinkie Geo** perhaps the same name as *Trunkie* below but Orkney dialect *trinkie* is a small ditch; 432850; Map Page X.

**Tring Geos** Swona; ON *þröngr* narrow; *gjá* ravine; compare *Trunkie Geo* below; 384840; Map Page XII.

**Trundi Geo** ON *þröndr* castrated boar; *gjá* ravine; 463833; Map Page XII.

**Trunkie Geo** 1. ON *þröngr* narrow; *gjá* ravine; 429857; Map Page X.

**Trunkie Geo** 2. see above for derivation; 468833; Map Page XI.

**Tumal** field-name; ON *tún-völlr* home field; such fields were not divided in the old system of land holding but were permanently attached to the dwelling; 451865; Map Page XIII.

**Tumol o Banks** Burray, 1750; see *Tumal* above and *Banks*.

**Tumol o Columbus** (sic) Grimness; 1750; vanished; apparently adjacent to St. Colm's Chapel.

**Tumol o Crapygoe** Burray, 1750; see *Tumal* above; ON *krappr* narrow; *gjá* ravine.

**Tumol o Ourigar** Burray, 1750; see *Tumal* above and *Ourigar*.

**Tumol o Bruntland** Burray, 1750; see *Tumal* above; ON *brent land* land cleared by burning; see *Bruntbigging*.

**Tumol o Milldam** Burray; 1750; see *Tumal* above.

**Tumol o Holy Graves** Burray; 1750; see *Tumal* above; location uncertain; perhaps near *St. Lawrence's Church*.

**Tumol o Whitestane** 1750; see *Tumal* above; location unknown.

**Tumulus** 453879; Map Page VIII.

**Turn Peak** coastal feature; perhaps ON *púfa-n* mound; Eng. 'peak'; 477922; Map Page VI.

**Turri Geo** ON *þari* seaweed; *gjá* ravine; 433848; Map Page X.

**Turriegeo** a house recorded in 1668; vanished; it must have been adjacent to the above coastal feature.

**Twinly Kirk** Swona; the site of a small chapel; Orkney place-names usually represent ON *púfa-in* the mound, as 'twin' as in *Twi(n) Ness* in Shapinsay, Westray and North Ronaldsay; prehistoric and later constructions were often sited on promontories; in this case it was a chapel; ON *hlíð* is probably 'cliff' in this instance; 381838; Map Page XII.

**Upper Attley** Widewall 1881; vanished; (*Upper Rattley* on OS map; see also *Atla*).

**Upper Barswick** see *Barswick*; 439863; Map Page X.

**Upper Berriedale** vanished, but position is known; also known as *Wilfred Kennedy's* and *Little Berriedale*; see *Berriedale* for derivation; 467929; Map Page VI.

**Upper Bigging** Widewall; vanished; see *Bigging*.

**Upper Biggings** Swona 1841; empty; same place as *Inverbiggings*; see *Bigging* for derivation.

**Upper Blanster** St. Margaret's Hope; vanished; see *Blanster*; 443925; Map Page IV.

**Upper Braehead**; vanished; see *Braehead*; 453905; Map Page VIII.

**Upper Breck** Widewall; vanished; see *Breck*; 443913; Map Page IV.

**Upper Cara** occupied; see *Cara*.

**Upper Collie** vanished; now a field-name on *Kirkhouse*; see *Collie*; 444918; Map Page IV.

**Upper Faulds** Burray; also known as *Overfaulds* and *Eastlynn*; occupied; 479964; Map Page II.

**Upper Field** *Cletts*; 460908; Map Page XI.

**Upper Gaira** Sandwick; derelict; see *Gaira*; 445890; Map Page VIII.

**Upper Haven** Grimness 1871; vanished; see *Haven*.

**Upper Kirk Geo** 432849; Map Page X.

**Upperknow** Quindry, Ronsvoe and Hoxa district 1851; vanished; see *Knowe*.
**Upper Lochhouse** Burray; occupied; 473965; Map Page II.
**Upper Lythes** Eastside; see *Lythes*; 458896; Map Page VIII.
**Upper Mayfield** 445843; Map Page X.
**Upper Mill** Sandwick 1861; vanished.
**Upper New Bigging** vanished; 428908; Map Page IX.
**Upper Olad** Sandwick; vanished; see *Olad*.
**Upper Quoydam** Widewall; vanished; see *Quoydam*; 429903; Map Page IX.
**Upper Rattley** Widewall; see *Upper Attley*; 428908.
**Upper Rockarry** Quindry, Ronsvoe and Hoxa district 1861; vanished; see *Rockarry*.
**Upper Serrigar** derelict; see *Serrigar*; 442877; Map Page VIII.
**Upper Tarland** 1. Burwick; see *Tarland*; 445841; Map Page X.
**Upper Tarland** 2. Brough; see Tarland; 445839; Map Page X.
**Upper Thurrigar** see *Thurrigar*; 455845; Map Page XIII.
**Upper Stone** South Parish 1861; vanished; see *Stone*.
**Uppertown** 1. Hoxa; occupied; 417939; Map Page V.
**Uppertown** 2. a house; occupied; an old tale hints that criminals were burnt at the
    stake near here; see *Weems Castle* for a reference to this; 418937; Map Page V.
**Upper Westshore** Burray village; new house; Map Page VI.

*Upthra, Swona; five members of the Norquoy family lived here on this six acre croft in
1920; by 1927, the holding had been abandoned.*

**Upthra** Swona; derelict; the highest house on Swona, standing at an elevation of
    20m.; Scots 'up through', with the meaning 'the higher (house)', paralleling the
    old house names Ap-trow and Doontrow in Birsay, the latter meaning 'the lower
    (house)'; 390846; Map Page XII.

**Upthra/Upfra Loch** near the above; 390843; Map Page XII.
**Urie Head** Barswick, perhaps Ork. dial. *orry* small; 434866; Map Page X.

**Valhalla 1.** Burray; occupied; fanciful house name; 484969; Map Page II.
**Valhalla 2.** St. Margaret's Hope; occupied; Map Page IV.
**Vamh** Hoxa; in *The Orkney Poll Taxes of 1690*, the name *Overvome* is recorded
 which is likely to be the same place; in Stromness Parish such a place-name is
 written Quholm; compare Whome on Flotta; ON *hvammr* grassy slope; 410928;
 Map Page V.
**Vensilly** ON *fen* marsh; ON *selja* willow; 457918; Map Page XI.
**Vensilly Hill** see above; 455919; Map Page XI.
**Vestlay Banks** Burray; occupied; origin unknown; 452968; Map Page I.
**Viewfield** St. Margaret's Hope; occupied; Map Page IV.
**Viewforth** Burray; occupied; 475971; see also *Fossil Museum*; Map Page II.
**Viga/Vigga/Viggie** 1736; vanished; the site of an old subscription school; a
 puzzling name; there was another Vigga (now called Barnhouse) in Birsay and
 a similar place-name in Holm; there are Viggar place-name in Burness in
 Sanday and North Ronaldsay; Viggar in Sanday has 'kirk' places in the vicinity
 and Vigga in Holm is in the Paplay district; these locations point to a derivative
 of ON *vigja* to consecrate a piece of ground; ON *garðr* enclosure; 450855; Map
 Page XIII.
**Vigil** South Parish 1841; vanished; may relate to a lookout post at the time of the
 Napoleonic War.
**Vikna** St. Margaret's Hope; occupied; named after the island of Vikna in Norway;
 when an adjacent house was built it was named *Naeroy* after an island close to
 Vikna!; Map Page IV.

**Waaness** Burray; a new house built on the site of *Swannie's;* despite the appearance
 of this name suggesting an Old Norse origin, the indications are that a previous
 owner renamed the site 'Waaness' perhaps through a misunderstanding when
 told locally, 'Hid's 'Swannie's', ie. 'Hid's Waaness'!; 457973; Map Page II.
**Wapping** Grimness 1891; vanished; transferred name from *Wapping*, London.
**Warbister Hill** Swona; the highest point on the island, 41m. above sea level; ON
 *varð*a beacon; *bólstaðir* farm; there could never have been a farm here at any
 time; *bólstaðir* must have its original meaning 'animal shelters'; 389842; Map
 Page XII.
**Ward Hill** dates from a time when beacon fires alerted the population to a danger
 and where watch was kept; there is an interesting reference in the *Orkneyinga
 Saga* to what was apparently this hill (see the chapter on 'Hills and Streams' in
 the Introduction); there are at least seven Ward Hills in Orkney; a searchlight,

one of at least twenty on the island was positioned here during World War II; see *Ball Hill*; ON *varða* beacon, 456887; Map Page VIII.

**Ward Hill Radar Station** vanished; during World War II this station was manned by R.N. (Royal Naval) personnel and was guarded by soldiers from different regiments e.g. Gordon Highlanders and South Wales Borderers; a number of A.T.S. (Auxiliary Territorial Service) also served here; later in the war R.A.F. (Royal Air Force) personnel manned the station; this camp also served as a recuperating centre for those torpedoed at sea in the vicinity of the islands; 456886; Map Page VIII.

**Wardhill** formerly *Sharnymire*; occupied; named from above feature; 459890; Map Page XI.

**Ward Point** Burray; ON *varða* beacon, indicating that, at one time, watch was kept on *Weddell Sound*; 474983; Map Page II.

**Wards** field-name on *Kirkhouse*; Sc. *ward/waird,* an enclosed piece of land; an alternative explanation is that the field is named after a previous owner with the surname 'Wards'; this family name has existed in the South Isles since the 17th century; 444914; Map Page IV.

**Wards Park** new housing development, St. Margaret's Hope; there are 8 occupied houses here; built partly on the site of *St. Margaret's Chapel*; Map Page IV.

**Warebanks** Burray, 1627; occupied; a large camp for Italian prisoners of war employed on the construction of the *Churchill Barriers* was established here during World War II; Orkney dialect *ware* seaweed; 475982; Map Page II.

**War Memorial** South Ronaldsay; located in St. Margaret's Hope and inscribed with the names of thirty-seven local men who gave their lives in two World Wars, the statue of the Seaforth Highlander is probably the finest of the Orkney

*The impressive South Ronaldsay War Memorial.*

War Memorials; the commission for the design was given to Alex Carrick, a well known Scottish sculptor whose mother was a Leith from St. Margaret's Hope; it was unveiled on 21st August 1921; 449932; Map Page IV.

**Wart** 1. Burray, 1821; see below.

**Wart** 2. the highest point of land in the west of Burray; the name of this hill has never been recorded but it can be guessed from the house name above; see *Little Wart*; see also *Wart (The)* below for derivation; 461964; Map Page II.

**Wart (The)** South Ronaldsay; ON *varða* beacon; see *Ward Hill*; 433936; Map Page IV.

**Wasbister** occupied; the most westerly of three farms set close together, the others being *Midbister* and *Isbister*; ON *vestr-bólstaðir* the western farm; 444902; Map Page VIII.

**Waston** Burray; see *West Town*.

**Waterfall** the *Berriedale Burn* falls over the cliffs at this point; 463875; Map Page XIII.

**Waterside** St. Margaret's Hope; occupied; formerly *Lairdene*; this large house has in its time performed three important services: 1. as a draper shop. 2. as a temporary solicitor's office when a solicitor from Low's practice called to do business with clients. 3. as a Dental Surgery when Dunnett, a Kirkwall dentist, visited the island; Map Page IV.

**Water Sound** now spanned by *Churchill Barrier No. 4*; a number of vessels have been wrecked in this stretch of water; 1. schooner *Ann* of Chester in 1874. 2. a fishing vessel (name unknown) of Gravesend in 1817. 3. schooner *Triumph* of Liverpool in 1874; see *Blockships 3*; ON *sund* channel; 460950; Map Page VI.

**Watersound** Burray; occupied; 476957; Map Page VI.

**Watersprings** 482925; Map Page VII.

**Waterview** Burray; 468968; Map Page II.

**Watrie Hall** 1750; vanished; it lay near *Flaws*; 'watrie' = 'watery'; there is a Waterhall near Dounby.

**Wavecrest** Burray; occupied; fanciful name; 476965; Map Page II.

**Wayside**; Eastside; occupied; 465892; Map Page XI.

**Weddell** Burray; 1492, 1500, 1821; occupied; ON *vaðill* shallow water; 478984; Map Page II.

**Weddell Bay** Burray; 476984; Map Page II.

**Weddell Fish Farm** originally a salmon farm but now 'probably the smallest fish farm in the world' operating on environmentally friendly principles, concentrating on, and experimenting with, shoals of halibut, cod and sea trout (*salmo trutta*), the latter fish being farmed in only three localities in Britain; 477986; Map Page II.

**Weddell Sound** Burray; now spanned by *Churchill Barrier* No. 3; the drifter *Rose Valley* of Inverness with a cargo of torpedoes sank in the eastern approaches in 1943; see *Blockships 2*; see *Weddell* for derivation; ON *sund* channel; 475985; Map Page II.

**Weddell Point** Burray; 473984; Map Page II.

**Weemys** see *Wheems*.

**Well Park** St. Margaret's Hope; occupied; Map Page IV.

**Wells o Swona** dangerous whirlpools off the south-east coast of *Swona*; ON *vella* to boil; approximately 379833; Map Page XII.

**Wells o Tiftaly** whirlpools between *Lother Rock* and *Muckle Skerry*; which are caused apparently by undulations in the sea bed; ON *vella* to boil; ON *þýfðr* hillocky; ON *hlið* gate, used in the sense of passageway; compare *Lippa*; 445805; N.B off the maps supplied.

**Weems** see *Wheems*.

**West Broch** Burray; one of two brochs which gave the island its name; both this broch and *East Broch* must have been quite distinctive in Norse times; an early excavation here revealed walls twelve and a half feet thick; now a grass covered elevation in a field known as *Ayresdale*; 483987; Map Page III.

**Weems Castle** Sandwick, on Castle Taing; believed to be the remains of a broch; known locally as *Lady Weem's Castle*; there is much confusion over the origin of the name applied to this feature; the name has apparently been transferred from a mansion house which was said to have lain in what is now the farm yard of *Mucklehouse*; (this happens also to be the site of the *Rood Chapel*); if we are to believe the tale which was recorded by George Low in his *A Tour through Orkney and Shetland, 1771,* it was occupied (possibly in the 16th century) by a Lady Wemyss; the story relates that she had a French maid who became pregnant to one of her servants; both maid and servant robbed their mistress, murdered her and her daughter and set fire to the house to destroy the evidence; both were caught and burned at the stake *on Kirkie Hill*; there may be a grain of truth in this; in 1471 William St. Clair was given the Earldom of Ravenscraig in Fife in exchange for the Earldom of Orkney—and Ravenscraig Castle is just along the coast from (East) Weems Castle in Fife; this castle may have had some association with the Sinclairs since in *Storer Clouston's Records of the Earldom* he includes in the Appendix an Inventory of Sinclair charters which was found in the Wemyss (sic) Castle charter chest; 434888; Map Page VIII.

**West Cara** Grimness; occupied; see *Alma*.

**Westend** Burray village; occupied; Map Page VI.

**West End** as the name suggests, the 'west end' of St. Margaret's Hope; Map Page IV.

**West End House** St Margaret's Hope; occupied; Map Page IV.

**Wester Birth** Swona; a big sea which comes in with varying stages of the flood tide to the west of the island; Faroese *burður* drift of current; approximately 380845; Map Page XII.

**Wester Bows** Swona; underwater reefs off *The Brook*; ON *boði* reef; 388850; Map Page XII.

**Wester House** Swona 1841; vanished; probably one of the *North Houses.*

**Wester House** Sandwick 1861; vanished.

**Westerlea** Burray village; occupied; it serves as the local Post Office; Map Page VI.

**Westermill** Burray; 1627, 1821; originally Westermeil; ON *vestr* west, *melr* sand; Westermill today lies some distance from the shore; the original dwelling must have lain near the *Ayre o Westermill*; 472958; Map Page VI.

**Wester Shoals** *Pentland Skerries*; 459784; Map Page XIV.

**Westhill** Burray; a district; 462955; Map Page VI.

**West Field** a field; 469916; Map Page XI.

**West Flaws** vanished; it was called *Flaws* in 1841, *Petrie House* in 1861 and *Mrs Miller's* in 1871! Mrs Miller operated a small school teaching reading and writing in the 1850s/1860s; it is also referred to as *Miller's School*; see *Flaws* for derivation; 453856; Map Page XIII.

**Westlea** 1. St. Margaret's Hope; occupied; formerly *Burn House*; Map Page IV.

**Westlea** 2. Sandwick, occupied; 437897; Map Page VIII.

**West Links** Burray; a house; 475955; Map Page VI.

**West Masseter** occupied; see *Masseter*; 446865; Map Page X.

**West Quoy** see *Whass Quoy*.

**West Shaird** Sandwick; occupied; *West Shaird* and *East Shaird* are almost one mile apart!; Sc. *shaird* a small portion, a variation of Eng. 'shard'; 430898; Map Page VIII.

**Westshore** 1821; Burray village; occupied; the jetty near here was the traditional ferry crossing point to South Ronaldsay; see *Cara Ferry*; 468954; Map Page VI.

**West Summerlea** Burray village; occupied; Map Page VI.

**West Town** Burray; sometimes applied to *Burray village* to contrast with *Northtown* and *Southtown* but this is not an old name.

**West Windi Skerry** Swona; ON *sker* reef; the schooner *Annie Marie* of Leith with a cargo of coal was wrecked here in 1925; 384835; Map Page XII.

**Wha Taing** Burray; 'wha' points to an extremely old Norse word related to Swedish dialect *hvaa*, foam; small deposits of copper ore may be found on the beach here; ON *tangi* point; 444962; Map Page I.

**Whale (The)** relates to a whale shaped rock; 469893; Map Page XI.

**Whaas Geo** 1. ON *hvass* a word used of the wind whipping up the sea; compare *Blow Geo* and *Windi Geo*; *gjá* ravine; 469834; Map Page XII.

**Whaas Geo** 2. see above; 443837; Map Page X.

**Whaas Geo** 3. see above; 393848; Map Page XII.

**Whass Quoy** wrongly marked on the O.S. map as *West Quoy*; see *Whass Geo 1* for interpretation; this exposed triangular piece of land seems to have been at one time a convenient place to quoy (ON *kvía* to enclose) sheep; the name Whass Quoy suggests that *Manse Taing*, which forms the apex of this triangle, was originally 'Whass Taing'; 475915; Map Page XI.

**Wheems** 1821; Eastside; occupied; also spelt 'Whims' and 'Weems' in records; a difficult name to interpret; perhaps ON *hvammr* grassy slope with Eng. plural; compare *Vamh*, Hoxa; 466916; Map Page XI.

**Whisky Waal Corner** the southern corner of *Bobby's* field; there is a well in the locality; the reference seems to be to the concealment of illegally distilled whisky at a time when such a practice was common; 429934; Map Page IV.

**Whistlebere**, Paplay; now called *Whistlebrae*; occupied; there are *Whistlebare* place-names in Sanday and Eday; Sc. 'whistlebare' originally poor quality, exposed land; 464913; Map Page XI.

**Whistlebrae** see above.

**Whitehouse** Eastside 1871; occupied; there are several Whitehouse place-names in Orkney, the suggestion is that they are built of stone and lime rather than turf; contrast the Highland 'blackhouse'; 458908; Map Page VIII.

**Whitelums** in *The Trance*, St. Margaret's Hope; reputedly one of the oldest houses in the village; 'white lums'= Sc. 'white chimneys'; at one time half this house was called *Nona*; Map Page IV.

**Whities** Herston, 1821; vanished; perhaps from the family name 'White' recorded in South Ronaldsay in the 17th century as 'Whytt', but more likely a clipped form of 'Whitehouse'.

**Widewall (Bay)** this bay is mentioned in the *Orkneyinga Saga*; when Earl Harald and Earl Rögnvald decided to attack Earl Erlend 'They went out on the Pentland Firth (from Thurso) taking the course for South Ronaldsay. They landed at Widewall and went on shore'. (Erlend was meanwhile in Barswick!); a number of vessels have been wrecked here; 1. the sailing vessel *Aurora* of Gothenburg, Sweden with a cargo of iron and deals, 1761. 2. *George* of Aberdeen in 1812. 3. *Janet and Mary* of Ullapool in 1812. 3. *Jean* of Liverpool, 1833. 4. American barkentine *Marengo* with a cargo of coal and glass in 1840. 5. sloop *Lady Janet Traill* of Thurso in 1792. 6. *Nelly and Ann* a sailing vessel in 1807. 7. *Primrose* of South Shields with a cargo of flax and logs in 1771. 8. brigantine *Sir Sydney Smith* of Stornoway from Karleshamm, Sweden with a cargo of iron and deals and bound for Liverpool, 1808. 9. brigantine *Stockton* of Isle of Man, 1833. 10. sloop *Barbara and Agnes* of Stornoway, 1830. 11. the *Kirkham* of Whitehaven in 1792. 12. vessel (name unknown) with a cargo of hemp and tar in 1771. 13. sloop *Alexie/Alexa* of Inverness in 1831. 14. *Pomona* of Aberdeen with a cargo of coal in 1819; the original ON form in the *Orkneyinga Saga* suggests ON *viðr* wide, *vágr* bay; the Eng. word 'bay' is unnecessary; 420925; Map Page V.

**Widewall** 1500, 1595, 1821; now district name; 438909; Map Page IV.

**Widewall Cottage** occupied; 448910; Map Page IV.

**Widewall Garage** St. Margaret's Hope; see *Garages*.

**Widewall View** see *School 6*.

**Wife's Geo** Burray, an intriguing name which at first suggested some dramatic occurrence in the past—perhaps the discovery of the body of an unknown woman here; the truth is that when the Norwegian brigantine *Frithjof* of Tonsberg was wrecked on *Burray Ness* in 1876 the figurehead (a woman in this case) was washed up in this geo; 499958; Map Page III.

**Wildcat Hole** coastal feature; 'wildcats' have not been recorded in Orkney in historical time; refers probably to wild, domesticated cats; 480923; Map Page VI.

**Wilfred Kennedy's** see *Upper Berriedale*.

**Willie Kirkness's** see *Manse Cott*.

**Willowbank** St. Margaret's Hope; occupied; a common fanciful name; Map Page IV.

**Windbrake** St. Margaret's Hope 1861; (also in 17th century); occupied; there are Windbreck (sic) place-names in Birsay, Deerness and St. Ola and a Vinbrake in Birsay; Windbrake in South Ronaldsay is early associated with the Cromarty family; see *Windbreck* below for origin; 443927; Map Page IV.

**Windbrake Cottage** occupied; 443927; Map Page IV.

**Windbreck** 1. Liddel 1492, 1500, 1841; occupied; the early recording of this name suggests that it translates as ON *vindr* wind, with the meaning 'exposed to the wind'; ON *brekka* slope; later called *Scholt*; now *South Liddel*; 463836; Map Page XII.

**Windbreck** 2. Burray; occupied; 462956: Map Page VI.

**Windhill** Burray; 463965; Map Page II.

**Windi Geo** Eng. 'windy'; ON *gjá*; 434842; Map Page X.

**Windi Mire** Eng. 'windy'; Sc. *mire* marsh; compare *Blos Moss*; 458872; Map Page XIII.

**Windie Knowe** Holland, 1750; vanished.

**Windmill** 1. the remains of a windmill built sometime in the 1790s may yet be seen; 471908; Map Page XI.

**Windmill** 2. nothing remains of this windmill which currently lies under a boat winch on the *Ayre o Burwick*.

**Wind Turbine** Burray; a 44m. high 850 kw. turbine on Northfield farm; 482983; Map Page III.

**Windward** Herston; empty; 422918; Map Page V.

**Windybrae** Eastside 1891; vanished; Sc *brae* hillside.

**Windy Ha** Burray; occupied; houses which were built on elevated sites in Orkney often had the adjective 'windy' ascribed to them; 464965; Map Page II.

**Wind Wick** ON *vindr* wind; *vík* bay; 460871; Map Page XIII.

**Windwick** 1821; occupied; the name is derived from the bay on which it stands; one of a number of place-names which provided Orkney surnames; John Windwick lived in South Ronaldsay in 1509; 460871; Map Page XIII.

**Windwick Dam** 458860; Map Page XIII.

**Windy Knowe** near Holland perhaps same name as *Windybrae*.

**Windywas** vanished though position is known; Sc. 'windy walls' used by the Scots to describe a poorly built house; compare Sc. 'Laird o Windywaas', a tramp who lived in derelict houses; 453902; Map Page VIII.

**Wing Skerry** see *Wing* below; ON *sker*, reef; 434838; Map Page X.

**Wing (The)** ON *vaengr* wing, as in Eng., used metaphorically to describe something extending outwards, in this case the landmass; there is also The Wing in South Walls; 436838; Map Page X.

**Windward** Herston; occupied; 421917; Map Page V.

**Wooldrage's** see *Dinki Bows*.

**Workshop** St. Margaret's Hope: a popular tourist venue; the *Loft Gallery* is on the floor above; Map Page IV.

**Workshop Flat** St. Margaret's Hope; occupied; Map Page IV.

**Yard House** St. Margaret's Hope 1861; location uncertain; may still exist under another name; Map Page IV.

**Yarpha** Grimness; 1821, 1851; vanished; there are Yarpha place-names in Sanday, Deerness and Orphir; ON *jörfi* gravelly soil; see also *Lower Yarpha*.

**Yeldabreck** Burray; occupied; a transferred name from *Yeldabrek* below; 475958; Map Page VI.

**Yeldabrek** Burray 1492, 1500; a vanished farm in the north of the island; ON *geld*, barren, of an animal but used metaphorically of poor land in Orkney place-names; it was pronounced 'yeld' in dialect and also carried the original Norse meaning; an old Orkney saying for example was '*A yeld soo wis niver good tae grises*' meaning 'a barren woman has no time for children'; there is a Yeldabreck place-name in Birsay, a Yeldavill in Harray and Yeldadee in Sandwick in the West Mainland; see also *Youlday* below.

**Yetham** St. Margaret's Hope; occupied; Map Page IV.

**Yorbrandis** 1500, 1595; ON *jörð* land; ON personal name *Brandr*; see *Brance* 485938; Map Page VII.

**Youlday** 1736; vanished; ON *geld*, barren, the 'day' element represents; ON *dý* bog; compare Yeldadee in Sandwick in the West Mainland; see also *Yeldabrek* above.

# Section 3

# Maps of South Ronaldsay and Burray

*Maps are reproduced from Ordnance Survey Explorer 461, Orkney, East Mainland, South Sheet, Scale 1:25 000, 2003 with the permission of Ordnance Survey on behalf of HMSO, Licence No. 100043901.*

I

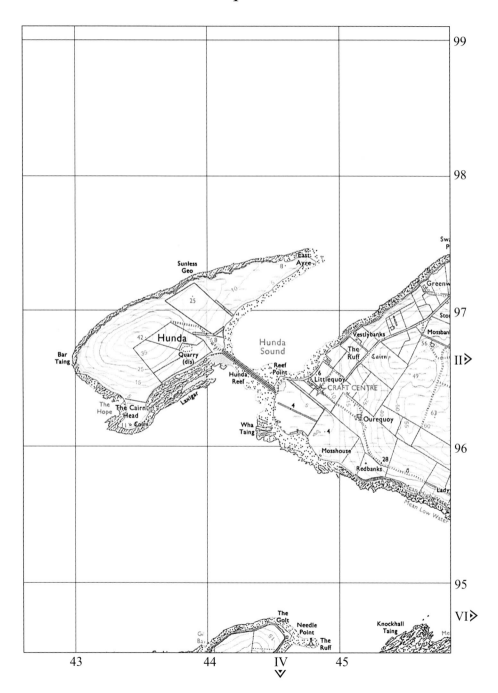

99

98

Sw
P

Greenw

97

Sunless
Geo

East
Ayre

8

10

6

25

Stor

Mossban

Hunda

42

Bar
Taing

35

Hunda
Sound

Vestlybanks

56

The
Ruff

II

Quarry
(dis)

8

Cairn

25

15

Reef
Point

49

Hunda
Reef

6
Littlequoy

CRAFT CENTRE

63

The
Hope

The Cairn
Head

Laxigar

4

5

60

Cairn

Ourequoy

55

96

Wha
Taing

4

Mosshouse

Redbanks

28

8

ean High Water

Lady

Mean Low Water

95

VI

43

The
Golf

Needle
Point

The
Ruff

Knockhall
Taing

Me

44

IV

45

Pier
Kirk
Point
13
Kirk
Poin
100
Churchill Barrier No 2
Blockship
Glimps
Sker
Jetty
5
Sheep
Dip
Glimps Holm
32
Dulse
Skerry
Brough
Geo
99
Sheep Pens
Broch
(rems of
15
10
Weddell Sound
Tarri
Clett
P
Weddell
Point
5
Churchill Barrier No 3
Blockship
Ward
Point
Weddell
Bay
10
Weddell
Warebanks
30
Penang
98
Gillietrang
Norton
North
III
37
Northtown
Swannies
Point
Echnaloch Bay
35
35
Swannie
Greenwell
Lookout
Tofts
30
10
Viewforth
Stoneyhall
Nearhouse
Lowerhouse
Hillbank
34
Gallowshill
Valhalla
97
Heatherhall
34
Newhouse
Lochside
So
Mossbank
Heathervale
Tillydelph
Klondyke
Hilltoft
23
Echna
Loch
Chapel Cottage
49
Hillside
Greenvale
Loch-House
Wayecrest
Kirklea
Midhouse
South-
house
Burray
80
Millfield
Faulds
63
Bloomfield
Slap
Summerton
Upper
Faulds
Ws
requoy
Inger Cottage
59
Howe
East
Lynn
Southbreck
96
Braehead
Cellardyke
Berryhill
Bruntland
Littlewart
Ardage
31
26
Windbreck
Hillfield
Westermill
Sch
Lurdy
Ladywater
Blinkbonny
Ourigaire
17
Burray
Village
Sutherland
Westhill
46
VI
47
48
28
nks
I
Cairn
E
banks

# III

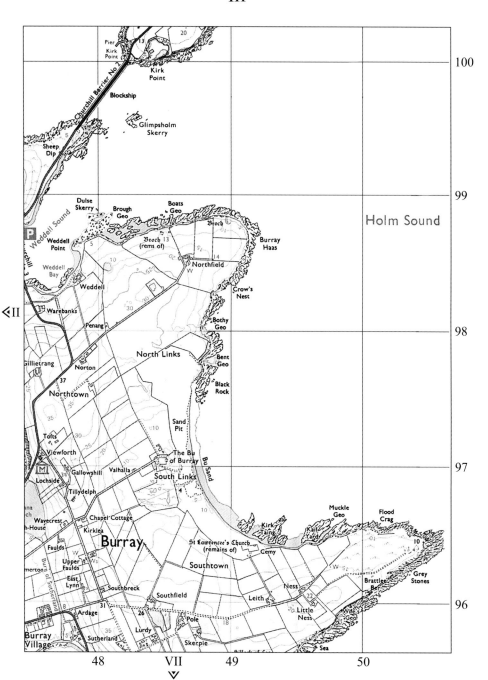

Pier
Kirk
Point
13
20

Kirk
Point

Churchill Barrier No 2

Blockship

Sheep
Dip

5

Glimpsholm
Skerry

100

Dulse
Skerry
Brough
Geo
Boats
Geo

Weddell Sound

P

Weddell
Point

5

Broch

Broch 13
(rems of)

Burray
Haas

14

Northfield
W

Holm Sound

99

Weddell
Bay

10

Weddell

30

Crow's
Nest

◁II

Warebanks

Penang

30

Bothy
Geo

98

Gillietrang

North Links

Norton

Bent
Geo

37

Black
Rock

Northtown

35

Sand
Pit

10

Tofts

30

25

Viewforth

20

Gallowshill

Valhalla

10

The Bu
of Burray

Bu Sand

Lochside

South Links

Tillydelph

50

4

Muckle
Geo

Flood
Crag

Chapel Cottage

Wavecrest
h-House

10

Kirk
Taing

Kaill
Yard

01

10

Kirklea

Faulds

Burray

St Lawrence's Church
(remains of)

Cemy

Grey
Stones

Upper
Faulds

merton

Southtown

W

Brattlee
Ber

East
Lynn

Southbreck

Ness

97

Ardage

Burn of Sutherland

31

26

Southfield

Pole

18

Leith

Little
Ness

22

Wife
Geo

Burray
Village

35

Sutherland

Lurdy

Skerpie

Sea

96

48

VII

49

50

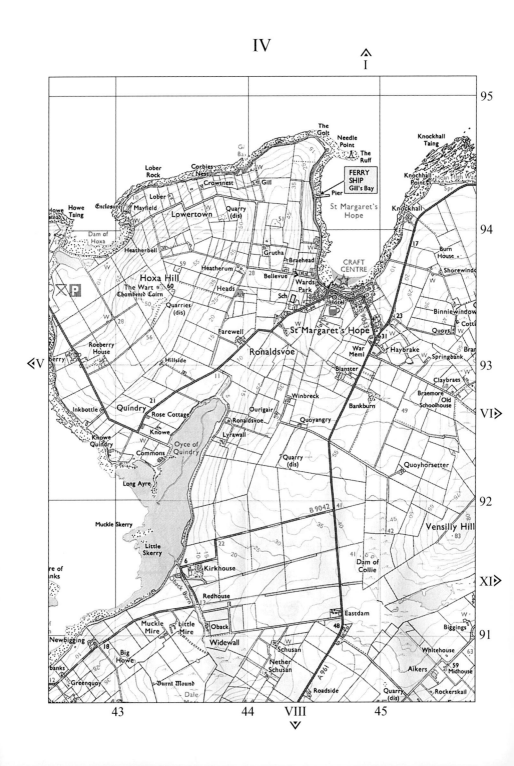

V

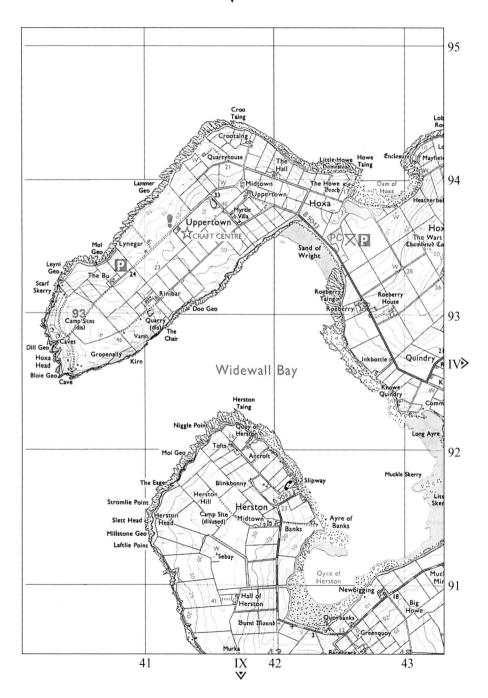

IX

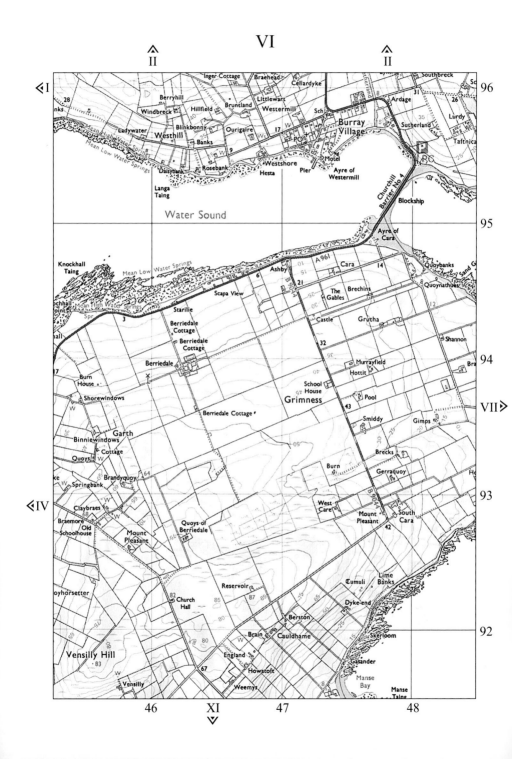

Inger Cottage  Braehead  Cellardyke  Southbreck
Berryhill  Littlewart  31
Bruntland  Westermill  Ardage  26
Windbreck  Hillfield  Sch  Sutherland  Lurdy
Ladywater  Blinkbonny  Ourigaire  17  W  Burray  Village  Taftnica
Westhill  Banks  9  POS
Daisybank  Rosebank  Westshore  Motel
Hesta  Pier  Ayre of
Westermill
Langa
Taing
Churchill
Barrier No. 4
Blockship

Water Sound

Ayre of
Cara

Knockhall
Taing
Mean Low Water Springs
Cara  14  Quoybanks
Ashby  A961  Quoynathues
6  B9061  21
Scapa View  The  Brechins
Gables
Starilie  Castle  Grutha  Shannon
Berriedale
Cottage
Berriedale
Cottage  32
Berriedale  Murrayfield
Burn  Hottit
House  Shorewindows  School
House  Pool

Grimness  43
Berriedale Cottage  Smiddy  Gimps
Garth
Binniewindows  Brecks
Cottage
Quoys  Burn  Gerraquoy
Brandyquoy  64
Springbank  West
Care

Claybraes  Mount  South
Braemore  Pleasant  Cara
Old  42
Schoolhouse  Mount  Quoys of
Pleasant  Berriedale

Lime
Banks
Cumuli
oyhorsetter  Reservoir  Dyke-end

Church
Hall  87  Berston
Brain  Cauldhame  Skerloom
Vensilly Hill  80  Gasander
83  England  Manse
67  Bay  Manse
Vensilly  Howatoft  Weemys  Taing

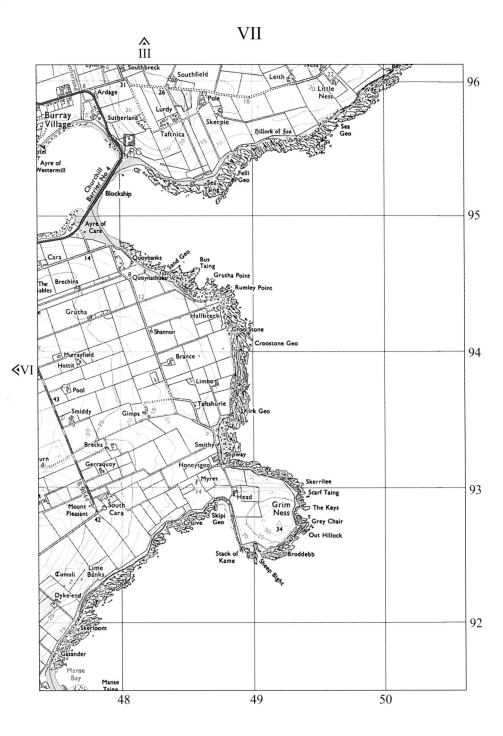

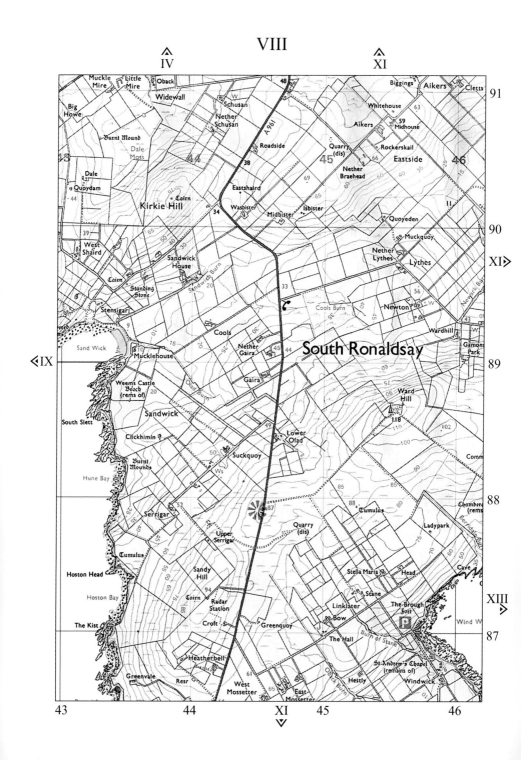

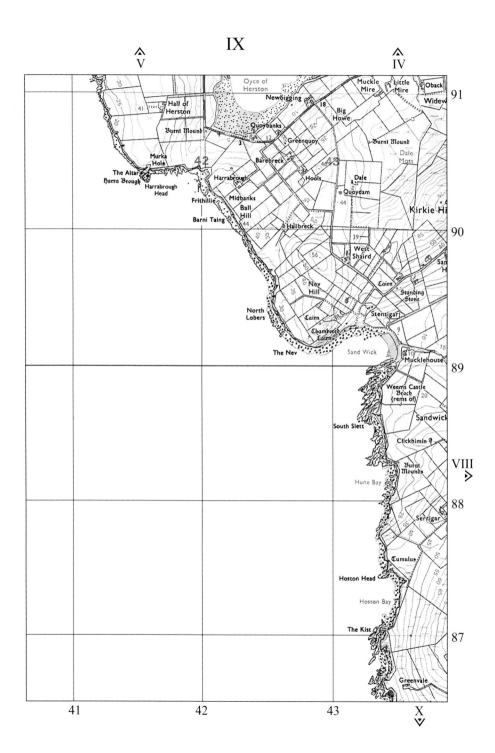

^
V

^
IV

Oyce of
Herston

Muckle
Mire

Little
Mire

Oback

Widew

91

Hall of
Herston

Newbigging

18

Big
Howe

41

Burnt Mound

Quoybanks

Greenquoy

Burnt Mound

Dale
Moss

12

Murka
Hole

42

Barebreck

43

The Altar

Harra Brough

Harrabrough
Head

Harrabrough

Hools

Dale

Frithillie

Midbanks

Quoydam

Kirkie Hi

Ball
Hill

44

Barni Taing

44

Hallbreck

90

West
Shaird

39

56

San
H

Ney
Hill

Cairn

Standing
Stone

North
Lobers

Cairn

Stensigar

Chambered
Cairn

9

The Nev

Sand Wick

15

Mucklehouse

89

Weems Castle
Broch
(rems of)

20

South Slett

Sandwick

Clickhimin ?

Burnt
Mounds

Hune Bay

88

Serrigar

Tumulus

Hoston Head

Hoston Bay

The Kist

87

Greenvale

41

42

43

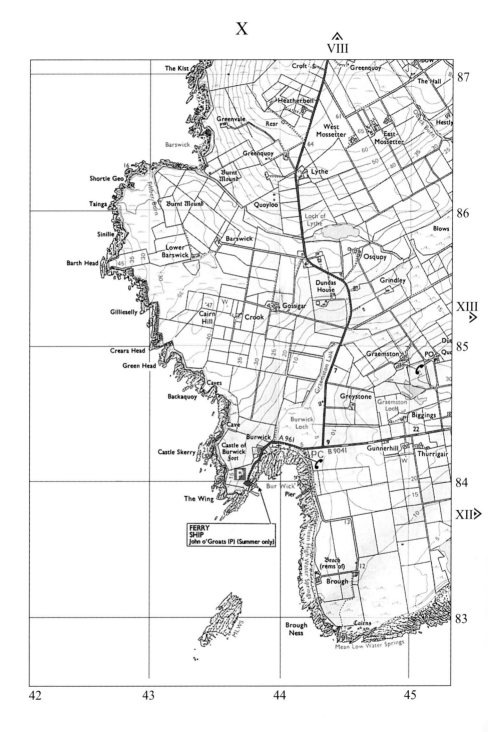

87

The Kist

Croft

Greenquoy

The Hall

Heatherbell

Greenvale

Resr

West
Mossetter

61

East
Mossetter

65

Hestly

60

Barswick

Greenquoy

64

50

40

35

30

25

Shortie Geo

Burnt
Mound

Lythe

16

86

Tainga

Burnt Mound

Quoyloo

Loch of
Lythe

Sinilie

Barswick

Blows

Lower
Barswick

Osquoy

Barth Head

45

35

30

Grindley

Dundas
House

52

Gillieselly

Cairn
Hill

'47
W

Crook

Gossigar

15

85

Creara Head

40

35

26

20

10

Graemston

PO

Du
Qu

Green Head

7

30

Caves

Greystone

Graemston
Loch

Backaquoy

Cave

Burwick
Loch

Biggings

22

Burwick A 961

9

Castle Skerry

Castle of
Burwick
fort

PC

B 9041

Gunnerhill

Thurrigair

W

P

20

84

15

The Wing

Bur Wick
Pier

10

FERRY
SHIP
John o'Groats (P) (Summer only)

13

Broch
(rems of)

12

Brough

83

Cairns

Brough
Ness

Mean Low Water Springs

42          43          44          45

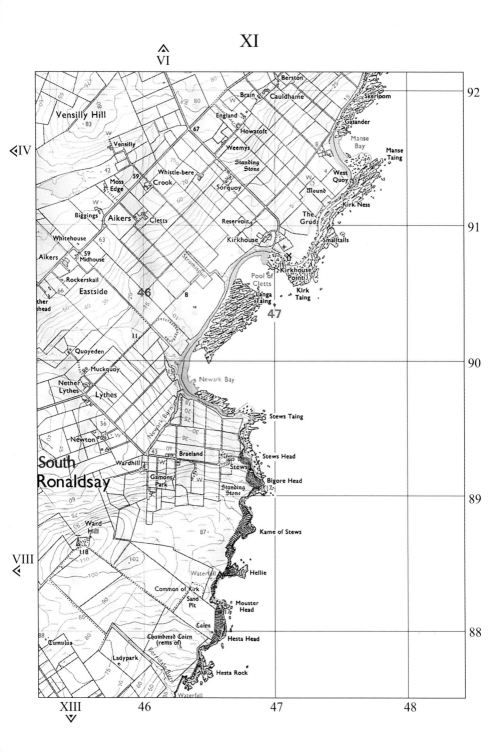

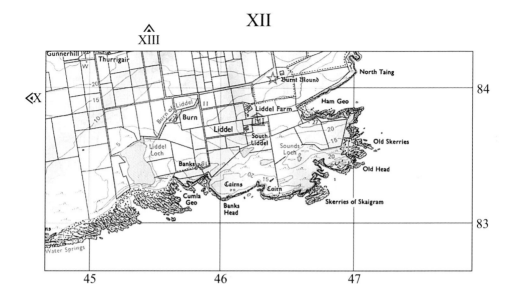

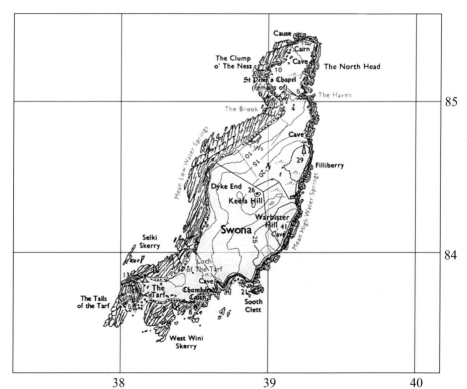

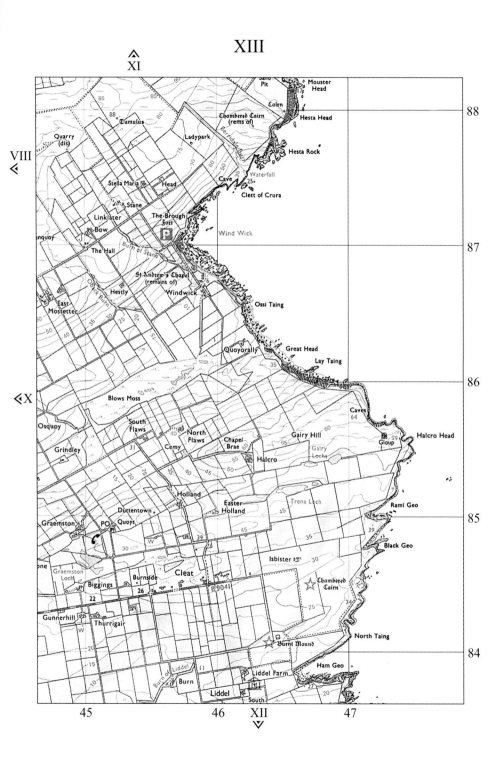

## VIII

88

Sand Pit

Mouster Head

Cairn

Chambered Cairn (rems of)

Hesta Head

Tumulus

Ladypark

Hesta Rock

Quarry (dis)

Waterfall

Cave

Clett of Crura

Stella Maria

Head

Stane

The Brough Fort

Linklater

Bow

P

Wind Wick

87

The Hall

Burn of Stane

nquoy

St Andrew's Chapel (remains of)

Hestly

Windwick

East Mossetter

Ossi Taing

86

Quoyorally

Great Head

Lay Taing

X

Blows Moss

Caves 64

Gloup

Halcro Head

Osquoy

South Flaws

North Flaws

Chapel Brae

Gairy Hill

Grindley

Cemy

Halcro

Gairy Lochs

Holland

Easter Holland

Trena Loch

Rami Geo

85

Duttentown

Quoys

Graemston

PO

W

Black Geo

Isbister

Graemston Loch

Cleat

Chambered Cairn

one

Biggings

Burnside

B 9041

Gunnerhill

Thurrigair

W

Burnt Mound

North Taing

84

Ham Geo

Burn of Liddel

Burn

Liddel Farm

Liddel

South

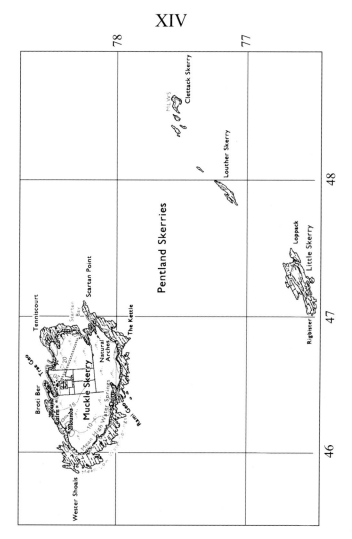

Clettack Skerry

MLWS

Louther Skerry

Pentland Skerries

Loppack

Little Skerry

Rigbister

Scartan Point

Tenniscourt

Scartan Bay

The Kettle

20

Natural Arches

Muckle Skerry

Broti Ber Geo

Mound Cairn

Mounds

Mean High Water Springs

Rani Geo

Wester Shoals

78

77

48

47

46

# References

## Maps

**Ordnance Survey** *South Ronaldsay and Burray, Six Inches to one Statute Mile*; 1877.
**Ordnance Survey** *Explorer 461, Orkney, East Mainland, South Sheet, Scale 1:25 000*; 2003.
**Blaeu's Map** 1654.
**Mackenzie's Map** 1750.

## Index

**J T H** (initials only supplied), *Orkney Place-Names Index, 1958/59, 1 inch to 1 mile; Ordnance Survey Maps*, 1977, unpublished typescript.

## Texts

**Anderson, J.** *Orkneyinga Saga,* Edinburgh, 1873.
**Barry G.** *History of the Orkney Islands*, Edinburgh, 1808.
**Ben, J.** (trans. M. Hunter), *A Description of the Orchadian Islands, 1529*, Stromness, 1987.
**Campbell, A. J.** *Fifteen Centuries of the Church in Orkney*, Kirkwall, 1938,
**Clouston, J. S.** *Records of the Earldom of Orkney, 1299-1644,* Edinburgh, 1914.
**Clouston, J. S.** *James Sinclair of Brecks*, Proceedings of the Orkney Antiquarian Society, Vol. XV, 1937-1939.
**Craven, J. B.** *Church Life in South Ronaldsay and Burray in the 17th Century*, Kirkwall, 1911.
**Esson, G. L.** *The Defence of South Ronaldsay in Two World Wars* (unpublished typescript); 2005.
**Esson, G. L.** *For Freedom and Honour,* Finstown, Orkney; 2001.
**Fenton, A.** *The Northern Isles: Orkney and Shetland*, Edinburgh, 1978.
**Gorrie, D.** *Summers and Winters in the Orkneys,* London, 1868.
**Gray, P.** *Howe Saga*, privately printed, Bristol, 2004.
**Hewison, W. S.** *This Great Harbour - Scapa Flow,* Kirkwall, 1985.
**Hossack, B. H.** *Kirkwall in the Orkneys*, Kirkwall, 1900.
**Irvine, J. M.** *The Orkney Poll Taxes of the 1690s*, privately printed, Kirkwall, 2004.

**Jakobsen, J.** *The Place Names of Shetland,* London, 1936.

**Lamb, G.** *Naggles o Piapittem—the place-names of Sanday, Orkney,* Kirkwall, 1992.

**Lamb, G.** *Testimony of the Orkneyingar,* Orkney, 1993.

**Lamb, G.** *Orkney Family Names,* Orkney, 2003.

**Lamb, G.** *Education in Orkney before 1800* (unpublished typescript).

**Lloyd's List of Orkney Shipwrecks** (unpublished).

**Low, G.** *A Tour through the Islands of Orkney and Shetland, 1774,* Kirkwall, 1879.

**Macdonald, J.** *Churchill's Prisoners,* 1942-1944, Kirkwall, 1987.

**MacGregor, G.** *Descriptive Notes on Orkney—South Isles;* Kirkwall, 1893.

**McLaren, P. N.** *Census of South Ronaldsay, Burray, Swona and Pentland Skerries,* 1821, (unpublished).

**Marwick, E.** *The Folklore of Orkney and Shetland,* London 1975.

**Marwick, H.** *Orkney Farm Names,* Kirkwall, 1952.

**Marwick, H.** *The Place-Names of Rousay,* Kirkwall, 1947.

**Omand, D.** (Ed.) *The Orkney Book,* Edinburgh, 2003.

**Picken, S. D. B.** *The Soul of an Orkney Parish,* Kirkwall, 1972.

**Royal Commission on Ancient Monuments**, Orkney; H.M.S.O. Edinburgh, 1946.

**Sauermilch, N. F.** *Scapa Flow im Wandel der Zeiten,* Bremen, 2004.

**Smith, J.** *The Church in Orkney,* Kirkwall 1907.

**Torfaeus, T.** (trans. A. Pope) *Orkney, Caithness and the North,* Wick, 1866.

**Tudor, J. R.** *The Orkneys and Shetland,* London, 1883.

## Video

**Findlay, J. S.** *Swona—Memorial to a lost way of life,* Viking Videos, Kirkwall, 2004.

## Web Sites

**www.rcahms.gov.uk** this site will lead the reader to details of all the recorded archaeological sites in Burray and South Ronaldsay; registration is compulsory but use of the site is free; readers should note that all 'Burray' entries are under 'South Ronaldsay'

**www.scotlandspeople.gov.uk** publishes details of all census information relating to South Ronaldsay and Burray but a subscription is required.

**www.southronaldsay.net** in addition to containing much information useful to genealogical researchers, this free web site provided by Lisa Conrad also includes, courtesy of the Annal family, the complete 1821 Census which has many house/farm names otherwise unrecorded.